OXFORD STUDIES IN
SOCIAL AND CULTURAL ANTHROPOLOGY

Editorial Board

AGE, MARRIAGE, AND POLITICS
IN FIFTEENTH-CENTURY RAGUSA

OXFORD STUDIES IN SOCIAL AND CULTURAL ANTHROPOLOGY

Oxford Studies in Social and Cultural Anthropology represents the work of authors, new and established, that will set the criteria of excellence in ethnographic description and innovation in analysis. The series serves as an essential source of information about the world and the discipline.

OTHER TITLES IN THIS SERIES

Age, Marriage, and Politics in Fifteenth-Century Ragusa

DAVID RHEUBOTTOM

OXFORD
UNIVERSITY PRESS

OXFORD
UNIVERSITY PRESS

Great Clarendon Street, Oxford OX2 6DP

Oxford University Press is a department of the University of Oxford.
It furthers the University's objective of excellence in research, scholarship,
and education by publishing worldwide in

Oxford New York

Athens Auckland Bangkok Bogotá Buenos Aires Calcutta
Cape Town Chennai Dar es Salaam Delhi Florence Hong Kong Istanbul
Karachi Kuala Lumpur Madrid Melbourne Mexico City Mumbai
Nairobi Paris São Paulo Singapore Taipei Tokyo Toronto Warsaw

and associated companies in Berlin Ibadan

Oxford is a registered trade mark of Oxford University Press
in the UK and certain other countries

Published in the United States
by Oxford University Press Inc., New York

British Library Cataloguing in Publication Data

Data available

Library of Congress Cataloging in Publication Data
ISBN 0-19-823412-0

1 3 5 7 9 10 8 6 4 2

Typeset by Best-set Typesetter Ltd., Hong Kong
Printed in Great Britain
on acid-free paper by
Biddles Ltd.,
Guildford and King's Lynn

PREFACE

The seeds for this project were planted almost twenty years ago with a small study in Dubrovnik's historical archives of fifteenth-century dowry records. The topic of dowry was already familiar since I had previously studied dowry transactions during several periods of anthropological fieldwork on kinship and marriage in a contemporary Macedonian village. I reasoned that a familiar topic would provide a bridge into a kind of research with which I had no previous training or experience—archival research. That initial summer project in the Dubrovnik archives led to a series of further small archival research projects and then to one very large one—the examination of the political careers of members of Dubrovnik/Ragusa's entire ruling class.

My earlier fieldwork in Macedonia had taught me that any meaningful understanding of the region also required an understanding of its history. A few years after that fieldwork I had joined a small group of historians and anthropologists at Johns Hopkins University who were interested in exploring some of the connections between history and anthropology. We hoped to move from history and anthropology to a historical anthropology or an anthropological history. Through a challenging and exciting programme of joint teaching and research seminars, we made some progress, but I also came to realize that I would not understand the 'historian's mind' and manner of working until I did some historical research of my own. The small project on dowries in fifteenth-century Ragusa, which began after I had moved to Manchester, was to be the first step towards developing that understanding.

The University of Manchester has very generously supported this work over the years with a series of grants in 1976, 1984, 1987, and 1990 which has enabled me to visit the archives in Dubrovnik for short periods. In 1978 I received a grant from the ESRC (then the SSRC) which permitted me to devote the entire academic year to archival research. I am very grateful to both of these institutions for their support. Added to these have been a number of separate private visits. These occasions have permitted me to amass a considerable body of material. The volume of this material has, in turn, permitted me to explore certain kinds of issues in very great detail, especially some aspects of developing political careers. It also meant that I had to become proficient in computer programming and the design and implementation of database systems.

The study of political careers took an unexpected turn at a critical juncture. Historians have known that the well-to-do urban merchants of the late medieval and early Renaissance period married comparatively late in life. Their brides, however, were much younger. This is one of the characteristics of what has become known as the 'Mediterranean Marriage Pattern'. Since most of Ragusa's governing élite were also successful merchants, I began to investigate the age at marriage in Ragusa. The result was unexpected. They married even later than had been reported for Florentine notables. The Mediterranean Marriage Pattern was present in an even more exaggerated form than had been found elsewhere. This prompted me to explore some of the structural implications of the pattern. And this, in turn, led me into demography and certain other specialist areas in which I had no previous interest or expertise. But once committed to this line of enquiry, unanticipated connections between social history and social anthropology began to emerge.

In the course of this work I have made some chastening discoveries in analysing these data with the assistance of the computer. Some concern the specific subject matter and these issues will be discussed in the chapters of this book. But there were other discoveries which concern the manner of working and these merit special mention because they are likely to fall outside of most anthropologists' experience. First, many impressions and cherished hunches about life in fifteenth-century Ragusa/Dubrovnik, gleaned from hours of reading in the archives, have proved upon later and closer analysis of the materials to be unfounded. It would be too embarrassing to reveal just how many hypotheses have met this fate. It would also be embarrassing to admit just how many weeks have been spent in fruitless attempts to salvage some of the more interesting ones. The certitude attached to some impressions is difficult to dislodge even when the disconfirming evidence is strong. I confess that there were mad moments when I was tempted to jettison some awkward data in order to cling to an attractive idea. I have been ruefully led to appreciate the historian's sometimes tiresome concern with sources and documentation.

Even with very ample documentation and the power of the computer to store vast amounts of information and to process it very quickly, it was often excruciatingly difficult and time-consuming (and sometimes impossible) to demonstrate what I 'knew' to be the case. This was the second discovery. Over the course of this project I have written many hundreds of computer programs to carry out various tasks of analysis. Many contained only a dozen lines of code. Others, like those which analyse kinship and affinal relations, or those which do record linkage, are lengthy and complex. Over the years I have had to become a skilled programmer and enjoyed the process. But trying to program the computer to carry out some procedures has been both humbling and humiliating. The computer is a willing and able assistant, but it is also exceptionally stubborn and stupid. It forces one to be absolutely clear and absolutely explicit about how, and in what order, the steps of analysis are to proceed. This too has been chastening. I now believe that computer programming should be part of the training of every anthropologist.

Finally, it is a pleasure to acknowledge the many debts that I owe and the many kindnesses I have received. In the Historical Archives of Dubrovnik, Professor Dr

Mato Kapović and his staff were always most welcoming and helpful. Few who do not regularly use archives can appreciate the importance of those scholars who compile catalogues, prepare printed sources, or write works of reference. In the course of my studies I depended upon many such works, but I must especially acknowledge my dependence upon, and respect for, the biographical research of Irmgard Mahnken, and Branislav Nedeljković's recension of the *Liber Viridis*— true monuments of scholarship. I owe a very personal debt to Dr Zdravo Šundrica who patiently coached me in basic palaeographic skills during my early days in the archives. Many colleagues from the reading-room in the Dubrovnik archives have offered comradeship, good advice, and many practical suggestions. Bariša Krekić and Susan Mosher Stuard have been particularly helpful and supportive and, as will become clear, I have drawn much inspiration from their writings.

In the very early stages of the enquiry, the Computer Support Unit of Manchester's Faculty of Economic and Social Studies prepared the data in machine-readable form and Margaret Irvine wrote several bespoke programs for data analysis. Through discussions with Margaret, I became aware that she was having to make important programming decisions about the treatment of my data which I did not understand and whose implications I could not fathom. As a result of these discussions, I understood that if I wished to exercise control over the questions posed of the data and the answers received, I would have to learn to write my own computer programs. Many of those programs were subsequently written in the command languages of the (initially) dBase II™ and (subsequently) 4D™ database applications. Other programs have been written in the Pascal and Smalltalk languages. With respect to other computing issues, I have benefited from numerous conversations over the years with Michael Fisher and Janet Bagg at the University of Kent and from a summer project working with Ilia Kouznetsov of the Computer Graphics Unit of the Manchester Computer Centre on advanced visualization software for the social sciences.

Various aspects of the Ragusan research have been presented to seminars at Manchester, Kent, Durham, Edinburgh, Cambridge, and Harvard. The seminars and day conferences at the J. K. Hyde Centre of Late Medieval and Renaissance Studies at Manchester have been an especially valued forum. I very much appreciate the comments and questions of participants at these seminars. Marilyn Strathern and James Weiner read an early draft of the manuscript and posed a number of awkward, if very helpful, questions. Bariša Krekić's comments on matters of detail and historiography have been especially appreciated. The errors which still remain are my own. Years ago Alfred Harris taught me that clarity and simplicity in scholarly writing are not to be despised. I have tried to follow his advice and example. John Davis has encouraged both this project and my involvement with computing over many years. At one timely moment he saved the project when it appeared to be floundering. I am very grateful for his advice and support. Finally, Sheila Gooddie has offered love and encouragement throughout the long period of writing. I dedicate it to her.

CONTENTS

LIST OF MAPS

LIST OF FIGURES

LIST OF TABLES

1

Introduction

Ragusa: The Study of a City-State

During the fifteenth century Ragusa/Dubrovnik survived when other city-states were collapsing or were being swallowed up by larger territorial states. Not only did it remain intact, but this classic little city-state also managed to preserve the institutional arrangements of an earlier age. Braudel has argued that fifteenth-century Ragusa was unique in the Mediterranean for it represented the 'living image of Venice in the thirteenth century' (1972–3: 339–41). What made it stable and enduring was an aristocratic republicanism. This was embedded in the culture of its ruling élite and in their governing institutions.

What makes Ragusa unique as an object for anthropological study is a relatively small population and an extraordinarily well preserved set of historical records concerning them. These archival sources allow us to examine the interplay between patrician politics, kinship, and marriage over the course of a half-century stretching from 1440 to 1490. It is the combination of rich archival materials, a small population, and the unusually long period of 'observation' which makes it possible to see how the trick of apparent stability was achieved.

Located on the eastern shore of the Adriatic Sea, Ragusa had a total population of about 30,000 living in its territory of which about 5,000 lived within the city walls. Those outside lived in neighbouring towns and in peasant villages. Its total territory consisted of a very narrow strip of coastal mainland and a handful of islands. From the fifteenth century until it was conquered by Napoleon, it was an independent city-state. Its independence, however, was always fragile. In earlier periods it had been a Venetian territory. Somewhat later it was a subject of the Hungarian crown. In our period, when the Ottomans were in the final stages of subduing the Balkans, it was allowed a tenuous independence in return for an annual tribute. Ragusa may have been tiny and precarious, but it was also very wealthy and influential. This stemmed from its far-flung trading empire. Both this trade and the terms of trade were dominated by the small patrician élite who numbered about 1,000 souls. These patricians also dominated the government.

Ragusan government consisted of offices and councils held exclusively by patrician males. The structure of government appears to be very stable over time. While this study concentrates on the second half of the fifteenth century, the same arrangement of offices and councils was in place for about a century before our period began and it was to continue for several more. If the structure of government appears stable, so does the ruling oligarchy. By 1440 the ranks of the patriciate had been 'closed' to outsiders for over a century. It was to remain closed for a further two. There was, therefore, a relatively simple and stable system of offices and councils and a closed population of eligible office-seekers.

There was also a framework of rules and procedures for allocating patricians to office. This framework shows every sign of being intentionally egalitarian. Within the closed monopoly association of the patriciate each male was to have his turn and no one, or no group, was to dominate. All offices were elected through secret ballot, the term of office was generally for a year (or less), incumbents could not succeed themselves, and close agnates could not vote for one another. This ensured a very rapid circulation of office-holders. But, as we shall see, the system was neither simple, egalitarian, nor entirely stable.

At the heart of government was the Great Council. Only patrician males could sit on this council. It was the principal legislative body and it made all of the crucial decisions regarding trade and diplomacy. It was the engine of government. Members of the Great Council elected the head of state (the Rector), from their own ranks. They also elected members of the Senate (or Council of Appeal), members of the Small Council who advised the Rector, judges of the several courts, and all of the other office-holders of the state.

At the top of the governmental hierarchy was the Rector followed by his Small Council and the Senate. These offices were held by elderly men who had long experience of government. At the bottom were a number of very junior posts such as that of Scribe in the Customs House. The latter were held by young men just beginning their political careers. In between there was a broad swath of about sixty other offices. Most of these had multiple incumbents. All of the incumbents for all of these offices and councils were selected from the ranks of the Great Council through a process of nomination and secret ballot. Therefore the major regular business of the Great Council was filling all these offices and councils. As we shall see, the number of elections actually held was much greater than sixty. Because of sharp competition for offices, multiple ballots were often needed to fill a single vacancy. And because of deaths and other happenstances, vacancies occurred at irregular intervals through the year. Elections, therefore, dominated council business. They provided a never-ending agenda.

Year after year, the same offices come up and they come up about the same time each year. Whatever else may have been going on in a very turbulent world outside the council chambers, the routine inside was an unrelenting grind of elections. Outside there may have been war and plague, inside there was the unending round of nominations and balloting. Elections, of course, had their own drama. At stake were careers, reputations, and family wealth. The outcomes could reward friends, humiliate enemies, recoup financial loss, administer snubs, send a rival to temporary oblivion, place an ally in an influential position, derail career aspirations, and so on. The Transactions of the Great Council (*Acta Consilii Maioris*) from 1440 to 1490 contain a very full record of these elections and other governmental business. The 7,000 ballots that I have been able to analyse may appear on the pages of the Transactions as routine business, but each outcome furthered or thwarted various plots and plans. Since many offices had several incumbents, staffing the hierarchy required the services of about 160 men annually. For reasons having to do with the ways in which records were kept, it is difficult to tell exactly what proportion of the patriciate might have been required to fill them. Over the entire half-century, it appears that about 270 men were eligible for office in an average year. Therefore about 60 per cent of the eligibles held office in any given year.

To be eligible one needed to be male, over 18 years of age (raised to 20 in 1455), the legitimate agnatic descendant of one of the thirty-three patrician 'houses' (*casata*, sing.), and, unusually for the area and period, the child of a patrician mother. The Ragusa patriciate was stable, closed, and endogamous. Therefore, if the structure of government appears very stable, so does the patrician élite who monopolized its offices. Ragusa's Foxes, like those of Venice, proved themselves adept at maintaining power (Pareto 1963: §2178). It appears that the same elements who dominated the polity in 1440 were also firmly in control fifty years later in 1490. Looking at the composition of the patriciate, it appears that there is no revolutionary movement between hierarchy and egalitarianism. In Paretian terms there was no circulation of the élite in fifteenth-century Ragusa. The same set of houses governed the state at the beginning of the period and at its end. Although some houses had died out, the patriciate remained closed and no new blood was allowed in.

Indeed, the period of stability appears much longer than this. In a study of the élite covering the fourteenth century as well as the fifteenth, Krekić (1986) has examined the concentration of power among the various patrician houses. Looking at the five highest offices in the government, he showed how these tend to be monopolized by members of a few houses. These also turn out, not coincidentally, to be the largest. Krekić reports that in the fifteenth century, one of these, the Goçe, held 12 per cent of the top offices. In contrast, another house, the Palmota, held only 2 per cent. It seems clear, therefore, as Krekić argues, that the Goçe held far more power and influence than the Palmota. Moreover, there is a remarkable consistency over the period of the two centuries. Amongst the top ten houses of the fifteenth century were seven houses that had also been amongst the top ten in the fourteenth century. Krekić does not elaborate upon the association between house size and the concentration of power, but it seems a reasonable implication of his analysis to suggest that the largest houses might have used their voting strength to elect their own members into high office. I shall refer to this possibility as the ruling houses thesis.

Remarkably, a very similar pattern is to be found among the Ragusan patriciate as late as the seventeenth century. Again looking at the highest offices for that period, Petrovich (1974) finds that they tend to be dominated by the largest houses.[1]

[1] He refers to them as 'clans' throughout and uses the Serbo-Croatian term *vlastela* in lieu of 'patrician' (Petrovich 1974: 514, 798).

Not only this, the powerful houses of the seventeenth century tend to be the same ones which dominated government in the fourteenth and fifteenth centuries. The Goçe were still the most prominent, followed by the Bona, Sorgo, Gondola, and so on (ibid.: 588–9). However, Petrovich adds to Krekić's analysis with an interesting observation. The large houses, he finds, hold the high offices roughly in proportion to their size. Examining the period from 1592 to 1667 decade-by-decade, he finds that there are considerable differences in the degree of under- or over-representation amongst the houses. These differences, however, tend to disappear when the period is examined as a whole. Thus, Petrovich shows that while the larger houses tend to hold more high offices than the smaller ones, they do not hold proportionally more. His findings, therefore, do not support the contention that large houses might have used their numerical strength to dominate the government. Indeed, Petrovich makes a different argument. He emphasizes Ragusa's political culture and points to the moral obligations of public service as well as the jural limitations on office-holding. Parenthetically, he does not explore the reasons why house representation waxed and waned through the three-quarters of a century that he studies. The analysis of such variation through the second half of the fifteenth century will be one of the central features of the present book.

Petrovich also suggests that there is no direct connection between the concentration of high office in a few houses and the number of marriages between these houses (ibid.: 631–9, 800). In fact in the seventeenth century there are surprisingly few marriages at all. Only about half of the patrician men married. This is related, he suggests, to the late age at marriage for men and very high dowries. On average Ragusan men of the seventeenth century did not marry until they were over 40 years old. High dowry costs, in turn, meant that many women remained unmarried and entered convents. In examining the marriage data and comparing the various houses with one another, Petrovich concludes that a ruling clique within the patriciate did not exist.

In the materials to be examined below, we will find, as Krekić did, that large houses tend to dominate the highest offices. And, like Petrovich, we will also see that the various houses hold offices in numbers that are roughly proportional to their voting strength. Therefore, we might also conclude that particular houses cannot be said to dominate government. In sum, the initial impression might be that there is no circulation of the élite or within it. A similar conclusion also seems to apply to political office and the structure of government. The government of 1440 consists of the same councils and offices as that of 1490. And, as just outlined, they seem to be dominated by the same kinds of people. This suggests a remarkable self-supporting egalitarian system with a marked continuity of culture. It might be suggested, therefore, that there is little evidence of historical process. But further analysis will suggest something quite different. There was a clique that dominated the government, there was circulation within the élite, and there were also changes in the structure of government.

Beneath the placid surface there was process aplenty. For one thing we will find that the numbers of politically active men increased dramatically through the latter half of the fifteenth century. Associated with this increase in numerical strength came significant changes in the age structure of the Great Council. These demographic changes hold significant implications for patterns of office-holding and for the distribution of power within various sections of the Great Council. For another thing, there were also changes taking place in the structure of government itself. There was, as Krekić's study of the concentration of power suggests, a hierarchy of offices and councils. But the analytical task of isolating a hierarchy will prove to be surprisingly difficult. Patricians of the period (and subsequent scholars) may have thought that there was a well-ordered hierarchy, but a close analysis will show that there were considerable areas of ambiguity. As we shall see, the reasons for this have to do with the passage of office-holders through various offices.

This leads to a re-examination of the notion of 'office'. In this respect this work presents a challenge to the ways in which anthropologists and historians regard office-holding and politics. Following the Weberian paradigm, offices have been understood within anthropology as positions which form a more-or-less orderly arrangement or structure. Prospective office-holders succeed to these positions and as incumbents acquire the authority to govern. As Goody has put it, 'offices are not simply a restricted category of roles; they are usually indivisible units within an "establishment", a table of organization' (1966: 1–2). In this study we draw attention to two assumptions behind such a view. First, the use of the terms 'establishment' and 'table of organization' suggests some kind of (uniform?) conceptual space in which offices are ordered *vis-à-vis* one another. This may be a locational space defined in terms of relative power or status. In this study we shall attempt to discover just what kind of space it is that Ragusan offices are arranged in. A second assumption in the conventional view of office is that such establishment units endure. Offices endure while persons—a succession of office-holders—move through them. In this study an alternative and complementary perspective is suggested. This rethinking has involved adding notions derived from space-time geography (Giddens 1984; Munn 1983, 1986) to more traditional 'West African' models of office (Fortes 1962; M. Smith 1974; Drucker-Brown 1989).[2] This requires a more processual understanding; it sees offices both as a product of those persons who pass through them as incumbents and, at the same time, it also views persons as being a product of those offices through which they move in their office-holding careers. This view treats the 'space' of office, not just in terms of locational co-ordinates defined by governmental functions or rights and duties, but also as a validational one for those who seek and hold office.

Finally, there is the lingering and curious problem of those large houses who

---

[2] I am indebted to Marilyn Strathern for a conversation about the 'oddness' of West African notions of office and their influence on anthropological thought.

numerically dominate in the lists of top office-holders yet who do not turn this to their own advantage. If they do not, it is not because of high-mindedness. Historians, like anthropologists, easily become advocates of those they study. The infatuation with a particular period, its people, and the place where they live can easily lead to blinkered partisanship. But if patricians could be civic-minded and selfless, they were not always so. Power could corrupt in Ragusa as elsewhere. Queller (1986) has shown that even serene Venice could not free itself of bribery, graft, backhanders, fiddling on expenses, embezzling public funds, influence peddling, and trafficking in state secrets. Sleaze in government is not a late twentieth-century invention. A muckraking inquiry has not yet been devoted to Ragusan politics, but even a casual stroll through the archival sources suggests that there was occasional scandal and corruption (Šundrica 1973).

If patricians were not always paragons of civic virtue, neither can the benign character of large houses be attributed to the effectiveness of legislation. The inability of large houses to flex their political muscle was not restricted to Ragusa. Chojnacki has noted that in Venice too the largest and wealthiest houses did not use their size to their advantage. The reason, he suggests, is that Venetian *casate* had no singular interest. Members found themselves split on both sides of most important issues (Chojnacki 1973: 67). There is similar evidence for Florence.[3] But if members of the same house occasionally found themselves on opposed sides, it seems unlikely that they would be split on the issue of supporting their agnates in their quest for office.

The right to hold office was no guarantee that any particular patrician would actually hold office. Eligibility was one thing, getting elected was another. Holders of offices in Renaissance city-states were elected through various systems of balloting. These electoral procedures were often very elaborate. The system in Venice for electing a new doge is probably the extreme example (see Finlay 1980b: 141–2). While ducal elections were particularly labyrinthine, selection procedures for other offices were also intricate. Even the nomination procedures were elaborate, but this did not stop abuses. More elaborate procedures were followed by ever more clever and brazen methods of circumventing them. Circumvention, in its turn, was followed by further legislation threatening draconian punishments. None of these had much effect (Queller 1986: 54–84). In Venice electioneering, influence peddling, vote buying, bribery, and other types of corruption went on unabated. What was at stake?

While the great bulk of the population of Florence, Venice, Ragusa, and similar states could not hold office and were thereby disenfranchised, they could attempt to influence those who enjoyed the franchise. The intricacy behind nomination and election procedures was intended to prevent or limit this. But the disenfranchised were only one source of danger. A more pressing one was factionalism. At stake was the unity of the dominant élite and, perhaps, the state itself. In Venice 'even

---

[3] See, for example, the very divided loyalties of the Soderini brothers discussed by Clarke (1991).

the faintest hint of political parties was not be tolerated' (ibid.: 76). Venice's special council for state security, the infamous 'Council of the Ten', had sweeping powers and it could act with terrible dispatch even against the most powerful. For example, within two days of hearing rumours of a conspiracy involving the doge, Marino Falier, the Council of the Ten had him beheaded on the spot where he had sworn his oath of office. They also hung the gibbeted bodies of his co-conspirators outside the Ducal Palace as a very public warning. The danger of sedition within the élite was thought to be so serious that, except for groups of close kinsmen or for wedding feasts, Venetian nobles could not hold dinner parties for fear of being involved in a conspiracy. Not even gatherings for a baptism were above suspicion.[4]

Complex electoral procedures were intended partly to prevent factionalism. They were also intended to prevent the concentration of power in only a few of the enfranchised. It was, of course, recognized that some of the élite would dominate political affairs. Venetians, for example, called such men the 'First' (*Primi*) (Finlay 1980b: 26). Varying combinations of ability, experience, influence, education, social standing, longevity, and wealth would bring such men to the top. Scrutinies, nominations, and elections were not intended to prevent this. Indeed, it was desired that men of ability should rise and exercise power. But they should not be able to pass on their influence to their offspring or be influenced by them. The exercise of power should not become dynastic. Venetians were sufficiently worried about dynastic influence for it to be an advantage for a ducal candidate to be *senza fioli* ('without sons') (ibid.: 134).

There is a paradox in this. In his discussion of the importance and rise of the city, Max Weber presents a close analysis of Venice's patriciate. His comments on Venice might also apply to Ragusa. He argued that the patrimonial tyranny of the urban patriciate required 'very strict mutual control of the noble families over each other' (1968: 1271). It also required a culture of solidarity whose benefits would be patently obvious to every patrician. Among these benefits were the huge monopoly profits that they might enjoy through their association. This solidarity of interests compelled the integration of the individual nobleman into the collective which exercised the tyranny (ibid.).

The collective interest should only operate at the level of the élite as a whole. It could not tolerate monopolistic interests within the various sections of the élite. In the case of Venice, Weber argued that internal monopolies were prevented by a series of administrative measures: (1) a competitive and overlapping separation of administrative powers, (2) a mutually controlling division of functions between officials, (3) short terms of office, and (4) a political court of inquisition charged with supervising both the political and personal conduct of the patricians (ibid.).[5]

---

[4] On the Falier conspiracy, see Lane (1973: 181–3). On dinner parties and baptisms, see Queller (1986: 77). The 'Council of the Ten' is discussed in Wurthmann (1989).

[5] A supervisory power over both the political and personal conduct of the patriciate did not appear in Ragusa until 1477 with the establishment of the *Proveditori de la terra* (Weber 1968: 1271–2).

The short terms of office, coupled with a desire to give as many persons as possible a chance to serve, enhanced solidarity within the patriciate. But, Weber argued, these devices also stifled the development of a truly professional officialdom (ibid.: 1272).

There is evidence of all four of these administrative techniques in Ragusa. Severally and in combination they undoubtedly made it very difficult for cabals within the patriciate to dominate the instruments of government, but this is somewhat different from Weber's argument that they helped 'compel the integration of the individual into the collective' and promoted a 'solidarity of interest'. There was some solidarity of interest in the Ragusan patriciate, but there were also considerable and bitter differences.

An ethos of civic service, multiplicity of interests amongst groups of agnates, and various administrative devices might make it more difficult for large *casate* to wring other advantages from their numerical superiority, but they are not the only reasons. There were others. We will point to one associated with the age structure of the *casata* itself. This, again somewhat paradoxically, concerns the Mediterranean Marriage System.

Anthropology in the Archives

Anthropology boasts a rich legacy of studies on politics and kinship. One more monograph, developing upon classic themes, should elicit little surprise if it dealt with Africa, Indonesia, or New Guinea. But such a study devoted to the late-medieval/early-Renaissance European city-state calls for further comment. For one thing, why should an anthropologist encroach upon the familiar ground of European history? This is a patch of intellectual territory that has been intensively cultivated by skilled and specialist historians. It is not immediately obvious what advantage would be found in an anthropological account. For another thing, such a study set in the second half of the fifteenth century would have to depend entirely upon archival sources. It could not be based upon intensive anthropological fieldwork and participant observation. What would be the possible advantage to an anthropological study of having to rely upon archival sources?

Archival materials on Ragusa/Dubrovnik are incredibly rich. As Fernand Braudel observed, 'they afford an opportunity to observe the extraordinarily well-preserved spectacle of a medieval town in action. For reasons of registration or through legal disputes an amazing collection of documents has survived' (1972–3: 1258–9). This is certainly true of Ragusa in the second half of the fifteenth century. Governmental records abound. The deliberations of the three governing councils are contained in three series: the *Acta Consilii Maioris*, *Acta Minoris Consilii*, and *Acta Consilii Rogatorum*. For this period the deliberations of the Major Council are found in ten manuscript volumes (Vols. 6–15), the Minor Council in seventeen (Vols. 8–24), and the Senate in twenty (Vols. 7–26); about 5,000 manuscript pages in total. There are separate series of volumes containing chancellery records, decrees, judicial records, and so on. The documentation concerning domestic and commercial affairs is, if anything, even more copious. Various contracts and agreements in the series *Diversa Cancellariæ* and *Diversa Notariæ* which Braudel alludes to exist in the tens of thousands. The volume of primary materials is staggering. All of the manuscript sources consulted for this study are contained in the Historijski arhiv u Dubrovniku (Historical Archives in Dubrovnik).

Like many local communities in which anthropologists live and conduct research, fifteenth-century Ragusa was relatively small. While it is difficult to gauge the precise size of the entire patrician class, a reasonable estimate of the number of men, women, and children at any particular moment would be about a thousand souls. In scale this is equivalent to a medium-sized village with a high density of interaction. Using the very rich source material, it is possible to know the names of almost everyone within the patriciate and a great deal more about most people.

In addition to the size of its population and wealth of source material about them, Ragusa and its patrician community hold another advantage. The day-to-day deliberations of the councils, outcomes of various votes, and the details of its governance are all available for scrutiny. This permits a study which would probably not be possible in a contemporary state, nor would it be practically feasible in the case of a larger historical one. Yet here in small compass is a complete state. It is the combination of these three features—the small size of the community, very rich documentation, and detailed records on the day-to-day operation of government—that make Ragusa an excellent subject for anthropological study.

The small size of Ragusa's patriciate, and the great volume of material about it, enable us to examine it whole. We can examine large houses and small, powerful houses and weak. Because this class was 'closed', both with respect to marriage and to the holding of office, it presents itself as a relatively self-contained universe for examining the relationship between kinship, marriage, and politics. This has both advantages and disadvantages. One disadvantage is that the degree of overlap might make it more difficult to discover the relationship between variables. But I suggest they could probably not be discerned at all if we were limited to a sample of houses, marriages, or office-holders. The total class perspective helps to obviate the very tricky problem of sampling. Or, as we shall see below, it removes it in some respects while introducing it in others. As a consequence of this total class perspective, this study must make use of very large quantities of data.

While these are important advantages, there are also disadvantages which may not be as familiar to anthropologists as they are to historians. For one thing the sheer magnitude of source material can be a handicap. Tens of thousands of manuscript pages are a treasure trove, but there is little way of knowing in advance of reading it whether any single page contains anything of interest. Amongst their other qualifications, historians also need good eyesight, well-upholstered bottoms and long periods of time for reading in the archives. Another disadvantage of archival work is that crucial volumes in a series of records are often missing: for example, in Ragusa the volumes of the *Pacta Matrimonialia* containing marriage settlements are lost for the period from 1464 to 1495. While some of the missing data can be reconstructed from other sources, the gaps present serious problems for analysis. Similar gaps occur in many of the other sources. In addition, certain types of information may be missing altogether. Family memoirs provide a most interesting example. About 500 of these *ricordanza* survive for Florence and the rich information these contain has provided materials for a number of studies (see, for example, Jones 1956; Philipps 1987; Klapisch-Zuber 1988b). None survive for Ragusa in our period. But in this respect it seems that it is Florence, not Ragusa, that is unusual. In Venice only one *ricordanza* is known to survive (Grubb 1994: 386).[6]

Nor, apparently, did Ragusans preserve diaries or personal correspondence. Again, to draw another comparison with Florence and Venice, there is nothing like the very revealing letters that Allesandra Strozzi wrote to her exiled sons about family matters and local affairs in Florence. Nor is there a Ragusan diarist such as the remarkable Venetian Marino Sanuto who compiled fifty-eight volumes of his personal diary—an astonishing forty thousand manuscript pages (Finlay 1980b: 10). For Ragusa of our period, there is not a single page of *ricordanza*, diary, or correspondence which survives.[7] It seems probable that some of these sources once existed, but they have since vanished. There are an enormous number of bits and pieces of evidence concerning the imponderabilia of everyday life in Ragusa that can be gleamed from wills, minutes of council meetings, legal disputes, and the like. While these can be assembled into a picture of daily life in the city-state, they still lack one vital ingredient. They are not presented through the integrated perspective of a native informant and they lack the distinctive colourings and shadings they would be given by a participant in that cultural world.

If Ragusa possesses a series of advantages which recommend it as a research site for historical anthropological enquiry, the choice of the period of study from 1440 to 1490 was made for a series of much more pragmatic reasons. Local historians in Dubrovnik advised me to concentrate on the mid-fifteenth century when I first began to study dowry records. They suggested that this period held some advantages for a novice in archival research. For one thing, in comparison to later periods, the manuscript hand of its notaries is quite legible and regular. Important 'charter' texts tend to be written in a style that palaeographers call Gothic Textualis while

---

[6] Grubb argues that Venetian noble families were memorialized on an aggregated basis in collective public documents. He suggests that they had no need for the atomistic, single-family private accounts of the Florentines (1994: 379–80). This issue will be returned to when we examine the issue of Florentine, Venetian, and Ragusan *casate* as 'lineages'.

[7] The archives contain two account books. One, by Jacobus de Gondola, deals largely with patricians and covers the period from 1457 to 1465. The other, probably wrongly attributed to Polo de Poça, contains accounts from about 1444 to 1460. Internal evidence suggests the latter book is in the hand of Jakob Matheus de Georgio (*Privata* 1, 2).

the great bulk of governmental documents are written in a more informal hand called Gothic cursive (Bischoff 1990). These styles would make the task of reading somewhat easier, especially for an anthropologist with no palaeographic training.[8] The qualifying 'somewhat' is important. While some notaries wrote in a neat hand, others—usually the ones that I needed to read—did not. Even the hands of the fastidious could degenerate into illegible scrawls towards the end of what must have been a frustrating and tedious day. The languages of the documents are Latin and Italian. Some, like the dotal bequests (*Carta Dotalis*) and wills (*Testamenta*), begin in Latin with standard legal formulas but then quickly retreat into vernacular Italian for the details. The documents also make extensive use of abbreviations and shorthand. While these add to the formidable difficulties in deciphering late-medieval manuscripts, there are published handbooks of abbreviations to assist in the process (Cappelli 1973; Pelzer 1966). In addition to these research aids, a dictionary of late-medieval Yugoslav Latin was also in the process of being published (Kostrenčić 1973). All of these would help to overcome some of the very considerable problems of a novice working with late-medieval manuscripts.

But there were further reasons for choosing a period beginning in 1440. There exists an excellent account of Ragusa written in the 1430s. Philippus de Diversis de Quartigianis de Lucca had been a grammar teacher in Ragusa. It was suggested to me that his 'Situs Ædificiorum, Politiæ et Laudabilium Consuetudinum Inclytæ Civitatis Ragusii' (1440/1880–82) would be a particularly valuable contemporary source.[9] But perhaps the most important reason for choosing this period was that it marks the terminus of Mahnken's genealogical research on the early Ragusan patriciate (1960). Her exhaustive and meticulous study represented a kind of *Who's Who* of the fourteenth-century patriciate. Although her study included some material from the late fifteenth century (and, in some cases, the early sixteenth), it was less detailed than for the period of the fourteenth. Since the second volume of her study contained the genealogies of the several patrician 'houses', it was pointed out that I would be able to both build upon her scholarship and extend it (see Appendices B and C). It was also suggested that my earlier anthropological field-work experience on kinship questions would be a bonus. Thus 1440 marks the beginning of the study period. The end is 1490.[10] Even though this account is based upon archival sources, I would like to insist that this is an anthropological study of an early-Renaissance/late-medieval society. This brings us to the final, and most significant, theme of this book.

---

[8] Here I gratefully acknowledge the advice and tutoring given to me in the archives by Zdravko Šundrica. In the early days of my research, he patiently coached me as I falteringly and tortuously read out for him line after line of text.

[9] See also Božić (1973, 1983).

[10] In the first stage of this enquiry, only the two decades from 1440 to 1459 were studied. This proved to be too narrow a time span. It proved inadequate, for example, to capture entire political careers. Therefore the window of observation was subsequently expanded.

Time and Process

In this account time is not a backdrop. It emerges as a crucial analytical element. In one sense it could not be otherwise. With an ethnographic present which stretches over half a century, the need to explicitly consider time and sequence becomes absolutely compelling.[11] This is not a novel suggestion. Rosaldo has pointed out how the extension of the ethnographic present caused his perception of the Ilongot 'to shift at its very foundations' (1980: 18). In his case the extension was from a period of months to the length of a person's lifetime. But it was not only his perception of the Ilongot which shifted, it also provoked a fundamental transformation in his view of the anthropological enterprise and its relationship to history. When Rosaldo wrote, the courtship between history and anthropology was still in its early stages. The relationship has since developed apace and generated an extensive literature charting its progress and problems. Today there are multiple connections between the various kinds of anthropology and the several types of history.

Yet it is fair to say that those who are attracted to the other discipline seem to be most fascinated by work whose subject matter and analytical perspective is similar to their own. It is not surprising, for example, that anthropologists should be attracted to Ginzburg's studies of witchcraft and agrarian cults or Le Roy Ladurie's analysis of affairs within a heretical peasant village (Ginzburg 1983, Le Roy Ladurie 1978). However, anthropologists have been much less interested in Le Roy Ladurie's studies of French grape harvests or his investigations into the heights of recruits to the French army (1979). When anthropologists look to the work of historians, it tends to be work which examines an 'ethnographic present' within a historical setting and where chronology is not a major element in the analysis. But this is paradoxical, for chronology is the defining characteristic of history.

As Cohn, one of the pioneer figures who has reintroduced history to anthropology, puts it, 'Chronology . . . is the basic methodological assumption which underlies the practice of all historians' (Cohn 1981: 228). It is a chronological ordering which provides 'the capacity to sort events, ideas, persons, and lives into before and after statements' (ibid.). Behind this crucial assumption lies another. It holds that time can be objectively measured and divided into units such as days or centuries. Things like events or persons are then assigned to particular units and on this basis are arranged into a 'before and after' sequence for study. Both assumptions are also crucial to the present analysis.

---

[11] Paradoxically, the selection of this particular period in the late fifteenth century for study is not especially significant. Were similar sources of information available, this book might equally (say) have focused on the period from 1600 to 1650. This is one respect in which this study differs from a historical one. Thus, while 'time' is of great significance to this analysis, it would be possible to argue that the notion of 'period' is not. This is, of course, an overstatement but it points up one reason why this is an anthropological account, not a historical one.

Within social anthropology, however, a different assumption is made. Following the radical distinction established by de Saussure between diachrony and synchrony, the ordering of events, persons, or similar things into a temporal sequence is not held to be significant. Indeed, the fundamental methodological assumption of anthropology is that ethnographic data exist in a relatively homogeneous, timeless analytical space—the 'ethnographic present'. In Lévi-Strauss's apt phrase, anthropological material requires a temporal dimension in which to unfold, but then this dimension is dispensed with. In this sense anthropological methodology becomes the instrument 'for the obliteration of time' (Lévi-Strauss 1966: 15).[12] But what, it might be asked, about anthropological studies of process? Do these not place sequence—before and after—into the foreground of analysis? The study of the so-called developmental cycle within domestic groups might be cited as one example. In the latter case the various forms of domestic group found in a society are said to be, to use Fortes's famous phrase, 'the crystallization, at a given time, of the developmental process' (1958: 3). This process, however, is cyclical (ibid.: 2) and the 'given time' refers to a particular period—generally conterminous with the ethnographic present. The passage of time within the ethnographic present, the sequencing of events, is not considered relevant. Moreover, since the process is thought to be cyclical, the period of time which occurred before the ethnographic present is not particularly relevant to the analysis except as a form of scene setting.

With respect to the notion of process, one must also refer to Leach's *Political Systems of Highland Burma* (1954). Leach's study has been the subject of extensive commentary. I refer to it here, not only because it shares the same empirical theme as the present study—the structural basis of political alignments, particularly those associated with ties of kinship and affinity—but also because of its explicit concern with two further issues which are central to the present work. These are issues, I suggest, which have not been explored by Leach's commentators.

The details of the Kachin ethnography are now part of anthropological folklore and need not be summarized here. Leach's argument, based upon the details of Kachin kinship and marriage, is highly original and sophisticated. But there are difficulties. The Comaroffs have discussed a number of these in their review of the relationships between history and social anthropology (1992: 22–7). Leach, however, points to two critical issues which the Comaroffs do not discuss. These are, to use Leach's terms, the problem of 'process in time' and the problem of 'adequate proof' (Leach 1954: 4).

In the case of the Kachin the problem of 'adequate proof' arises because 'the recorded facts . . . are so fragmentary as to be capable of almost any interpretation' (1954: 227). This statement, characteristic of Leach's throwaway manner, contains several problems. One implication is that 'more facts' are needed. Presumably if

---

[12] In this famous passage Lévi-Strauss is referring specifically to music and myth.

there were more, they would rule out some possible interpretations, leaving a residue of more plausible ones. Unfortunately, as Leach explains, sufficient historical material on political alliance in Highland Burma was not available to test his argument.

In their absence Leach does not examine the transition between *gumsa* and *gumlao*. No evidence about processes is adduced and such historical materials as exist are shown to be broadly consistent with the state of affairs within a *gumsa* order or a *gumlao* one. In place of an analysis of process, Leach instead invokes a psychology of resentment. This, like his utilitarianism, is one of the more irritating shortcomings of the analysis (Comaroff and Comaroff 1992: 23). In this respect his retreat into crude psychology has close parallels with Pareto's discussion of the circulation of 'lions' and 'foxes' to which he refers (Leach 1954: xi). These terms refer to the dynamics that Pareto perceived between elements in the governing class and the subject class, a dynamic associated with the willingness of each class to use violence to obtain its ends (Pareto 1963: §2178).

Today, the absence of archival materials or published sources from the past need not be such an obstacle. Studies do not necessarily depend upon pre-existing archival sources. They may, like Rosaldo's examination of Ilongot headhunting, use various imaginative techniques to generate their own set of records (1980). One difficulty, however, as Rosaldo points out in another connection, is that 'even the most brute of brute facts [is] . . . culturally mediated' (ibid.: 17). This truism has an interesting twist. The 'past' as narrated by informants is likely to be filtered through present-day understandings and preoccupations. But a second type of mediation is also at work, this one based upon the first. The techniques that the anthropologist devises to reconstruct source material about the 'past' are mediated by the understandings which the anthropologist has learned about the culturally mediated 'present'. The difficulty lies in the self-confirming nature of the techniques. Present-day understandings are used to devise techniques which then generate materials. Because the materials have no existence independent of the techniques which have generated them, they cannot disconfirm those understandings.

Ragusan archival sources are also 'mediated'. In this case they are mediated by the interests of those who had them written. But I would argue that materials like the Ragusan sources have a degree of independence which reconstructed materials do not. If archival sources such as minutes of council meetings or dowry bequests can be regarded as anthropological fieldnotes, those fieldnotes have been selected, but not created, by the anthropologist. They are thus different from reconstructed sources, but not necessarily superior to them because of that. Judgements about superiority would depend upon their use; on questions about their selectivity, about the thoroughness and sensitivity of interpretation, about the salience of the questions posed of the materials, and so on. Because of the independent quality of original archival source material (as opposed to reconstructed sources), there are other differences which follow from this.

Archival sources are public in a manner which fieldnotes generated through most anthropological fieldwork are not. Archival sources may be independently consulted by many different investigators. Because of this, the interpretation of the sources is open to debate. There is much more besides which might become the subject of debate such as their authenticity, translation, provenance, and so on. Moreover, the investigator has the obligation to document the source of particular pieces of information so that others may refer to the original. Fieldnotes, on the other hand, are often aids to memory. In matters of interpretation, their creator has the 'I was there' claim to authoritativeness as well as the power to limit access. Even if the anthropologist were to cite the date and source of particular items of information, this information cannot be independently assessed by later investigators. Archival sources confer no such rights of authoritativeness.

Archival sources are finite and limited even if, as in the case of Dubrovnik's historical archives, those limits are extraordinarily broad. They may thereby provide sufficient materials for dealing with the problem of 'adequate proof or disproof' if they are both rich and of sufficient chronological depth. Leach was later to publish a study of a village in Sri Lanka based upon fieldwork which contained copious amounts of material, enough he suggested to allow the reader to independently pose and test alternative interpretations (1971). Like the present study, Leach's Sri Lankan study made use of numerical summaries of data. Largely due to the pioneering work of the Manchester School, most contemporary anthropologists have come to appreciate the necessity of numerical summaries of data and their statistical treatment for certain types of enquiry.[13]

It is necessary to add that Ragusa in the fifteenth century was, as the records make clear, the centre of a highly 'numerate' merchant culture. One of its sons, Benedetto Cotrugli, the Ragusan consul to Naples, was the author of the influential *Della mercatura et del mercante perfetto* (1573), completed in 1458. His *Perfect Merchant* was a comprehensive guide to business practice, including a very clear explanation of double-entry bookkeeping.[14] Enumerating, counting, and accounting were cornerstones of a merchant's life. Students in schools studied *leggere, scrivere, et abbaco*, where 'abbaco meant solving practical mathematical problems on paper' (Grendler 1989: 308). This involved using arithmetic (including decimals), algebra, and geometry to help solve business-related problems (ibid.) And, when that merchant élite entered the council chambers of government, attention turned to the counting and tabulating of ballots. It was an age of a highly 'numerate mentality' (Burke 1987: 119).

The Dubrovnik archives make it possible to examine the relationship between

---

[13] In this respect I am puzzled by the Comaroffs' advocacy of an 'antistatistical and anti-aggregative' anthropology (1992: 20). Leach, of course, was neither anti-statistical nor anti-aggregative (Leach 1971; see also Fuller and Parry 1989: 12).

[14] Stuard makes the important point that Cotrugli's book is much more than a practical manual of business. It also includes important chapters on the morality of business and the foundations of a well-ordered life in the family (Stuard 1992: 209–12).

success in obtaining office and the (kinship) basis of support in very great detail indeed. It would be extremely difficult to accumulate this volume of material in the normal course of a traditional anthropological field research project. Furthermore, the same archival sources may be returned to time and again whereas one can never return to the same anthropological fieldsite (or home). Moreover, as research interests change and develop, the archival researcher may broaden, or contract, the window of observation over subsequent visits.

This leads to the second and more important issue that links Leach's analysis of the Kachin with this study of Ragusan élite politics. This is the problem that Leach raises in *Political Systems of Highland Burma* (1954) concerning history. He asserts that an adequate assessment of his theory would not only require sufficient 'facts', but historical facts. Why historical facts? Leach's answer is clear. It is because 'any theory about social change is necessarily a theory about historical process' (ibid.: 227).

In the following analysis of Dubrovnik's patriciate, we have the advantage of a great plenitude of 'facts', most of which can be dated. This permits us to arrange them into a before-and-after sequence. And this, in turn, creates a multitude of analytical possibilities. In the simplest case, we can treat the entire half-century as a single 'ethnographic present' and begin a first-order analysis of structures of kinship, marriage, and politics. From this we can then proceed to a second-order analysis by treating various sub-periods within the half-century as a succession of 'ethnography presents' in order to see how similar structures, and relationships between structures, may alter over time. In this respect, as Rosaldo has suggested, structural summations are treated 'an an analytical starting point, rather than as an encapsulating conclusion' (1980: 20). These sub-periods may then be further subdivided or aggregated in order to explore particular connections. Finally, particular processes can be examined over time to assess their effects. This may suggest the isolation of other limited periods for special examination. These, in turn, may reveal other processes, and so on. The lengthy period of study, therefore, permits a variety of windows of observation to be opened to examine the interplay between structure and process. But it is only by having a sufficient 'number of facts'—to adopt Leach's rather unfortunate terms—that we will be in a position to test (adequately 'prove or disprove') the possibility of various relationships between them. 'In the last analysis, it is by humbly inspecting the most minute particulars that the route to the universal is kept open' (Dumont 1970: 3). However, it is important to emphasize that this is an approach to analysis, a type of meta-methodology. It is not a 'theory about social change' or even less 'a theory about historical process' (Leach 1954: 227). As a 'theory' it only amounts, to use Elton's apt phrase, to 'one damn thing after another' (1967: 40).

2

Ragusa: Trade and Territory

Location

Dubrovnik lies on the eastern coast of the Adriatic Sea at nearly the same latitude as Barcelona and Rome (Carter 1972: 9). The old city lying within its encircling walls is so small and jewel-like that it is difficult to grasp its importance in the Mediterranean world of the fifteenth century. Whether one regards Dubrovnik as part of the Mediterranean world or as part of the Balkans depends on whether one stands atop its Minčeta Tower and looks upward and inland towards Mount Srđ and the unending white wall of mountains, as Braudel refers to them, which separate the coastline from the Balkan interior, or turns around and looks at the flat horizon of the Adriatic Sea (1972–3: 125). Perched on its rocky promontory jutting out into the sea, Dubrovnik does not seem to belong to either world. Mount Srđ, which dominates the city from a height of 412 metres, is part of the chain of Dinaric Alps which runs the entire length of the Dalmatian side of the Adriatic coast. The mountains rise sharply from the water's edge all along the considerable length of the coast. Their ridges run parallel to the coast like a series of knife-blades. As one looks inland, the successive ridges of mountains, each higher and more forbidding than the last, extend into the Balkan interior as far as the eye can see. The new-fold limestone mountains are both hard and resistant to erosion, yet they are also very porous. Water dissolves the limestone and percolates down into enormous underground drainage systems. Heavy seasonal rainfall disappears quickly. While there are occasional narrow fertile valleys beyond the ridges, much of the terrain is stark, extremely rugged, and covered by dry scrub with sharp ribs of limestone protruding everywhere. Therefore, not only is access to the hinterland difficult, but the hinterland itself is hard and uninviting.

In only five places along this entire coastline is the wall of mountains breached. Dubrovnik/Ragusa is very close to one of these access points into the interior. This route into the interior winds its way past Mount Srđ up to the Brgat Pass, which is located almost due east of the city, and then travels down towards the Popovo valley, the town of Trebinje, and the interior beyond. Ragusa was also only a short journey away from a second access point. This second route begins at the mouth of the Neretva River further up the coast to the north and west. The Neretva provides entrée into Bosnia and Serbia. Therefore, one of Ragusa's advantages was its location in relation to two of the five major routes into the relatively inaccessible Balkan interior.[1]

A second advantage concerns Ragusa's position at the end of the long string of islands on the Dalmatian side of the Adriatic Coast. As the crow flies, it is over 500 km. (305 miles) from Umag on the Istrian Peninsula in the north through the coastal islands to Ragusa. These islands are extensions of the Dinaric Alps and offer protection to shipping from the ravages of sudden and capricious storms. By contrast the Italian coastline on the opposite side of the Adriatic is relatively featureless and has few natural harbours or places of safe anchorage. The *bura*, cold north-easterly winds blowing seaward from inland, aid sailing towards the Mediterranean but are particularly dangerous along the Italian coast. In Ragusa, on the other hand, in addition to its seafaring advantages the *bura* is associated with health and well-being. Diversis, for example, claimed that the *bura* rid the city of plague in April 1433 (1880: 17). Contrasting warm, wet winds from the south, known locally as *jugo* (*Scirocco* in Italian), bring high waves and rainy squalls (Vidović 1984: s.v. 'jugo'). These winds can be dangerous for sailors and are locally associated with illness and death. These two winds divide the Adriatic into two areas. If one draws a line across the Adriatic running from the north-west towards the south-east, the part along the Dalmatian coast is called the *sopra vento*, above the wind. The part on the Italian coastline is called *sotto vento*, under the wind (Tadić 1968: 8). In addition to the *bura* and *jugo*, there is also a third wind, the *maestral*. This is a mild north-westerly of the summer months which aids shipping moving up the Dalmatian coastline or crossing the Adriatic. Although the temperature in the summer months can be unpleasantly hot, this is moderated in the daytime by the relatively cool winds blowing inland from seaward. The evenings in turn are made pleasant by cooler masses of air descending back towards the sea from the mountains. These summer breezes also free the city from swarms of insect pests. The prevailing sea currents also assist shipping moving up the Dalmatian side of the Adriatic. The direction of flow is counter-clockwise, from east to west. Thus, the currents flow from Ragusa up towards Venice and thence back down along the Italian side of the Adriatic.

Because of these advantages, and the hazards to shipping along the Italian coastline, most shipping of the period moving from Venice through the Adriatic to the Mediterranean chose to ply the Dalmatian side of the Adriatic. Beginning in Venice and after making an open run across the Gulf of Venice, boats would then have a lengthy and secure island-hopping journey down the Dalmatian coast. Ragusa was often the last protected point along the chain of islands before vessels had to venture into open seas on their way to distant ports. The small city harbour was made more secure during our period when St Luke's Tower was reinforced and a massive curtain wall and breakwater built. The harbour contained a small arsenal

---

[1] The other three begin on the coast at Split, Kotor, and the mouth of the Bojana (see Carter 1972: 136–42).

with a covered shipyard and three berths for the state's men-of-war. Because of the harbour's small size, the nearby area of Gruž was developed to expand harbour and shipbuilding facilities. Ragusa therefore was advantageously situated with respect to both sea and overland trade.

Trade

Ragusa's significance in this period can be gauged by its role in the spice trade. At the peak of that trade, when between one-and-a-half and two million English pounds of pepper were being imported annually into Europe, European merchants maintained five permanent trading houses (*fondachi*) in Alexandria. The Venetians maintained two. The French and Genoese had one apiece. The Ragusans also had one. Furthermore, Ragusa was one of the three major trans-shipment ports (*scalas*) leading into Italy and Germany, Messina and Venice being the other two (Lane 1940: 587). This comparability with France, Genoa, and Venice is difficult to grasp. Ragusa was a small city with only a small population. At the time it only had a twentieth of the population of Venice and a fraction of that of Genoa (Mols 1974: 22 and 42). Yet this small city was a major commercial centre and it played a vital role in the geopolitics of the region. Its patrician élite were not only active in managing its economy and in determining its trading policy, but were also legislating and implementing the nimble diplomacy which Ragusa maintained between Christian West and Ottoman East.

Caravans under control of Ragusan traders ventured into the interior carrying fabrics, salt, wine, honey, oils, spices, and manufactured goods. By the middle of the fifteenth century, textile production had grown to become one of the most successful economic activities. In the 1440s local production is estimated to have reached 4,000 'pieces' annually.[2] This new industry, which had been heavily financed by Florentine capital, had attracted a variety of Italian and Spanish merchants and importers to the city.[3] Ragusan merchants are known to have travelled as far afield as England. Their first recorded sailing to England was in 1443 to buy woollen cloth. Exports in textiles found a booming market in the Balkan hinterland. Indeed, the lucrative trade in Ragusan cloth prompted Venice to enact a series of protectionist measures to safeguard her own textile industry.[4] Both states took a very active interest in both cloth production and trade. In Ragusa the dyeshops were once in both state and private hands, but as the industry became

[2] The estimate comes from *Enciklopedija Jugoslavija* 3: 139; cited in Carter (1971a: 12). 1 *peca* (*pezza*, in Italian) = 3.2–3.8 metres (Elder 1934).
[3] On the role of Florentine merchants and capital in Ragusa, see Krekić (1976, 1978); on their role in Venice, see Goldthwaite (1980: 38). On Ragusan cloth production and the textile trade, see Krekić (1976), Roller (1951: 5–91), Carter (1971a), and Dinić-Knežević (1982). On relations between Ragusa and Aragon, see Spremić (1971); between Ragusa and Puglia, see Popović-Radenković (1957–8); on merchants from Prato in Ragusa, see Popović (1959).
[4] On Ragusan merchants in England and Venetian protectionism, see Carter (1971b).

more important, dyeing became a state monopoly, and the state enacted a series of measures to control and protect its domestic industry.

The production of salt was also a state monopoly. Large salt pans were located at Ston, Gruž, Zaton, Šipan, and Mljet. It was also imported from other sources in the Mediterranean, especially Corfu (Gelčić 1955). The official and unofficial trade in wine was also very important. Each year five officers were elected by the Great Council to try to stamp out the trade in contraband wine.[5] Four armed vessels tried to intercept this illicit trade. The Great Council elected the captains of the armed vessels and the Small Council decided where they were to go. In 1485, for example, the Small Council sent two young men in their twenties out on patrol: Marinus Marco de Lucari (ID 1305) was to patrol below Trsteno while Savinus Nicola de Babalio (ID 2451) was sent to Cavtat.[6]

Returning caravan trade from the Balkan interior brought meat, hides, fur, wax, fat, cheese, ores, and precious metals. Since wagons or teams of oxen could not traverse the rugged and treacherous tracks, caravans consisted of pack-horses. The smallest viable caravan contained two horses, each carrying a load of about 140 *oka* (180 kg.). Large caravans might have up to one hundred horses, but most had twenty-five horses or less. The journey from Ragusa to Niš took about fifteen days in good weather. Niš was an important link on the great road between Belgrade and Istanbul, which was a further fifteen days' journey beyond. The peak of the caravan traffic was in late autumn. In winter the passes were blocked by snow. At other times good pack-horses were in short supply, especially during spring sowing and summer harvest when their peasant drovers were required on the land. There were particular shortages from June to July and from September to October. In addition to the caravan trade Ragusan merchants also invested in large herds of cattle. These were herded in the mountains on behalf of their owners by Vlach shepherds. After being fattened in summer pastures on the upper reaches of the River Drina, they were driven down in the autumn to the city, from where the live animals, meat, and animal products were shipped across the Adriatic to Italian markets aboard Ragusan vessels (Petrovich 1974: 342n.).[7]

Of the minerals lead and copper were very important, but they were overshadowed by the trade in silver. At various commercial and mining centres, Ragusa maintained merchant colonies of her traders. One of the most important was at the mining settlement at Srebrenica. It was administered by patricians and consisted of merchants and other tradesmen as well as miners and goldsmiths. Since Ragusans served as contractors, financiers, and customs officials as well as the

[5] These were the *Officialis contrabanoris vini*. On the elections of the *Contrabanoris vini*, see *Acta Consilii Maioris* 15: fo. 59v (hereafter *Act. Maior.*). For the election of the captains: ibid. and *Acta Minoris Consilii* 22: fo. 4v (hereafter *Act. Minor.*).
[6] Hereafter the names of persons will be followed by an identification number. These numbers refer to Appendix C and they help to distinguish between several people who may have the same name.
[7] With good weather and favourable winds a boat could cross the Adriatic in about twenty-four hours (Carter 1972: 149). Large, especially made Ragusan vessels of close to 1,600 tons carried animals across the sea to Italy (Petrovich 1974: 346n.).

owners of mines, their influence was pervasive.[8] They even managed to impose their own currency as the major medium of exchange. When the Serbian mining centre at Novo Brdo fell to the Turks in 1466–7, it had a population of about 40,000 (Carter 1972: 234). This was about eight times the size of Ragusa itself and comparable to the population of the entire city-state with all of its outlying villages and towns. The inhabitants of these mining settlements were often known as 'Saxons', a term descriptive of those who had originally been granted mining rights, but which later was extended to all the inhabitants of autonomous mining settlements (Ćirković 1987: 161n.).

These mining centres were vast, and so was their significance to the geo-economy of Europe. At their peaks the mine at Novo Brdo in Serbia produced about 9 tons per annum while the Bosnia mine at Srebrenica produced about 5–6 tons. In contrast, it has been estimated that in the middle of the fifteenth century no other major European mine produced more than 2.80 tons per annum.[9] Most of the Balkan silver produced in Ragusan-controlled mines was carried by Ragusan caravans to the port before being shipped abroad on Ragusan vessels. Silver was made into jewellery and tableware as well as coins.

As the Ottoman Turks consolidated their control over the Balkan interior, the Ragusan authorities became increasingly concerned about maintaining the state's privileged trading position. In 1458 two patrician envoys, Paladino Givcho de Gondola (ID 1216) and Paladinus Petrus de Lucari (ID 1314), were sent to negotiate with a representative of the Sublime Porte. An agreement was struck in Skopje with Mahmud Pasha Andjelović, the Beylerbey of Rumelia, representing Sultan Mohammed II. In return for a tribute of 1,500 ducats, Ragusa was allowed autonomy within the Ottoman Empire. This proved to be a masterstroke of good fortune. It guaranteed safe conduct for Ragusan merchants throughout the consolidated Turkish lands. Prior to conquest these had been a patchwork of various political units, often warring amongst themselves and always extorting whatever the traffic would bear. Under Ottoman rule all the principal markets were unified and all dues abolished. As Biegman emphasizes, Ragusa had 'an especially favoured position in that the customs duties it paid were the lowest existent within the Empire' (Biegman 1967: 27). When the Turks closed the Black Sea to Venice and Genoa in the fifteenth century, Ragusa was the only Christian nation allowed to maintain commerce with Moldavia and Tartary.

Within the Balkan interior, each wealthy Ragusan colony could boast of its own church and consul. There was an extensive network of such colonies, each with its own administrative system headed by a *knez* (or 'prince'). By the 1460s there were close to thirty such colonies in the Balkan hinterland. Their number and position waxed and waned over time depending upon trading conditions. In Turkish lands

---

[8] For an account of the entrepreneurs Jacomo (ID 565) and Nicolinus de Zrieva (ID 569) (Jakov and Nikolin Crijević), in a company concerned with commerce and mining in the Balkan interior between 1452 and 1457, see Krekić (1964).

[9] These figures are from Krekić (1979: 250–1), quoting from studies by Ćirković and Nef.

colonies were established in Sarajevo, Novi Pazar, Prokuplje, Skopje, Travnik, Mostar, and Belgrade (Hrabak 1952).[10] Such colonies were important, relatively self-contained outposts of Ragusan interests. They provided a home-away-from-home for Ragusan merchants. Within the colony transactions were governed by Ragusan law and negotiated in Ragusan currency. These colonies not only served as a temporary home and conduit of commerce, but they also fed back valuable information to the centre at Ragusa about local crops, market conditions, customs and tariffs, political conditions on the ground, troop movements, local disturbances, and the latest diplomatic manœuvres and intrigue.

Similar colonies were also found overseas. On the Italian side of the Adriatic, there were colonies with consuls in Ancona, Bari, Barletta, Crotone, Otranto, and Venice. Other colonies were found at Alexandria, Catánia, Iraklion, Istanbul, Siracusa, and Thessaloniki. Ragusa maintained colonies as far east as Akkerman and Silistria (Petrovich 1974: 394; Mitić 1973). The latter were reached by the *extra Culfum* sea route which passed south from Ragusa along the Albanian coast to Corfu where it split into two further routes. One of these went to Sicily and Western Italy, the other went around the Peloponnesus to Crete. The second route then split again into two further routes: one went northwards into the Aegean and thence to the Black Sea, the second continued east to the Levant or headed south to Alexandria. Northwards from Ragusa, the *intra Culfum* passed through the Korčula channel and then followed the Dalmatian Islands towards Venice. While this island route gave some protection from the vicious winds, the same islands and inlets harboured pirates which were a plague to shipping at various times. Venice suppressed the pirate centre at Omiš in 1444, but later the Uskoks, Christian refugees from Turkish lands, continued to harass shipping and caravan traffic alike.

Ragusa's maritime prosperity did not depend solely on the transport of cargo, but on all aspects of shipping. Ragusa's shipyards produced vessels, and her villages and towns provided ship's masters and crews.[11] Some vessels, particularly those taking the northern route up the *intra Culfum*, were small, but the city also produced larger ships of 70–90 *kola* capacity. (A *kola*, a measure of ship tonnage, is equal in volume to about 2,000 litres of wheat.[12]) Profits from shipping were large and both patricians and commoners, sometimes jointly, owned vessels. Both were also involved in maritime insurance. Funds invested in a vessel were repaid in about a year's time from the profits.

The state received customs duties on merchandise imported from Turkey and

---

[10] Cited in Tadić (1955: 242).

[11] While detailed studies of shipping for the period 1440–90 are not available, some estimates of the importance of shipping can be gained from the next century when Ragusa boasted about 180 ships, 200–250 ship's masters, 5,000 seamen, and a merchant marine worth 675,000 ducats. R. Davis has pointed out that Ragusa's merchant fleet at the time outranked England's (1962: 2, as quoted in Carter 1972: 312). Cf. Tadić (1948, 1958).

[12] One *kola* is equivalent to about one-and-a-half tons in deadweight tonnage as used in shipping. A *kola* (Serbo-Croatian)/*carro* (Italian) equalled 19 Venetian *star*. A *star* is equal to 98.4 litres. On the problem of estimating cargo capacity and weights in the late medieval period, see Lane (1964).

exported to it. There was also a caravan duty imposed at a rate of 1 per cent of the value of each caravan Finally, there was a duty on merchandise transported aboard Ragusan ships. The state received further income through its salt and wine monopolies. Indeed, the volume of trade through Ragusa was so great and the income from customs so profitable that the city had little need to tax its inhabitants on their incomes. As a result Ragusa lacks a series of regular tax documents, such as the famous Florentine *catasto*, which might be used to estimate personal wealth.[13] Patrician wealth, indeed the wealth of the entire city-state, depended largely upon trade. The size of the Ragusan territory was quite small and the land did not produce enough to provision even its small population. Although many patricians owned estates outside the city walls, sold wine from their vineyards, and collected taxes from the headmen of their villages, the major source of patrician wealth came from commerce. Overland and maritime commerce were high risk/high profit activities for individual patricians. Over time they generated huge private fortunes. At the level of the state, tariffs on this trade plus income from state monopolies swelled the government's coffers. Therefore as a class the patricians used the lever of their monopolistic position to gain multiple benefits. They benefited, first, from their own holdings and enterprises. Next they benefited from having exclusive access to the profits from state-run monopolies. Finally, and certainly not least, they benefited from being able to determine and manage the terms of trade.

Territory

With the incorporation of Konavli (*Canal*) in the early part of the century, the city-state had reached the territorial limits it was to maintain until the republic ended in 1808. On the mainland this territory extended from the tip of Pelješac Peninsula (*Puncta Stagni*) in the north to the end of the Konavli plain in the south, a distance of about 135 km. The coastal areas, both north and south of Ragusan territory, were in the hands of the Venetians. Although the Pelješac Peninsula is mountainous, its 355 sq. km. also includes some very fertile land. Once the lands of the Pelješac were firmly in the hands of the Ragusans, they were partitioned among its citizenry. Three-quarters were granted to the patricians and the remaining quarter to other townsfolk (Carter 1972: 124). The Pelješac Peninsula is joined to the mainland by an isthmus with two massively fortified towns: Ston (*Stagno*) looks south-east towards Dubrovnik through the Koločep channel while Mali Ston (*Quel mare*), on the other side of the isthmus, faces north-west up the Neretva channel. High curtain walls with towers join the two. There are large salt pans at Ston. Mali Ston had a small arsenal with covered berths for three ships. At the very opposite end of the territory is the fertile plain of Konavli, acquired from

---

[13] On the Florentine *catasto*, see Herlihy and Klapisch-Zuber (1985).

neighbouring lords in the first part of the fifteenth century. The plain is about 22 km. long but only 2.5 km. wide. The eastern portion of the plain had been acquired in 1419 from Duke Sandalj Hranić and the western portion in 1426/27 from Radoslav Pavlović (Fine 1987: 486). Between these two extremes lay the heart of the republic: the narrow strip of coastline with the city of Ragusa almost in the middle.

Therefore, travelling from north to south through Ragusa's major settlements, one would enter Ragusan territory at the fortified settlement of Orebić (*Tersteníça*), on the western coast of the Pelješac Peninsula where the strait separating it from the island of Korčula is narrowest. Through this strait flowed most of the naval traffic plying the Dalmatian side of the Adriatic. Venetian fortifications at Korčula commanded one side, Ragusa dominated the other through Orebić. Further south at the neck of land linking the Pelješac Peninsula with the mainland are the towns of Ston and Mali Ston. Further along the coast on the mainland are the towns of Slano and Zaton (*Malfum*) with their harbours. From there the land route becomes very circuitous because of the detours around Zaton's inlet and the very large fiord-like Ombla Inlet (*Rijeka Ombla*). After these detours one reaches the harbour at Gruž (*Gravosa*) and the environs of Ragusa. By small boat the journey from Zaton to Gruž takes only a few minutes. Gruž was soon to become the site of the summer palaces of some of the city's notables as well as a major shipbuilding and harbour facility. After Gruž it is only a short journey across the neck of the Lapad Peninsula before one reaches the walled city itself.

Moving south past the city, limestone hills rise sharply, making overland travel difficult until one reaches Pelegrin Point. The town of Cavtat (*Civitas vetera*) is the next major settlement, with the Konavli basin beyond. Thus the city-state of Ragusa stretched from the tip of the Pelješac Peninsula to the foot of the Konavli basin. Yet none of this territory extends more than a few kilometres inland from the coast.

Offshore the state controlled a number of islands. Of the larger inhabited islands Lastovo (*Lagosta*) (53 sq. km.) was the furthest offshore and the most distant from the city. Mljet (*Meleda*) (98 sq. km.), the next furthest, lies off the Pelješac Peninsula. The next three, Šipan (*Juppana*, 16 sq. km.), Lopud (*Dalafota*, 5 sq. km.), and Koločep (*Calamota*, 2 sq. km.) run parallel to the coast. The small island of Lokrum (*Lacroma*, 0.8 sq. km.) lies just off the walled city itself.

The city, roughly pentagonal in shape, is entirely enclosed with walls. The encircling main wall is 1,940 metres in length and up to 25 metres in height. Towards the land side it is 4–6 metres thick and 1.5–3 metres thick towards the sea. These walls were completed by the end of the thirteenth century. In the fourteenth century fifteen towers were added, a bulwark was constructed, and the city moat was excavated. When Constantinople fell to the Ottoman Turks in 1453, an alarmed city began a hasty and massive fortification programme. An interior wall 22 metres in height and 4 metres thick was built from the Ploče Gate to the Minčeta Tower in less than two-and-a-half years. The Minčeta Tower, which

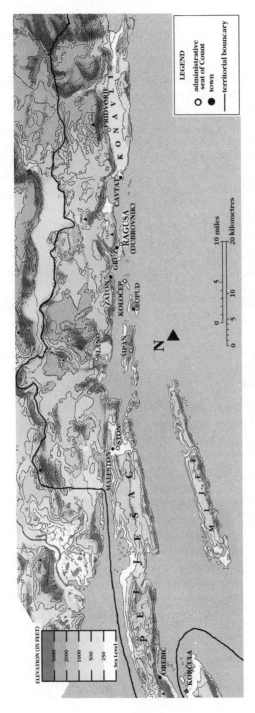

MAP 1. The Ragusan State: territorial boundaries *c.*1450. (The remote island of Lastovo is not shown.)

dominates the city, was rebuilt in its present form, construction began on the Bokar fortress outside the Pile Gate, towers along the city walls were strengthened, the walls of the Lovrjenac fortress outside the city and overlooking the small harbour were doubled towards the west and north, and the Revelin fortress was begun outside the eastern portion of the city to protect its eastern land flank. All of this was an enormous and hugely expensive undertaking (Beritić 1978).[14]

The city is bisected by the *Placa* (or *Stradun*), its main thoroughfare, which runs 292 metres from the Pile Gate and the Franciscan Church Monastery at the city's western entrance to the clock tower at the harbour end. The stone paving of the *Placa* was first laid in 1468 and follows the line of the city's main sewer. Although much of the city was reconstructed after the great earthquake of 1667, a number of today's houses lining the *Placa* retain features of the fifteenth century. The old city's political centre, however, was located on a street running at a right angle to the *Placa* near the harbour. Next to the clock tower was the Great Arsenal and a building which housed the chambers of the Great Council (destroyed by fire in 1817). Beyond them is the Rector's Palace. The original building was destroyed by a gunpowder explosion in 1435. The arcaded portico which one can see today was reconstructed in 1463 after a second explosion.

The city was divided into six districts (*sexteria*). Pusterna (*Pustijerna*) was the oldest of the six. It occupied the area which extends from the fort of St John (*Sv. Ivan*) to the Cathedral and thence to the sea wall. St Peter and Castellum made up the other two districts of the original section. The remaining three districts of St Blasius, St Maria, and St Nicolas were added in the latter part of the thirteenth century. Five of these six *sexteria* are on the south side of the *Placa*. The *sexteria* of St Nicolas occupies all of the area inside the walls lying north of the Placa (Krekić 1972: 63–9).

It is very difficult to estimate Ragusa's population in this period. Partial censuses of Konavli were undertaken in 1429 and 1463 and there was a listing of houses within Ragusa's walls made in 1481. A cursory analysis of this last *Cathasthicum* suggests that 81 of the 508 houses within the city were patrician homes (*Cathasthicum* 3: 'Case del Comune de Ragusi e terreni e affitti 1481'). Patrician households were scattered in all sections of the city and the households of agnates are not clustered in particular streets or even in particular neighbourhoods. In addition to their city residences, a number of patricians also had summer villas with gardens in other locales such as the one that the Goçe built at Trsteno (Grujić 1977: 44). Many city households were joint-family units containing married brothers or fathers with married sons. Similarly, many single dwellings were subdivided so as to provide lodgings for multiple families. Yet even if we assume that each dwelling within the city walls held about ten persons, the patrician population would only be about 800 and the total urban population would be

---

[14] Lovrjenac Fortress carries the inscription: 'non bene pro tot libertas venditure auro' ('Liberty is not for sale for all of the gold in the world').

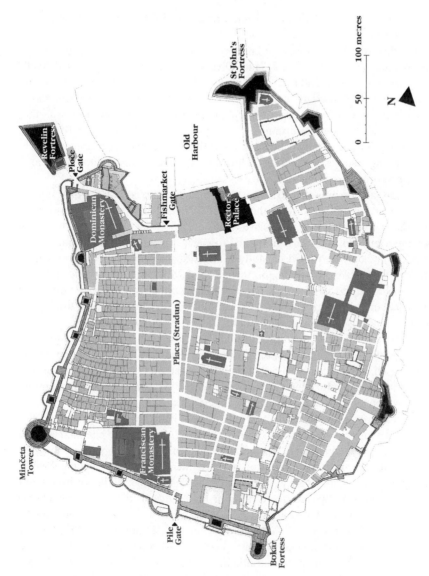

MAP 2. The walled city of Dubrovnik (Ragusa) today

about 5,000. The population of all Ragusan territories has been estimated to be about 40,000.[15]

Even this small population could not provision itself. The narrow strip of coast-line does not contain much arable land. Diversis stated that the city needed 70,000 *star* of wheat each year and local grain reserves lasted only four months (1881: 30). Since the nearby hinterland contained neither arable land nor convenient routes for the transport of bulky grains, cereal grains had to be imported by sea. This grain came a considerable distance from regions in Asia Minor, the Black Sea, Greece, and Southern Italy. Thus, trade and the maintenance of trading networks with outlying colonies was not just a lucrative sideline, it was absolutely essential in order to provision the population.

This population was divided into two broad categories with further subcat-egories. Starting at the bottom, the most disadvantaged section of non-citizens were slaves. While the traffic in slaves from neighbouring Slavic lands had been prohibited in 1416, Ragusans continued to engage in the slave trade and to own slaves throughout the period of study.[16] The vast majority of non-citizens were peasants. Some, like those living on the island of Mljet, held their own lands and were subject only to certain taxes. Most of the peasants, however, were unfree and owned labour obligations to their patrician lords. They endured 'hard work, poor pleasures, and the scrimmage of appetite'.[17]

The category of citizens (*cives civitatis Ragusii*) also contained subdivisions. The *cives de populo* (henceforth *populo*) constituted the bulk of the population within the city itself. The *populo* consisted of merchants, artisans, tradesmen, seamen, and other occupations. Outsiders who resided in the city on government contract and who were employed as chancellery officials, teachers, physicians, armourers, and the like were also included among the *populo*. Patricians, of course, were also citizens. All citizens were subject to the same set of domestic, commercial, and criminal laws. No distinction was drawn between *populo* and patrician in this respect. Neither did the differences between them necessarily include wealth. Some *populo* merchants were extremely wealthy, comparable to the wealthiest and most powerful of the patricians. Writing in 1440, Diversis divides the merchants into three categories. The poorest ('*perlabuchii*') deal in hens, eggs, and similar items. A middle group ('*comardarii*') trade in cheese and meat. The highest ('*supremi*') sell precious metals, textiles, spices, and other luxury goods. Patricians, he notes, also trade in luxury goods although some among them are poor and draw their living from rents.[18] But, however poor, the patricians could not engage in certain aspects of trade and commerce. They were prohibited by law, for example,

---

[15] Another means of estimating the patrician population is from the number of Great Council members. Assuming an equal number of adult males (council members) and females, and assuming that the under-age population equals the adult, the total number of patricians would be about 1,100 (cf. Krekić 1972: 33).

[16] *Liber Viridis*: Cap. 162 (hereafter *Lib. Vir.*); cf. Krekić (1972) and Stuard (1983).

[17] The phrase is Paul Theroux's.

[18] Diversis (1981: 4). The punctuation in this passage allows for differences in interpretation. Compare Stuard (1992: 87n.) with Krekić (1987a: 189–90).

because of 'honour and honesty', from trading in the fish market (*Liber Croceus*: fo. 58, hereafter *Lib. Croc.*). However, as I have indicated, the major difference between patricians and *populo* concerned access to the instruments of government. While patrician birth might confer status, it also gave access to those councils and offices which managed the essential commercial, diplomatic, and military affairs of state. Therefore we now turn to examine some of the institutions through which the patrician 'monopoly association' managed the apparatus of the Ragusan state.

3

Ragusan Government and the Quest for Offices

The Great Council

The Great Council was the centre of government. This council was the ultimate source of power in the state. Its members were summoned by the Great Bell about five times a month in their own chambers for regular meetings.[1] There they established governing ordinances, determined policy, and elected the numerous officials who staffed the state apparatus. Diversis says, 'here in short is all the power of the republic'.[2] Only adult patrician males over the age of 18 were eligible to sit on this body. Its membership had become exclusive in 1332. In that year the Great Council directed that a committee of three should draw up a list of sitting members and all those who might deserve membership. The latter were men whose fathers or ancestors had previously sat on council (Petrovich 1974: 561).[3] After Ragusa's Great Council closed, only legitimate male descendants of existing members could sit on the council. Legitimacy required a legal marriage between patrician father and patrician mother. Except for the courtesy admission of neighbouring rulers such as Count Vlatko Vukčić from Hum and Count Žarko Vlatković, the Great Council remained closed for over three centuries until 1667 when, after the ranks of the patriciate had been badly depleted, ten wealthy merchant families were permitted to purchase entry.[4] The patricians thought of themselves as a nobility with coats of arms. Their names bore the honorifics *Ser* and *Donna*.

The form and principles of Ragusa's government were consistent with the political philosophy of the period and practice found in Venice and Florence. That philosophy had seen a shift in thinking about the legitimate possession of *iuris-*

[1] '*Ad sonum compane more et loco solutis congregato*', as the ordinances put it (*Lib. Croc.*: Cap. 4, fo. 2).

[2] '*Hoc leges statuit, expensas disponit et concedit, hoc gratias et dona largitur, hoc cunctos officiales et in urbe et in districtu ac locis ei subditis eligit, mutat et revocat, et qui in illo nonfiunt, ab inferioribus sua auctoritate instituuntur. Hujus breviter est omnis Reipublicæ potestas*' (1881: 6; cf. M. Rešeter 1929a).

[3] In 1332 Ragusa was under Venetian domination. It is noteworthy that Venice's own Great Council (the *Serrata del Maggior Consiglio*) had 'closed' thirty-five years earlier in 1297 (see Lane 1971; Finlay 1980b: 41; Chojnacki 1994). Many Ragusan institutions and practices appear to be modelled after Venice. Chojnacki suggests that the Venetian patriciate was not permanently fixed by this event. Some houses died out and were lost to the ranks of the patriciate. Other houses, excluded earlier by the *Serrata*, managed to filter in sometime later (Chojnacki 1973: 54–8).

[4] '*Comes Vladissanus filius domini ducis Stephan*' and '*Comes Sarchus Vlatchovich*' (*Manuali Practici del Cancelliere* 1, *Specchio* I: fo. 386 (hereafter referred to as *Specchio*)). Count Vlatko's ties did not prevent his father from invading Ragusan territory in Konavli with Ottoman approval in 1451. As Fine remarks, treachery operated in both directions. Ragusa had tried to exploit a dispute between Count Vlakto and his father Herceg Stefan over the affections of a Sienese woman: cf. Fine (1987: 580, 588).

dicti—the power, as Azo, a leading Glossator of the Justinian *Codex* and teacher of the civil law at Bologna (d. *c*.1230), put it, 'of stating that which is lawful and right and establishing that which is equitable' (Azo 1966: 67; as quoted in Skinner 1988: 391). Following the rediscovery of Aristotle's works, political thinkers moved from thinking that all governments are the imposition of God's ordinance through a God-given hereditary lordship to considering the three alternatives outlined in Aristotle's *Politics*. These were monarchy, aristocracy, and a third form where 'the body of the people acts in the name of the common good' (quoted in Skinner 1988: 397). Aristotle thought that the best form might be a mixture. The government of Venice, esteemed for its stability and tranquillity (the *Serenissima*), was seen as a mixture. Venice was successful because of the rule by patricians—an aristocracy which was seen as a mean between monarchy and popular rule. The Doge represented principles of monarchy, the Great Council represented popular consultation, while the patricians represented aristocracy.

Ragusa's government was also a mixture, but a mixture in which the doctrine of popular sovereignty was most prominent. Drawing on the idea of *universitas*, a central idea in the Roman law of corporation, an entire group was thought of as acting with a single will and speaking with a single voice (Gierke 1987: 44). While there had been some earlier attempts at consulting all the citizens of Ragusa, by the fifteenth century consultation was restricted to the patriciate. Following growing humanist thought, civic success was held to rest upon *virtus*. This quality rests not in quiet contemplation, but in a Ciceronian active civic life. In Ragusa the expression of this cardinal virtue was not to be found in the pursuit of individual fame, but in the attainment of glory for the community.[5]

Patricians reserved unto themselves all the seats on the Great Council. This was the engine of government. It made all of the crucial decisions regarding trade or diplomacy or it delegated these decision-making powers to special sections of its membership. The rights and duties of these sections were determined within the Great Council itself and their members were drawn from it. The Great Council elected the Rector, or head of state, and all of the other office-holders of the state.[6] Almost all of these were selected from its own ranks. While the total number of such offices varied slightly over time, there were about fifty to sixty posts to be filled each year. Since many offices had multiple incumbents, the total number of patricians holding office in any single year was much greater than the number of offices. About 160 patricians held office in an average year.

While the number of Great Council members varied from year to year, an average of about 270 males sat on the Great Council between 1455 and 1490.[7] It

---

[5] See Kokole (1996) for a provocative analysis of the iconography of the Rector's palace and on the influence of classical antiquity within Ragusa.

[6] There are some exceptions which are discussed below.

[7] This yearly average includes all those who held office between 1440 and 1490, those who entered the council but did not hold office, and a few others who did not hold office and whose date of entry is unknown but who are known to have been alive.

is not possible from the sources to determine exactly who was attending the council in any given year or even how many men might have been eligible to attend. In the analysis which follows, I refer to men as being politically active. I consider a person to have been politically active in a given year if that person is known to have been alive in that year and if he would have reached the age of eligibility to sit on the council. The year 1455 is used as a benchmark because from 1455 onwards all new entrants and their date of entry are recorded in the Chancellor's Handbooks (*Specchio*: fos. 386v–394). From this data and from other evidence, it is possible to determine those who sat on the council after 1440 and their approximate year of entry.[8] Before 1455 a person had to have reached the age of 18 before being eligible for Great Council membership, but in that year the age for admission was raised to 20, with the additional provision that illiterates could not be elected to office. At that time there was unease among senior council members about the calibre of young entrants.[9]

In this analysis I concentrate on the routine of everyday government, but it would be very misleading to imply that the period from 1440 to 1490 was placid and uneventful. It was extremely turbulent, violent, and highly dangerous for Ragusan commerce. In this period the Ottoman Turks conquered Constantinople, assumed control over the Balkan interior, and began to extract periodic levies from Ragusa.

However, the Turkish conquest was fitful, subject to reversals, and was only consolidated over a considerable period of time. In the meantime an assortment of Hungarian, Serbian, Bosnian, Albanian, Greek, and Hercegovinian rulers, despots, lords, bans and hercegs came to power, formed alliances and broke them (both with one another and with the Turks), and waged war (against one another and the Turks). At the same time they fomented insurrection amongst their neighbours while unsuccessfully striving to suppress it at home. The chaotic Balkan political cauldron bubbled and churned. Ragusan commercial ventures in the Balkan interior were often very unsettled and highly risky. This, of course, also had important consequences for domestic industries. After the boom in the 1440s, for example, the textile industry floundered as warfare disrupted the Balkan markets. But later, as Turkish control was consolidated and stable trading conditions re-established, textile manufacturing revived.

But there was not only trouble abroad. In the same period Ragusa's relationships with her immediate neighbours were very fraught. In the early 1450s Ragusa found herself at war in Konavli with Herceg Stefan Vukčić-Kosača. These troubles, the almost constant warfare in neighbouring Hercegovina, and the famines which

---

[8] The dates of entry for the period from 1440 to 1455 are estimated from the dates at which men held their first office. From the careers of those who entered the Great Council after 1455, for example, we know that the office of *Lavorieri de pagamento in Ragusi* was held (on average) three years after entry. Thus if someone held this as a first office in 1447, we assume that his date of entry would have been around 1444.

[9] The age at entry had been 20 before 1348 when it was lowered to 18. There it remained until 1455. Ragusans calculated ages from conception (*a conceptione*), not from birth. See M. Rešeter (1929a: 10n.).

accompanied them brought refugees streaming into the city and its environs. Some had to be expelled by force (Krekić 1972: 100–1). Although Turkish domination of the Balkans created stability in trade, it also put at risk the uneasy relationship between patricians, *populo*, and peasantry. The Turkish practice of granting various privileges to individuals began to undermine the authority of the state over its people. By the late 1460s the problem had become so worrisome that the state intervened to ban the practice with heavy penalties of fines, imprisonment, or hanging for infringements.[10] If this was not enough, there were major plagues in 1466 and again in 1482–3.

Therefore, government offices to which patricians elected one another—such as those charged with securing safe and clean water, obtaining and dispersing adequate grain supplies, supervising textile manufacture and trade, or overseeing municipal fortifications—were much more than posts of honour and sources of income for idle patricians.

The Great Council met about fifty times a year and transacted about 250 items of minuted business. In this volume of activity, major items of governmental business such as the drafting of a new statute, or the dispatching of a diplomatic mission, account for only a small portion of the total number of items on the agenda. In 1470, for example, the minutes of only five meetings record decisions on such matters. Most day-to-day activities appear routine, even mundane. If the world outside was in turmoil, it was business as usual within the council chambers. One typical item of business was the granting of exemptions. These were both frequent and typical of Great Council business. For example, one meeting approved Petrus Çubriano de Lucari's (ID 1296) request to be allowed to return to Ragusa since his pregnant wife was near term. He was serving on the island of Lastovo as *Conte Lagosta*. The council approved his request for twenty days' leave with the note that Nicola Jacheta de Goçe (ID 858) had agreed to serve in his place.[11] Compassionate grounds were not the only reason for granting release from official duties. On another occasion a certain Clemenantis Mar(inus) de Goçe, serving in Stagno as one of the *Officiali lavorieri*, was given leave to return to Ragusa to pursue 'his opportunities'. Christoforus Givcho de Buchia (ID 397) agreed to serve in his place.[12]

Other frequent items of council business concerned the granting, or extending,

---

[10] *Acta Consilii Rogatorum* 19: fos. 278v, 279v, 290 (hereafter referred to as *Act. Rogat.*). The relationship between patricians, *populo*, and peasantry—although central to our understanding of Ragusa's history—is still imperfectly understood.

[11] It does not seem likely that Petrus returned to Lastovo since the Great Council elected Marcus Andreas de Zrieva (ID 637) as his successor only three days after it had approved his request (*Act. Maior*. 15: fos. 244v, 245). The minute of the Great Council actually lists him under his father's name, Ciprianus. Ciprianus de Lucari died in 1441. The *Specchio*, however, properly records Petrus de Lucari as *Conte Lagosta* (*Specchio*: s.v. *Conte Lagosta*).

[12] The Council was not always so generous: a similar request from Johannes Nicola de Caboga (ID 517) was refused several months later (*Act. Maior*. 15: fos. 248v, 259). I am unable to identify this Clemenantis (?) de Goçe. Perhaps the incumbent should be Benko Marinus de Gondola (ID 1182) (*Specchio*: s.v. *Officiali lavorieri de pagamente in Stagno*)?

of concessions such as Clemens Marino de Goçe's (ID 1020) right to trade in wine for three additional months, or requests to sell property in order to raise dowries. On 10 May 1490 the sons of the late Raphael Nicola de Goçe (ID 886) asked the council for permission to sell or pledge some of their goods in Trsteno in order to realize forty *hyperperi* for the dowry of their sister Petronella (ID 890) (*Act. Maior.* 15: fos. 245v, 250). The *hyperperi* (*hyperpera*, sing.) was Ragusa's 'ghost money' or money of account (Cippola 1956: 38–9).[13] The copper *follaro* and silver *grosso* were the coinage in circulation for everyday transactions (30 *follari* = 1 *grosso*, 12 *grossi* = 1 *hyperpera*).[14] Council minutes are full of items such as concessions, grants, land sales, and the like. Other minuted items concerned the granting of temporary discretionary powers to other offices or councils. But all of these various types of decisions, great and small, account for less than one-third of all council business. In examining the working of the Great Council, it is apparent that the most frequent and time-consuming item of council action was election to office.

Councils and Offices

The most important of these offices was that of Rector. He was head of state, signed official documents, received ambassadors, sentenced convicted criminals, and so on. Considerable discretionary powers were delegated to him (sitting together with his Small Council) in the conduct of government and diplomacy. Reflecting the dignity of the state and its special embodiment in the person of the Rector, his movements were restricted to the confines of the Rector's palace and the official precinct during his term of office. On public and official occasions he was physically separated from the official entourage by eight 'princes' (*knezaci*, the term used by the Slavic-speaking populace) who carried out his orders and protected his person.[15] In all the government documents he is referred to as the 'Lord Rector'.

Whatever powers and dignities the Great Council granted to the Rector with one hand, it took away with another. In most matters a Rector could not act without the approval of his Small Council. The Rector's term of office was only for one month and he could not be re-elected until two years had elapsed. Therefore over the period of a decade over fifty patricians would hold the highest office of the state. This represents a considerable circulation of power amongst the older male members of the patriciate.

The Small Council advised the Rector. It was made up of eleven members: six

[13] On moneys of account, see Lane and Mueller (1985: 7–9).

[14] 3 *hyperperi* = 1 ducat (Stuard 1992: 93). The classic work on Ragusan coinage and its monetary system is M. Rešeter (1924–5). A useful summary of Ragusan coinage, weights, and measures is presented in Appendix 1 of Carter (1972). The three coins in circulation are described in Diversis (1882: 3).

[15] Diversis, our source on this subject, uses the term '*chenesaghi*' in the Latin account (1881: 8). It is rendered as *knezaci* ('princes') in a Serbo-Croatian translation (Božić 1983: 26).

councillors (*Consereri del menor conselo*) directly elected by the Great Council and the five Justices of the Criminal Court (*Judici del criminal*). It acted as the executive committee of state dealing with a vast array of daily issues. This council's own jurisdiction included the naming of guardians, appointing certain officials on merchant vessels, naming the six nobles who were to serve for the month as Guards of the Night, and so on.[16] It had two other functions, however, which were very important. One lay in advising the Rector and, thereby, ensuring continuity in administration through the rapid circulation of Rectors. It also produced slates of nominees for a series of offices which the members of the Great Council then chose from. Members of the Small Council, of which eight were required for a quorum, held office for one year. After a term on the Small Council, two years had to elapse before a person could be re-elected. Like the Great Council, the Small Council also had its own chambers. Its members were summoned by three chimes of the small bell. In 1450 this bell called the Small Council into session on 174 occasions. Omitting the sabbath, the Small Council met every other day on Tuesdays, Thursdays, and Saturdays (Diversis 1881: 6).

In addition to the Great Council and the Rector with his Small Council, the third major institution of governmental decision-making was the Senate or Council of Appeal (*Pregato*). As its name indicates, one of its responsibilities was to consider appeals regarding laws and ordinances, but its influence and power extended far beyond the legislative and judicial. It permeated both foreign and domestic affairs. The Senate imposed the death penalty and it intervened in major domestic issues. It also shaped foreign policy. For example, it selected and dispatched envoys. Special subcommittees drafted instructions to ambassadors and envoys, and composed replies to messages from foreign heads of state. It also held certain elections, such as for those who would be responsible for the sale of salt from the state's salt pans (*Act. Rogat.* 25: fos. 82, 93, 102v, 105, etc.). But this brief description does not begin to capture the extent of its interests and powers. The forty-five members of the Senate, of which thirty-one were required for a quorum, consisted of the eleven members of the current Small Council, the eleven previous members, twelve Rectors sitting for eleven months after their term of office, five Civil Judges (*Judicieri del comone*), and a number of others directly elected by the Great Council (*Lib. Vir.*: Cap. 188). The number of directly elected members fluctuated somewhat from year to year but the average was about eleven. Prior to 1456 attorneys of the city and civil courts (*Advocati del comone* and *Advocati del proprio*) were also included in the Senate as a matter of right. After March of that year they had to be directly elected by the Great Council (ibid.: Cap. 472, '*Advocati non sunt de consilio rogatorum*'). The minimum age for membership in the Senate was set at 30. Members held their seats for one year. Like the members of the Small Council, they could not be re-elected for another two years.

The Rectorship and seats on the Small Council and Senate tended to circulate

---

[16] On the salt franchise and the guards, see *Lib. Vir.*, Cap. 89 and Cap. 5, respectively.

amongst the same set of men. Therefore, while no one could succeed himself as Rector, Councillor, or Senator, that does not mean that he was removed from the central organs of power for any length of time. Senior men circulated from one of these posts to the next. The three deliberative bodies of the state—the Great Council, the Rector with his Small Council, and the Senate—met frequently throughout the year. Whereas a young patrician who regularly attended sessions of the Great Council could attend up to about fifty meetings a year, an older man, sitting on all three councils, could attend over 250. He would be involved in discussions ranging from the fairly trivial, such as a private sale of a village plot, to the weightiest issues of state.

Associated with the three deliberative councils were a large number of elected administrative offices. In addition to the Rector, there were about sixty other offices that had to be filled each year. Since some of these offices, like that of the Judge of the Criminal Court, had multiple incumbents, the total number of Small Councillors, Senators, and other office-holders elected out of the Great Council in any single year was about 160. They covered such different areas of governmental function as defence, the administration of outlying areas, customs and finance.

A functional description of government and office is given by Philippus de Diversis in his account of Ragusa in 1440 (1880–1). He begins by describing the three governing councils, the courts, and the relationships between them. This priority in narrative indicates which institutions he thinks are most important. Then he describes some of the offices in terms of a set of enduring principles (*'principatu perpetuo'*). Some of these concern major functions of government and their associated offices such as trade and commerce (Principle One), defence (Principle Two), or public health (Principle Ten). Others concern particular offices rather than governmental functions. Thus in Principle Eight he discusses the duties of the *Raxone officiali* and in Principle Nine that of the *Massari de le biave*.[17] A final section concerns duties of a more occasional nature (*'de principatibus temporalibus, qui sunt utiles, sed non semper necessarii'*). While Diversis's account provides an interesting glimpse into the period through the eyes of a contemporary observer, it is very patchy and incomplete. Therefore, while we will borrow from it and refer to it from time to time, we will provide our own framework.

There was an elaborate judiciary with a Criminal Court with five judges, augmented to six after 1459 (*Lib. Virid.*: Cap. 492). These were known as the *Judici del criminal*, or *Judici de Rectori*. There was also a Civil Court with six judges (*Consoli de le cause civil*). The functions of this court were subdivided in 1459 into matters *de stabel* and *de mobel* (ibid.: Cap. 493). There was also a Municipal Court with five judges (*Judicieri del comone*). There were three elected municipal attorneys (*Advocati del comone*) and six attorneys for the Civil Court (*Advocati del proprio*). They all held their seats for one year and they could not succeed them-

---

[17] Diversis writes in Latin: *rationum officiales* and *massarii bladorum*.

selves in the same office until an interval of two years had elapsed. There was also a magistrate who handled small claims (*Vicario del Rector*).[18]

Administrative areas outside the city were governed by patricians who were sent out for terms of six months. These (and their seats) were, respectively, the counts of *Canale* (Konavli, at Pridvorje), *Isola de Mezo et de Calamota*[19] (Koločep), *Lagosta* (Lastovo), *Slano* (Slano), *Stago* (Ston), and *Zupana*[20] (Šipan). In addition further patricians were stationed as Castellans in Ston and Mali Ston (*Castellani de quelmar*) and as Captains at Orebić (*Tersteniça*) and Janjina (*Puncta/Ponta Stagno*).[21] There was a further Captain stationed at the castle of Sochol between the villages of Dunave and Dubravka in Konavli.[22] Two other sets of officials were also posted to Ston who held office for one year. These were the two Paymasters (*Officiali lavorieri de pagamento in Stagno*) and two Recorders (*Officiali lavorieri de scritta in Stagno*) for the labourers in Ston.

Within Ragusa's city walls there were comparable officials for the labourers, but in this case there were three Paymasters (*Officiali lavorieri de pagamento in Ragusi*) and three Recorders (*Officiali lavorieri de scritta in Ragusi*).[23] Armaments, too, had three Paymasters (*Armamento officiali*) and two Recorders (*Officiali de scritta de armamento*).[24] But this was just the beginning. Customs were handled by four officials (*Doanieri*) and by one youthful Recorder (*Scrivari over garcon dela dohane grande*).

The three *Massari de le biave* were responsible for the state's grain supply, mainly wheat, millet, and barley. They were responsible for procuring the supply, for ensuring the safe and legitimate unloading of grain cargo, for securing the state's warehousing, and for granting sale franchises (cf. Diversis 1881: 22 and 30). Krekić notes that shipowners were informed a year in advance when their turn for transporting grain would occur. In emergencies all local shipping could be requisitioned for transport, importers could be given a holiday from customs duties, and foreign grain could be confiscated (Krekić 1972: 107–8). Three youthful officials (*Biscoti*

[18] In 1478 the term of office changed from one year to six months (*Specchio*, s.v.).

[19] This post originates in 1457. Ordinarily there were two incumbents per year, each holding office for six months. But in some years (1461–3 and 1466–8, for example), only one *Conte* is elected.

[20] Prior to 1444, the term of office for the *Conte de Zupana* was one year. In that year it was changed to six months (*Specchio*, s.v.).

[21] After 1450 two Castellans simultaneously served in Mali Ston for six-month terms. The senior, who was older and who had a higher salary, served at the *Castel de sopra* (also known as the *Castel de suxo*). The junior served at the *Castel de sotto* (*Castel de zoso*) (*Lib. Virid.*: Cap. 413; *Specchio*, s.v. *Castellan de quelmar*). The term of office of the *Castellan de Stagno* was changed from one year to six months in 1479 (*Specchio*, s.v.).

[22] This castle was presented to the Republic in 1391 by the Counts of Hum. It stands at the edge of the mountains astride a route into the interior.

[23] There is a puzzling hiatus of a decade after 1479 when no *Officiali lavorieri de scritta in Ragusi* is elected (*Specchio*, s.v.).

[24] Only two *Armamento officiali* are elected from 1462 to 1480 and none between 1481 and 1488. Two are elected annually thereafter (*Specchio*, s.v.). Three *Officiali de scritta* are elected for the first time in 1471, then two are elected annually to 1480. Again, none are elected from 1481 to 1488. Two are elected annually thereafter (*Specchio*, s.v.).

officiali) were given responsibility for (military?) supplies of hardtack.[25] Three others had responsibility for the salt trade (*Salinari*). In terms of municipal services, other officials (in sets of three incumbents each) were responsible for roads and public ways (*Salezo officiali*),[26] weights and measures (*Fontigieri*), sewers (*Gatti officiali*, literally 'Cats Officials'), water supplies and fountains (*Aqueducto de la fontana officiali*), and supervision of the wool trade (*Lane officiali del arte della lana*).[27] There were also two attorneys elected to deal with the wool trade (*Advocati alla camara del arte della lana*).[28] The city had four official valuers (*Stime officiali*), four officers of the Mint (*Cechieri*),[29] four Registrars (*Camerlengi del comone*),[30] and five Overseers of Public Accounts (*Raxone officiali*). The three State Treasurers (*Texorieri de Sancta Maria*) held office for life.

Public health and sanitation were of great concern. The city contracted the services of physicians and surgeons. Most of these came to Ragusa from the West. Most were Italians or, to a lesser extent, Jews although in 1458 a Master Andrew from Constantinople was engaged and, somewhat later, two Greek physicians were employed. They were to treat all Ragusans without fee (Krekić 1972: 93–4).

A city orphanage, one of the oldest in Europe, was founded in 1432. It had three patrician supervisors (*Officiali Hospedal de Misericordia*).[31] A hospital for the poor, the *hospedal Grande*, again one of the oldest in Europe, had another three patrician Trustees elected from the ranks of the Great Council (ibid.: 109–10). Plague was a terrible danger and twice devastated the city within our period. A group of five *Cazamorti* were given extensive powers to deal with the threat. Special quarantine areas were established on Mljet and the tiny island of Mrkan (*Mercana*) and the *Cazamorti* were given sufficient power to control the movement of goods and persons coming from infested areas. In 1482 they even received Great Council approval to confine Daniel Marin de Caboga (ID 524) in a house in Gruž because he had travelled through a region where plague was suspected.

Various monasteries, convents, and churches also had Trustees who were elected for terms ranging from three years to life. These were the *Procuratori de San Blasio*; *Procuratori de San Piero, Lorenzo et Andrea*; *Procuratori de Sancta Maria Angellorum*; *Procuratori de Sancta Chiara*; *Procuratori de San Domenego*; *Procuratori de la Croma*; *Procuratori de Sancta Georgio de Canal*; *Procuratori de Sancta Crose de*

---

[25] This was one of the few patrician offices whose duties were not regulated by statute. It was established by a decision of the Great Council in December 1449 and the incumbents first took up their posts in 1450 (*Specchio*: fo. 48).

[26] This office is held intermittently between 1443 and 1469, with two, one, or no incumbents (*Specchio*, s.v.).

[27] See Roller (1951: 13–22).

[28] Two *Advocati* were elected annually from 1455 to 1480. None were elected from 1481 to 1486 and two annually thereafter (*Specchio*, s.v.).

[29] P. Rešeter 1891–2, cited in Mahnken 1960: 39.

[30] The number of *Camerlengi* was increased from three to four in 1454 (*Specchio*, s.v.).

[31] From 1470 the post was split into two, with two Recorders (*de scrita*) and two Paymasters (*de pagamento*) (*Specchio*, s.v. *Officiali Hospedal de Misericordia*).

Grauosio; *Procuratori del Monasterio de San Jeronimo*; and *Procuratori de San Francesco*.[32] There were other officials who were elected from the ranks of the patriciate on an occasional basis, such as *Ambassadori*, Captains of naval vessels (*Capitanio Barchetaris*), and other officials concerned with the contraband trade in wine (*Officiali contrabanoris vini*).

With all of these posts, one wonders if it was really necessary to have three-of-this or four-of-that. Were the duties sufficiently important, or onerous, to require so many incumbents? It is difficult to give a clear answer because in many cases we do not know exactly what the officials did, or the amount of time that they were expected to devote to their duties. As in so many areas, there is a surfeit of information about some aspects of office and a virtual famine about others. Over the years there was some tinkering with the fine print of regulations concerning offices. Age qualifications for offices could be raised or lowered, salaries adjusted up or down, intervals between the holding of certain posts adjusted, the numbers for a quorum changed, particular sequences of offices prohibited, and so on.[33] But it is still unclear just what many office-holders did.

Perhaps some of the bloating of offices was intended to enhance incomes or provide poor relief for indigent patricians. Two sons of Nicola Sarachin Bona (ID 297) were elected to be *Cechieri* in two successive years immediately following their father's death.[34] But if some posts were sinecures for poor patricians—jobs for the lads—the pay scales were not generous. At the bottom of the pay scale the *Biscoti officiali* had an annual salary of 10 *hyperperi*. In what appears to be the upper end, the *Conte de Canale* had 400 for six months. It is difficult to work out salary levels since there were many methods of remuneration. Some received straight salaries, some received fines or fees, and others had a small salary plus fees or fines. We cannot determine how much they received, or how significant that income was in comparison to other sources of wealth. But, with the exception of a few offices, it does not appear that the purpose of multiple incumbents was to do well by tending the public good.

Indeed, some of the posts were so unpopular that hefty penalties were levied on those who were elected but declined to serve. Several of the posts in Ston carried

[32] While Ragusa remained a most faithful servant of the Roman Catholic Church, the patriciate were also concerned to maintain their distance and independence. The Great Council decreed, for example, that no Ragusan was to be Archbishop of Ragusa (*Lib. Virid.*, Cap. 129).

[33] For example, the age of the *Conte de Lagosta* was raised to 35 in 1478 (*Lib. Croc.*: fo. 86v). The salary of the *Conte de Canale* was lowered from 500 *hyperperi* to 400 in 1427, and then to 300 in 1462 (*Lib. Vir.*: Cap. 212 and marginalia; *Lib. Croc.*: fo. 17). The interval of vacancy for all the various Counts and Castellans was changed from two years to three in 1486 (*Lib. Croc.*: fo. 86v). The number required for a quorum in the Great Council was reduced to eighty, albeit in the plague year 1466 (*Act. Maior.* 13: fo. 15v). Senators were prohibited from concurrently holding another office in the city (with a number of exceptions) in 1469 (*Lib. Croc.*: fo. 37v). But given these changes and others, it remains that over the spread of a century the framework of regulations concerning offices remained remarkably stable.

[34] Stephanus (ID 302) was elected in January 1479 and Jacobus in February the following year (*Specchio*, s.v. *Cechieri*).

penalties of 100 *hyperperi* for refusing service.[35] Remote postings were unpopular.
Ston was particularly unpopular, even dangerous, because of malaria, and a posting
there was regarded as punitive. There are other reasons why so many posts had
three or more incumbents.

There is the impression, difficult to document, that a conscious attempt was
made to have a range of experience in the posts. Bright new faces were often elected
at the same time as older hands who had served in the post on numerous previous
occasions. For example, when Nicola Corçi Goçe (ID 822) was elected *Doanieri* in
1472, 1473, and 1475, he was the most experienced of the four men elected on each
occasion.[36] There may have been an informal policy of using the system of multiple incumbents as a form of apprenticeship training in the craft of government.
The business of government was certainly very time-consuming. Only elderly
men, largely retired from the day-to-day duties of managing their family's commercial ventures, could devote themselves full-time to endless council sessions and
the responsibilities of office. Most men would need to keep a regular eye on commerce and farming. However, with three men sharing most duties, it would be possible to attend to governmental responsibilities at the same time as minding the
family's affairs. But there is an additional reason which is suggested by a final post,
the *Proveditori de la terra*, which was established in 1477.

The provisions of the legislation establishing the posts of Overseer (*Proveditori*)
(there were to be five incumbents) are very lengthy and detailed, with forty-five
major sections (*Lib. Croc.*: fos. 60–9). Two features stand out. One is the general
purpose of the *Proveditori*. Their duties involve scrutinizing the performance of
other office-holders and monitoring elections. They were, in other words, to elimi-
nate corruption in government. It was not that patricians would gain an unfair
advantage over others. That, after all, was what it meant to be a patrician. Rather,
the fear was that sections of the patriciate would misuse their monopoly rights to
gain an advantage over other patricians. The inscription above the entrance to the
Great Council chamber read '*Obliti privatorum, publica curate*', which means
'Having forgotten your private interests, take care of public affairs'. In relation to
this, the second notable feature of the *Proveditori* was that they were to be selected
from five different houses. This feature applied to a number of posts.[37] There was
the particular fear that agnates would connive to further the interests of their
house. Hence, close agnates were not permitted to vote for one another and two or
more agnates could not concurrently hold the same post. Therefore, having three

---

[35] The *Conte de Stagno*, the *Officiali lavorieri de pagamento in Stagno*, and the *Officiali lavorieri de scritta in Stagno*. The post of *Castellan* carried a penalty of 50 *hyperperi* (*Specchio*, s.v.).

[36] *Specchio*, s.v.

[37] The following should also come from different houses: *Advocati alla camara del arte della lana* (*Lib. Virid.*, Cap. 458), *Advocati del proprio* (*Specchio*, fo. 11), *Camerlengi del comone* (ibid., fo. 71), *Castellani de quelmar* (ibid., fo. 122), and *Consoli de le cause civil* (ibid., fo. 62), *Judici del criminal* (*Lib. Virid.*, Cap. 493), *Officiali lavorieri de pagamente in Stagno* (ibid., Cap. 352), *Officiali lavorieri de scritta in Stagno* (ibid.), *Raxone officiali* (*Specchio*, fo. 320), and *Stime officiali* (ibid., fo. 330).

or more incumbents in a post, particularly if they had to come from different houses, would facilitate mutual surveillance and make it difficult for any one of them to use the office to the advantage of their own house. The patriciate was a monopoly association, but it was also a very wary one.

The Structure of Government

If the holding of offices and council seats was highly important to Ragusans of the fifteenth century, what is not clear is how they represented all of these posts to themselves. Do the posts, as a totality, have a distinctive shape, form, or structure? Did the Ragusans of the period 'totalize' them in some fashion for themselves? Geometric metaphors have sometimes been invoked to describe the government of Renaissance city-states. Venice's government, for example, has been described as a pyramid with the Great Council as the base, the Senate as the middle, and the Signoria as the vertex. Yet, as Finlay notes, 'Venetians would have been surprised to see their government explained by tidy diagrams and orderly models' (1980b: 39). The arrangement of Venetian and Ragusan offices and councils was anything but tidy. Indeed, as Max Weber has emphasized, the overlapping jurisdictions, elaborate checks and counterchecks, tightly circumscribed powers, and elaborate methods of consultation had been built into the structure of government over the decades to prevent the accumulation of power (1968: 1271). One could conclude that cumbersomeness and complexity in governmental arrangement were seen as necessary features. They make the description and analysis of the 'shape of government' very difficult.

Instead of considering Ragusan offices and councils solely in terms of functions, let us assume that they might also have been ordered in some kind of hierarchy. This order is determined by the sequence in which offices are held by individuals over the course of their political careers. There are grounds for making this assumption. I have spoken of 'a hierarchy' of offices. It seems clear from archival sources that the patricians of the period thought that there was a hierarchy. We know that they were obsessed with order and precedence. Officials processed in order on state occasions. On the feast of the patron saint of the city, St Blaise (or Sv. Vlaho), they made their way in order from the Rector's palace to the Cathedral. There they were seated with the Rector first, followed by his Small Council, members of the Senate, and then the other officials. Unfortunately, I cannot find any source which spells out the sequence for those other officials. The book of state ceremonies does not tell us who was there or in what order. The *Specchio*, or Chancellor's Handbook, which is such a rich source of information, lists every one of the state officials—in alphabetical order!

In the absence of a contemporary account, I adopt a prosopographical perspective (Stone 1987). We know, for example, that age and seniority were important

TABLE 1. *Age of men at entry into Great Council*

Age at entry	No.	%
20	228	40.3
21	117	20.7
22	81	14.3
23	43	7.6
24	25	4.4
25	21	3.7
26	15	2.7
27	14	2.5
28	3	0.5
29	4	0.7
30	6	1.1
31+	9	1.6
TOTAL	566	100.0

Mean age at entry: 21.8 years
Standard deviation: 2.5 years

Source: *Specchio*: fos. 389–392v.

ordering principles for Ragusans. A number of posts had minimum age qualifications attached to them—and a few had maximums as well.[38] We also know that offices with 'higher' age qualifications were more bitterly contested. There is a relationship, as we shall see, between the seniority of an office and the majority needed to obtain it. That is, not only did more people cast votes in the balloting for the 'higher' offices, but the higher the office the more slender the majority of the winning nominees.

To obtain data on the hierarchical ordering of offices, I studied the office-holding careers of those who entered the Great Council from about 1436 to 1490. After 1455 the date when a patrician entered the Great Council is known and sometimes his age at entry as well. I therefore recorded the date of entry and age (where noted) for all individuals who entered between 1455 and 1490. These data show that the average age at entry to the Great Council was about 22 (see Table 1).[39]

Since a man might hold a particular office several times, it was important to determine the point at which he was elected to an office for the *first* time. Therefore, for purposes of analysis, successive holdings of the same office were eliminated from the individual orderings, leaving only an ordering of offices held for the first time by each of the 406 office-holding individuals. Moving from these individual career patterns to the hierarchy of offices, the next step was to

[38] The *Advocati alla camara del arte della lana* could not be over 45 years old, *Castellani de quelmar* could not be over 60, nor the *Castellan de Sochol* over 65 (*Lib. Virid.*, Caps. 458, 380, 408 respectively).
[39] A discussion of the methods is found in Rheubottom (1990). The data were obtained from the Chancellor's Handbooks (*Specchio*: fos. 386v–394).

determine the average point at which an office-holder was likely to hold an office for the first time. These average values provide a rank ordering of offices, a first approximation of an office-holding hierarchy (see Table 2).[40]

As we have seen, these several offices were involved with everything from sewers to statecraft. While a man did not become eligible to sit on the Great Council until the age of 20 in 1455, a few began their office-holding careers somewhat earlier when they were elected to be *Scrivari over garcon*. Those taking this post in the customs were sometimes under 18 years of age. But, aside from this, the first step on the ladder of offices came with election to the *Biscoti officiali*, *Cechieri*, or several other junior positions. With some notable exceptions, election to a first office came between three and ten years after entry to the Great Council. These offices no doubt gave valuable experience on the practical issues of day-to-day government to young men. Their experience in these posts would help them to make weightier decisions as their reputations and responsibilities increased. But elections to these early posts were largely unproblematic. Those who were elected received a substantial majority of the votes cast.

The responsibilities of higher-ranking offices were greater. So was the prestige of such posts. As patricians climbed the ladder of office, the fights for the honours of high office became more intense. The higher the office is in the hierarchy, the smaller becomes the majority of winning candidates. In the case of low-ranking offices like that of *Scrivari over garcon dela dohane grande* or *Biscoti officiali*, the average majority was 74 per cent. For mid-ranking offices like *Camerlengi* or *Massari*, the average majority drops to 68 per cent. The average majority in elections to the Rector or *Pregato* drops to 63 per cent. To hold high office a patrician had to have experience in many posts and would have spent many years in the Great Council. Election to the office of Rector, for example, came after the person had held office on about twenty-two occasions and had sat on the Great Council for over thirty years.

Elections and Competition for Office

Elections to these posts fill the council minutes. Every one of the meetings of the Great Council in 1470 included at least one election and two-thirds of all agenda items were elections (see Table 3). Elections must have dominated proceedings in Venice as well. Sanuto reported that the Great Council elected 831 posts of which 550 were within Venice and 281 outside. In addition Venice's Senate elected 150 officials of its own (Finlay 1980b: 59–60). In comparison, perhaps the four ballots held at the average meeting of Ragusa's Great Council was a modest amount of activity. The names of three candidates were put forward for most vacancies. For

---

[40] This table differs in some particulars from one published earlier (Rheubottom 1990). The present table contains additional information and a number of errors have been corrected.

TABLE 2. *Hierarchy of offices and councils (in ascending order)*

Rank	Office name[a]	Number of incumbents[b]	Years after entry
1	*Scrivari over garcon dela dohane grande* [recorder in the customs' house]	1	−1.5
2	*Biscoti officiali* [responsible for (military?) supplies of hardtack]	3	4.2
3	*Conte Lagosta* [the Count, or administrator, of the district of Lastovo]	1	7.0
4	*Cechieri* [officers of the mint]	4	7.1
5	*Castellan de Stagno* [commander of the fortress at Ston]	1	7.7
6	*Officiali de scritta de armamento* [recorder of workmen in the armoury]	2	7.7
7	*Officiali lavorieri de scritta in Ragusi* [recorder of workmen in Ragusa]	3	8.0
8	*Officiali lavorieri de pagamento in Ragusi* [paymaster of workmen in Ragusa]	3	8.4
9	*Salezo officiali* [official for roads and public ways]	3	8.7
10	*Armamento officiali* [paymaster of workmen in the armoury]	3	9.8
11	*Fontigieri* [official for weights and measures]	3	11.2
12	*Stime officiali* [official valuers]	4	11.8
13	*Advocati alla camara del arte della lana* [attorney to the wool trade]	2	12.3
14	*Capitanio de la ponta* [captain of fortification at Janjina]	1	13.2
15	*Castellan de quelmar, Castello de sopra* (also *de suxo*) [commander of the upper fortress at Mali Ston]	1	13.3
16	*Castellan de quelmar, Castello de sotto* (also *de zoso*) [commander of the lower fortress at Mali Ston]	1	14.4
17	*Conte de isola de Mezo et de Calamota* [the Count, or administrator, of the district of Koločep]	1	15.8
18	*Raxone officiali* [overseer of public accounts]	5	16.1
19	*Gatti officiali* [official for sewers]	3	16.4
20	*Officiali lavorieri de scritta in Stagno* [recorder of workmen at Ston]	2	16.6
21	*Camerlengi del comone* [Registrar]	4	16.7
22	*Procuratori de San Francesco* [trustee of a religious foundation]	3	16.8
23	*Vicario del rector* [magistrate of small claims court]	1	16.8
24	*Judicieri del comone* [judge of the Municipal Court]	5	17.0
25	*Castellan de Sochol* [captain stationed at the fortifications of Sochol in Konavli]	1	17.8

TABLE 2. (*Cont.*).

Rank	Office name[a]	Number of incumbents[b]	Years after entry
26	*Massari de le biave* [official responsible for the state's grain supply]	3	18.4
27	*Procuratori del Monasterio de San Jeronimo* [trustee of a religious foundation]	3	18.7
28	*Aqueducto de la fontana officiali* [official for water supplies and fountains]	3	18.8
29	*Officiali Hospedal de Misericordia* [supervisor of the city orphanage]	3	18.9
30	*Procuratori de Sancta Crose de Grauosio* [trustee of a religious foundation]	3	19.0
31	*Officiali lavorieri de pagamente in Stagno* [paymaster of workmen at Ston]	2	19.0
32	*Doanieri* [customs offical]	4	19.4
33	*Conte de Zupana* [the Count, or administrator, of the district of Šipan]	1	19.8
34	*Advocati del proprio* [attorney for the Civil Court]	6	20.2
35	*Procuratori del hospedal de Misericordia* [trustee of the orphanage]	3	20.9
36	*Salinari* [official responsible for the salt trade]	3	21.1
37	*Procuratori de la Croma* [trustee of a religious foundation]	3	22.4
38	*Procuratori de Sancta Georgio de Canal* [trustee of a religious foundation]	3	22.5
39	*Advocati del comone* [municipal attorney]	3	22.6
40	*Conte de Canale* [the Count, or administrator, of the district of Konavli at Pridvorje]	1	22.8
41	*Lane officiali del arte della lana* [supervisor of the wool trade]	3	22.9
42	*Conte de Slano* [the Count, or administrator, of the district of Slano]	1	24.4
43	*Procuratori de Sancta Maria Angellorum* [trustee of a religious foundation]	3	24.5
44	*Procuratori de Sancta Chiara* [trustee of a religious foundation]	3	24.5
45	*Procuratori de San Domenego* [trustee of a religious foundation]	3	26.2
46	*Cazamorti* [official concerned with the plague and public health measures]	5	27.2
47	*Procuratori de San Piero, Lorenzo et Andrea* [trustee of a religious foundation]	3	27.5
48	*Procuratori de San Blasio* [trustee of a religious foundation]	3	29.0
49	*Consoli de le cause civil* [judge of the Civil Court]	6	29.2
50	*Judici del criminal* [Criminal Court justice]	5	29.7

Table 2. (*Cont.*).

Rank	Office name[a]	Number of incumbents[b]	Years after entry
51	*Pregato* [member of the Senate, or Council of Appeal]	varies	30.1
52	*Consereri del menor conselo* [member of the Rector's Small Council]	6	31.2
53	*Rector* [head of state]	1	33.1
54	*Conte de Stagno* [the Count, or administrator, at Ston]	1	34.5
55	*Proveditori de la terra* [overseer of elections: monitored conduct of public officials]	5	34.8
56	*Procuratori del hospedal Grande* [trustee of the hospital for the poor]	3	35.8

Notes:

[a] Names of offices as given in *Specchio*: fos. 1–309. The *Texorieri de Sancta Maria* and the *Collegio de le Appellatione* are not included in this listing. The former held office for life. The latter body was not established until 1490.

[b] The number of incumbents are those holding office at any one time. See the text for variations and details.

some posts slates of nominees were first selected by the Small Council and then presented to the Great Council for election. These are the *Advocati de proprio, Armamento officiali de pagamento, Biscoti officiali, Cazamorti, Doanieri, Massari de biave, Salinari*, and those members of the Senate who were to be directly elected.[41] Our only source on election procedures, an eighteenth-century account, reports that each councillor was given a linen ball which he then deposited in an urn which had divisions for the pro and con votes (Carter 1972: 114).[42]

Elections were often bitterly fought. On 26 February 1450, for example, the Great Council met to elect a new Rector for the month of March. At this meeting five ballots were held. No one was elected. At the following meeting on 5 March, more ballots were held. Two more were required before Junius Dobre de Calich (ID 528) was finally elected with a vote of sixty-three in favour, fifty opposed, and three abstaining. In the seven ballots required for this election, eleven different names were put to the membership and seven of these names appeared on more than one ballot. The name of the eventual winner had appeared on five (*Act. Maior.* 9: fos. 102–3). During the same year some positions on the *Judici del criminal* became vacant. To fill four vacancies required sixty-five separate ballots spread over thirty council meetings. A total of thirty-five candidates from twenty

[41] Petrovich claims that each candidate on the slate of nominees was selected by a different body: these were the Great Council sitting as a whole and two *ad hoc* committees of six members each elected from the Great Council for this purpose (1974: 746–7). I can find no evidence of these nominating procedures, but it is the case that three candidates are generally put forward for each vacant post.

[42] This is very similar to the procedures in Venice (Queller 1986: 85–92).

TABLE 3. *Meetings of the Great Council in 1470*

Date	Items of transacted business	Number of ballots for offices	Number of persons voting (approx.)
2 January	2	2	133
3 "	8	6	115
5 "	6	6	148
8 "	7	6	114
12 "	6	4	103
15 "	5	4	117
18 "	5	3	107
29 "	5	3	132
26 February	9	6	135
28 "	10	7	148
12 March	6	3	134
15 "	4	3	153
28 "	6	3	143
30 "	6	4	125
2 April	12	6	104
28 "	7	4	113
28 May	8	6	120
8 June	7	4	109
18 "	7	4	103
28 "	11	4	99
7 July	8	5	103
30 "	10	5	100
8 August	6	3	104
11 "	2	2	113
27 "	7	4	85
26 September	7	3	101
10 October	3	3	133
15 "	6	3	168
18 "	6	5	121
29 "	5	5	unknown
30 "	7	7	158
14 November	3	2	111
26 "	8	4	135
1 December	1	1	202
3 "	2	2	179
4 "	1	1	167
5 "	4	4	149
11 "	4	3	173
12 "	4	4	147
14 "	3	3	147
17 "	1	1	104
18 "	3	1	121
20 "	4	4	106
22 "	3	2	102

Source: *Act. Maior.* 9: fos. 173–207.

different houses were put forward. The name of one of these candidates, Jacomo Marin de Gondola (ID 1228), appeared on thirty-four ballots before he was finally elected with a majority of one.

Rectors were regularly elected towards the end of the preceding month.[43] Some nominees might be holding another post at the time. If so, they interrupted their term of office to become Rector, and then resumed the post when their month as Rector was finished. When Piero Symcus de Bona (ID 143) was elected to be Rector for the month of April 1445, he was also elected to be *Advocati del proprio* at the same meeting (*Act. Maior.* 7: fos. 255v–256). Attendance at meetings to elect the Rector was often the highest for the month and it was not unusual for several inconclusive ballots to be held. In 1470 seven of the twelve end-of-the-month meetings required multiple ballots to elect the next Rector. The months of February, April, and October saw particularly fierce elections with at least nine inconclusive ballots. Elections to other high offices show a similar pattern. Hotly contested elections were a hallmark of the Great Council. Three vacancies on the Small Council required forty-five ballots spread over twenty-three council meetings and a single vacancy on the Senate required eleven ballots over seven meetings.

If the election of the next month's Rector was often contentious, at least such struggles were distributed evenly over the year. Most electoral activity, however, occurred around the beginning of the new year when a large number of offices had to be filled. Council meetings in December and January were largely given over to elections. December was particularly difficult since many posts had to be filled. Persons not attending council meetings in this month could be fined (*Lib. Vir.*: Cap. 465).[44] In addition to selecting a new Rector for the month of January, elections in December 1470 were for the eleven members of the Small Council (requiring five ballots), six *Consoli de le cause civil* (three ballots), five *Advocati del proprio* (one ballot), five *Raxone officiali* (one ballot), four *Doanieri* (one ballot), three *Officiali lavorieri de pagamento in Ragusi* (one ballot), and one *Judici del criminal* (one ballot). Elections of members of the Small Council consumed four entire meetings and part of the fifth (on 3, 4, 5, 11, and 12 December respectively).[45]

These ballots could be extremely time-consuming because three candidates were put forward for each open post. Thus, in the first ballot for the eleven Small Council posts, thirty-three names were listed but only five men were actually elected. Since Bartholo Çuan de Goçe (ID 972) and Sigismundo Raphael de Goçe (ID 914) were tied with ninety-one pro votes apiece, another ballot had to be held

---

[43] At one meeting in 1465 Rectors were elected for the two successive months of December and January. This was a plague year when other extraordinary measures also had to be adopted (*Act. Maior.* 12: fos. 228v, 229v).

[44] The fine was 25 *hyperperi*.

[45] Generally, the ordering of elections in December was from the more important offices to the less. In most years elections of the *Judici del criminal* preceded that of the *Consoli de le cause civil*. The two exceptional years were 1480 and 1485.

to resolve the tie. In the reballoting, Bartholo increased his vote and was elected with ninety-five pro votes. Sigismundo, his agnate, saw his support eroded to eighty-six in favour.[46] The following day another ballot was held to try to fill the six remaining seats and therefore the names of eighteen candidates were put to the Council. Only three men were selected on this occasion, so more ballots were required on the following day to fill the three remaining vacancies. In the event, however, only one person was elected, necessitating yet another ballot six days later. Two seats still remained unfilled. But once again the matter was not finally resolved since only one councillor was elected. A fifth and final ballot was needed to elect the last councillor.

It is worth noting that the size of the winning majority ranged between 136 and eighty-eight pro votes on the first ballot, between ninety-two and eighty-four on the second, and was in the high eighties in the third, fourth, and fifth. Therefore the size of the majority did not decline much as the ballots proceeded. Similarly, the interest in the election, judging from the number of members voting in each ballot, was also maintained over time. One hundred and seventy-nine members voted in the first ballot, 167 in the second, 149 in the third, 174 in the fourth, and 158 in the fifth. Given the time-consuming nature of the electoral process and the necessity of holding meetings over five days, this shows remarkable endurance amongst the electors as well as the general importance of the outcome.

Outside the two peak months around the beginning of the new year, elections were distributed fairly evenly over the year, except for the months of October and November which could have more since elections to posts in the administered towns of Stagno were held then. They concerned the *Officiali lavorieri de scritta* and *Officiali lavorieri de pagamente* and the *Castellan*. By being elected in October to take up a post in the new year, the new office-holder would have sufficient time to arrange his personal affairs and move. There tended to be few elections in the summer months. The Rector and his Small Council were given special powers during the grape harvest and did not need to call the Great Council into session except in case of emergency.[47] Therefore, many of the elections in the off months were to fill vacancies which had arisen because an office-holder had completed his term of office, had been elected to fill another office, had died, or was embarking on a voyage. Such occasions were largely unpredictable.

Elections for particular offices tended to be held at the same time each year, thereby giving an order and predictability to the governmental year. The holding

---

[46] Tied ballots were not resolved by awarding the office to the person receiving the least number of votes against. This vote was particularly close. Initially Bartholo de Goçe had ninety-one in favour, eighty-four opposed. Sigismundo de Goçe had ninety-one in favour, eighty-six opposed, and eight abstentions. The reballoting gave Bartholo ninety-five pro votes and eighty-one con. Sigismundo received eighty-six pro, ninety-two con (*Act. Maior.* 13: fo. 202v).

[47] The responsibilities of the harvest season, plus the discomfort of the heat in the chambers, meant that elections would not be held from 15 August to 15 September—'la qual cosa molto disconzava de persone et non era necessaria al ben comune' (*Lib. Vir.*: Cap. 290).

of so many elections late in December allowed a 'new' government to be associated with a new year. Thus, even though the ballots for some offices were held in December and sometimes earlier, the official term of office was often recorded as beginning on the first of January. This orderly routine to the official year corresponded to a folk model of order in which doctrines of harmony, unity, and balance were important. This same regularity, however, created possibilities for political manœuvre, since if one was elected to an earlier post, one could not be a candidate for a post being voted upon later. Thus, the opponents of a particular individual could prevent his election to a desired office by ensuring that he was elected to some post that was balloted on earlier. This action might clear the way for their own candidate. Similarly, by electing their own man to a post early in the election process, they could prevent him from being elected to a later office which he might not have wanted to hold. But while elections for particular offices tended to be held at about the same time, there was also a strong tendency for them to drift later and later into the year. The *Conte de Stagno* can be taken as an example. The *Conte* was elected for a term of six months. In 1480 Marinus Benedetto de Gondola (ID 1181) was elected on 4 May. The following year the next *Conte* was elected on 1 June. By 1482 the date had slipped back to 13 August. In 1484 the date had drifted to 6 October, and the following year it had moved further to 18 November. By 1488, nine years after Marinus de Gondola was elected, the date had returned to May. This drifting was apparently caused by the reluctance of the Great Council to elect a replacement until the sitting incumbent had finished his term of office.

Those who receive the most votes do not always take up office. An office-holder must always gain a majority of the votes cast, but sometimes others receive more votes than the person accepting office. The others may have refused office. A rather unusual case concerns the election of two *Lane officiali del arte della lana* in July 1485, when three of the six nominees received more votes than Nicola Çovan de Poça (ID 1640), who was elected and accepted (*Act. Maior*. 15: fo. 55v).[48]

Election business could be tedious. We have seen that virtually every meeting of the Great Council contained at least one. In sessions where many were held, the process must have appeared interminable. This is reflected in the manuscript sources. As one reads through the successive ballots of lengthy meetings, the details become sketchier and less accurate as one fruitless ballot follows another. Desperation and boredom lead to clerical sloppiness. In successive ballots the names of nominees are recorded in increasingly abbreviated fashion. Occasionally the names are mixed and at least once the clerk became confused over the month (*Act. Maior*. 12: fos. 217, 221)! But elections could also be high drama. There was much at stake.

---

[48] This case is unusual, but not unique (cf. *Act. Maior*. 14: fo. 189v; 15, fo. 244r).

4

The *Casata*

What is the Casata*?*

Only patricians were eligible to sit on the Great Council. This council had 'closed' its membership about 1332, becoming a hereditary body thereafter. Very little is known about the circumstances and even the date of the closing is uncertain.[1] It is known that a committee of 'three good men' had been given the task of drawing up a list of all currently sitting members and those others whose fathers or grandfathers had been members. Hereafter membership was restricted to these men and their legitimate male offspring. At the time of closing Ragusa belonged to Venice and was administered by a Venetian Count.[2] It is significant that Venice's own Great Council had become hereditary thirty-five years earlier in 1297.

Genealogical research on the fourteenth-century patriciate shows that members of Ragusa's Great Council were grouped into seventy-eight *casate* at the time of its closing (Mahnken 1960). Over the course of the following century a number of these *casate* (*casata* sing.) died out and by the late fifteenth century only thirty-three survived. Understanding of the term '*casata*' presents some problems. The *casata* was an important Ragusan institution but it is not quite so clear what this unit was or what part it played in the structure of government.

The term appears frequently in government documents, where it is found in a variety of forms such as '*casada*', '*chasata*', and so on. The *Specchio*—that indispensable handbook on government for the mid-fifteenth century—opens with an alphabetical list of all the thirty-three *casata* whose noble gentlemen were eligible to hold office.[3] A second section then lists all offices with their incumbents in order (with dates).[4] A third lists all men eligible to sit on the Great Council with dates

---

[1] Dubrovnik's scholars disagree about the date of the closing. There is no direct evidence. Nedeljković has argued that the closing took place sometime between 1319 and 1324, but certainly before 1325 (cited in Petrovich 1974: 560). He points to differences in procedures for making nominations to the Great Council between 1319 and 1325. Great Council records are lost for the period between June 1320 and June 1325. Krekić places it soon after 1332 (1972: 32). According to Mahnken it took place in 1332. She refers to legislation of 12 May of that year prohibiting patricians from engaging in the trade of butchering (1960: 29n. citing *Monumenta Ragusina*, V, p. 349).

[2] Ragusa became independent from Venice in 1358 in the aftermath of the war between Venice and Hungary/Croatia.

[3] It reads in its entirety: '*Queste sono le casade de le Çentilomi de la magnifica Citade de Ragusi qui descrite per alphabeto de ba bi be bo bi secondo apar per ordene ut infra*' (*Specchio*: fo. 1–1v).

[4] Under each office there is a brief description with references to specific statutes where the details of eligibility, tenure, payment, and responsibilities are spelled out.

of entry (after 1455) and their ages at entry (after 1472). In these lists each person is identified by their personal name and the name of their *casata* or surname. This format is followed in all governmental documents.

In Florence and Venice the term has been rendered by historians, with references to anthropological studies of unilineal descent groups, as 'patrilineal lineage' (Chojnacki 1985: 241–2; F. Kent 1977: 6–7; Klapisch-Zuber 1985: 117).[5] There are some good arguments for adopting the same terminology for the Ragusan *casata*. When the term *'casata'* appears in the statutes, it appears in a restrictive context where if two or more persons are holding a single office, then they should not be of the same *casata*. The two *Officiali lavorieri in Stagno* must come from two different *casate*, the three *Camerlengi del comone* should be from three, and so on. The wording is typically of the form: 'doi zentilomini de doe schiate over casade' (*Lib. Vir.*: Cap. 378). As in the preceding phrase, the terms *'schiate'* (Italian, meaning 'race' or 'stock') and *'casate'* are often found together and are used interchangeably (ibid.: Caps. 292, 337, 352, 360bis, 378).[6]

The implication is that if several agnates held the same office at the same time, they might use the opportunity to favour narrow *casata* interests over the broader interests of Ragusa herself. The restriction was scrupulously maintained. In the case of the three *Camerlengi del comone* we find that there are no instances where persons from the same *casata* hold this office at the same time although there are several occasions where they follow one another closely. In May 1445 Climento Antonio de Goçe (ID 1012) replaces Raphael Marin de Goçe (ID 877) as one of the *Camerlengi*. The following month Climento is replaced by Luca Çugno de Bona (ID 248). In the elections which follow, Luca de Bona in his turn is replaced by Marin Sarachin de Bona (ID 291) (*Specchio*: s.v. *Camerlengi del comone*). Thus Goçe follows Goçe and Bona follows Bona, but their terms of office do not overlap. In both of these cases the agnates are not closely related to one another. Of Venice Gaspara Contarini wrote 'that not onely in the Senate, but also in all other offices there shoulde not bee any more of one kindred or allyance, with the preservation of equalitie required' (quoted in Pullan 1971: 114). It is the combination of descent in the male line plus the implication of group interest which suggests that the Ragusan, Venetian, and Tuscan *casata* is a patrilineal descent group.

However, Jack Goody, the anthropologist who is most frequently cited by historians of Europe, has rejected such an interpretation. The lineages of Tuscany are, he insists, 'very different from the type of corporate descent group character-

[5] Elsewhere the Kents refer to the several members of the Peruzzi, one of the Florentine *casate*, as a 'kindred' or 'family', but the context makes it clear that these terms are loosely substituted for 'lineage' and 'clan' which appear elsewhere (D. and F. Kent 1981: 345). Kuehn also occasionally substitutes 'kindred' or 'family' (as in 'family line', 'family branch') for 'lineage' (1991: 153, 156). The literature on kinship and kin groupings in Italy is large and relates to a wide range of issues (see, for example, Visceglia 1993, Mineo 1995). I have concentrated on the work of F. Kent and Klapisch-Zuber because their work has been particularly influential in discussions among historians and anthropologists.
[6] For convenience here and in the analysis which follows I refer only to the *casata*, but the following remarks could apply to *schiate* as well.

istic of, say, African lineage systems' (1983: 232). Goody suggests that the Tuscan *casata* or 'house' is perhaps more akin to 'a descending, "ancestor-oriented" kindred' (ibid.). The brevity of this judgement has left historians bewildered. If the *casata* is not a lineage, why isn't it? And what difference does it make?

In a later work Goody elaborates on this summary judgement. In the course of a larger analysis of Eurasian marriage and domestic institutions, he contrasts the various types of 'lineage' found in China with those of Africa and India. Tuscan 'descent lines' are mentioned in passing. Although they only receive one paragraph of coverage, we learn that they are not lineages for the following reasons: (*a*) They 'were not formally constituted corporations in the same way [as Chinese endowed lineages], but groups of kin linked together by claims to status and estate in aristocratic and mercantile families' (1990: 77). (*b*) 'These groups existed in a society that was largely cognatic (bilateral) in its kinship organisation' (ibid.). This difference is qualified because, like the endowed lineages of China, Tuscan descent lines are also found among the rich rather than the poor. (*c*) 'They consisted of "descent lines" rather than the more extensive kind of group found in China, or in a different form in Africa, although in Italy branch lines were sometimes held together over the longer term by joint interests, including claims to property and status' (ibid.).

Therefore while Tuscan 'descent lines' come close to being proper lineages, they do not quite reach the mark. For those who might still find this somewhat obscure, Goody goes on to point out that a refinement of concepts concerning the lineage is badly needed. Not only do European *lignages* differ from lineages, but the lineages of China, India, and Africa differ from one another (ibid.: 78–9). We will refer again to Goody's three points when comparing the Ragusan *casate* with their Tuscan and Venetian counterparts.

In using the term 'house' to refer to the Tuscan *casata*, Goody has opened a further line of interpretation. It was Lévi-Strauss who drew the attention of kinship specialists to the noble houses of medieval Europe. These noble houses, like the Kwakiutl *numayma*, show certain anomalous characteristics which do not fit neatly into traditional classifications of kin groups. In contrast to 'lineages' and lineage-based societies, he offers the notion of the 'house' and house-based societies.

The paradox of the 'house' in Lévi-Strauss's view is that it transcends such theoretically incompatible principles as patrilineal/matrilineal descent, filiation/residence, hypergamy/hypogamy, close/distant marriage, and heredity and election (1983: 174). This suggestion has been taken up and elaborated in a number of studies. It has been proposed that perhaps even some examples of 'classic' African lineage systems are better understood as house-based systems (Kuper 1993; Carsten and Hugh-Jones 1995). Therefore, there is the additional possibility that the Ragusan *casata* might well resemble European noble 'houses' and that the Ragusan patriciate might show the features of a house-based system. This alternative will also be canvassed in the discussion which follows.

If there is some puzzlement about the differences between lineages, kindreds, and houses and about the significance of the differences, it is not restricted to historians. When Meyer Fortes published 'The Structure of Unilineal Descent Groups' in 1953—the key work on lineage which is often cited by historians of Italian city-states—the outlines of lineage systems were becoming reasonably clear. There had been studies of three systems which were to become classics. While the Nuer, Tallensi, and Tiv were quite different from one another, the studies of them provided a compelling series of how-to-do-it examples for subsequent generations to follow. But even amongst the so-called descent theorists there were, and still are, considerable differences on a broad range of fundamental issues such as 'cognatic descent', the relationship between alliance and descent, or that between filiation and descent.

But if descent theory once dominated the centre of kinship studies, and if kinship studies had the pride of the central place within social anthropology, they no longer do so. There have been important theoretical shifts within anthropology. The notion of 'society' and the morphological assumptions which underpinned studies of 'kinship', 'economy', 'politics', and 'religion' have come under intense critical scrutiny. The guiding idea of 'society' was supplanted by the notion of 'culture'. 'Culture' too has been criticized and deconstructed. It has now been eclipsed by other guiding ideas such as 'embodiment', 'agency', 'narrative', and 'memory'. As the discipline has come to terms with developments in such areas as practice theory, feminism, or phenomenology, the older debates about descent and lineage may now appear parochial with their roots embedded in a structural/functional paradigm and an Africa-centric ethnography. So far have theoretical interests shifted that today even some kinship specialists are not so certain about what a 'lineage' is. Therefore, viewed from the outside, it might appear that kinship studies within anthropology are in disarray.

But the questions which dogged descent theorists are still timely, particularly so to historians and social anthropologists who are attempting to determine the outlines of institutions of historic peoples. Relying heavily upon archives of written sources—and especially legal sources—the historical anthropologist must still painstakingly try to reconstruct the contours of institutions. It is here that questions like 'What is the *casata*?' are still very timely. There is, therefore, a double task in the discussion which follows. The first of these is to address the interests of historians of the late-medieval period, especially those who study politics and kinship in Italian city-states. To this end my account makes explicit and detailed comparisons between Florentine and Venetian institutions and Ragusan ones. The second task is to address social anthropologists, both kinship specialists and those who may feel that issues like 'descent' need no longer concern them.

The present account has a limited comparative frame. While concentrating largely on Ragusa, it also draws upon studies from Florence and Venice for comparative analysis. It does not attempt the broad comparison of lineage systems that Goody suggests is overdue. It has more modest objectives. In some respects the more limited comparison with Florence and Venice is inevitable. Studies of Ragusan politics, kinship, and marriage are still in their infancy. There are many topics that have been intensively studied with respect to Florence or Venice but about which almost nothing is known for Ragusa. Therefore, until research on comparable Ragusan institutions can be undertaken, the temporary alternative is to interpolate research findings from Venice and Florence. Similarly, the present study attempts some lines of enquiry which have not been attempted for Venice and Florence. Therefore, some of our findings will be used to make suggestions about the understanding of Venetian and Florentine institutions and practices. But this process of comparison and interpolation must be done with caution. We need to beware the Charybdis of exaggerating differences between these city-states while, at the same time, avoid the Scylla of a too hasty homogenization.

The first question that must be answered is whether the Ragusan and Tuscan terms '*casata*' refer to the same thing. Although the terms are identical, this may mask some important differences in Ragusan and Tuscan institutions that need to be explored. Once the question about similarities and differences is answered, there is the further problem of what kind (or kinds) of unit these *casate* are. This would help to tidy up the classification problem. Finally, and far more important than the question of terminological niceties, we need to discover what the similarities and differences between the *casate* mean for our understanding of Florentine, Venetian, and Ragusan institutions. Therefore, it may be useful to begin with the question of what language was in everyday use in Ragusa and the clues that this language vocabulary may provide about kinship usage and links between Ragusa, Venice, and Tuscany.

It is well-known that anthropologists borrowed terms like 'lineage' and 'agnation' from the vocabulary of Roman and later medieval law. Florentines, Venetians, and Ragusans also used this vocabulary—words like *lignaggio* and *agnatio*—to talk about units more colloquially spoken of as *consortia*, *domus*, *casa*, *schiatta*, *casato*, and *progenia* (cf. Kent 1977: 6).[7] But, although they used Latin legal vocabulary and ideas taken from Roman jurisprudence, this does not mean that the *casata* is identical to kin groupings found in ancient Rome. Neither does it necessarily follow that Roman kinship provides a good illustration of what anthropologists mean by a 'lineage system'.

Language and Kinship

Ragusa was a polyglot community. Four languages were in everyday use. A vernacular Slavic language was likely to have been the language of the streets and the domestic language. Servants and villagers (and slaves) from the interior would have spoken in a Slavic tongue. Since a number of patricians began in this period to

---

[7] In his text Kent tends to use the term 'consorteria' where I have used '*casata*' (cf. 1977: 229).

adopt Slavic forms of their surnames and since a number of them bore Slavic given names, it seems quite likely that they used the Slavic language in daily speech amongst themselves as well (cf. Krekić 1995). It is noteworthy that the Ragusan poet Đore Držić (born 1461, died 1501) wrote in the Slavonic vernacular. Đore and Marin Držić, poet and playwright, respectively, were from a non-noble line of the extinct noble Dersa *casata* (Carter 1972: 503–4).[8]

But if a Slavic language was the language of house and street, official council records make clear that Italian was also commonly used in the city. Legislation might commonly begin with Latin formulas, but the substantive enactments tend to be written in Italian. The same applies to more personal documents such as marriage contracts or wills. It would be implausible to argue that this Italian is merely the language of the notaries and completely unintelligible to those patricians having the documents drawn. It is known that Italian was the language of commerce and was also used in schools.

Latin is a third possibility. Learned patricians would be familiar with Roman practice from their reading of the classics as well as study of the law. One 'librarius' had a shop on the main street before 1463, there were a number of private libraries which are documented in wills, and there was an active circulation of books amongst members of the patriciate (Krekić 1994). Latin was also used in government documents. The minutes of the Great Council, for example, were kept in Latin. The suggestion that Ragusan patrician kinship might in some respects be modelled on Roman kinship might seem absurd, but it cannot be dismissed out of hand. The reason is a fourth possibility. This is 'Latine', the indigenous Ragusan language spoken amongst patricians. It is not altogether clear what 'Latine' is, although it has been suggested that it is a vulgar form of Latin which the forebears of the patricians adopted from the Dalmatian Romans (Božić 1948: 23).[9] Whatever its origins, 'Latine' was sufficiently important for the Senate to rule in 1472 that it should be the idiom of council discussions (*Act. Rogat.* 21: fo. 273). It does not appear, however, that this reactionary measure met with much success.

The issue of language has a direct bearing on our understanding of the *casata* and kinship in Ragusa. If Italian were the language of patrician family life, then we might expect that the Ragusan *casata* would be similar to the *casata* (say) in Florence and the Italian mainland. The analysis of one would have clear implications for the analysis of the other. But if the Slavic vernacular were the language of the family, then kinship forms among the patriciate might mirror those of the Slavic-speaking villages and hinterland of Ragusa. The use of Latin, or 'Latine', as the language of kinship would suggest other possibilities. Everyday language would point towards somewhat different ways of understanding what *casata* meant.

[8] See also Mahnken (1960: s.v. 'Dersa').
[9] Stuard suggests that it is a dialect of Italian (1992: 34). Some words are still current in the Dubrovnik dialect.

But the issue of the language impinges upon analysis in another way as well. While the patterns encoded in the Slavic vernaculaɪ, in Italian, and in Latin have a number of similarities between them, there are also differences. It is in this respect that the language used in daily life has a bearing on our understanding of Ragusan kinship.

What, then, was the language of kinship in patrician Ragusa? There can be no definitive answer at our present state of understanding, but it is possible to esti-mate likelihoods. The documents which survive as government records provide few clues. With respect to kin terms, for example, such documents as contain any information refer to only a very small number of kinship positions and the kin terms are presented in the language of the document itself: either Latin or Italian for the period. However, neither of these seems a likely candidate. As council records make clear, Latin was not well understood even by those who should have been well schooled in it. Italian was taught and used, but it was only taught to some and used in relatively specialized contexts. Diversus himself was a grammar master from Lucca. He mentions in his account, however, that Italian was not the lan-guage of everyday affairs in Ragusa (Petrovich 1974: 61n.).[10] It would be very sur-prising, therefore, if either Latin or Italian were the everyday language of kinship. It seems much more likely that the local Slavic language was the language of the patrician home. Patricians would certainly have been familiar with the forms of Slavic kinship idioms of their servants, neighbours, and peasants. But in the absence of firm evidence, this cannot be more than a suggestion. It should be noted that the language and practice need not have been either 'Italian', 'Slavic', or some-thing else. Within a polyglot community such as Ragusa sitting astride several cul-tural worlds, there might have been multiple idioms in daily use and patricians might have used them interchangeably.

In this respect the inferences which can be drawn from kinship terminology cut two ways. On the one hand terminological systems appear to change very slowly. Therefore, while we do not have analyses of terminological usage among fifteenth-century Ragusans, Florentines, or Venetians, analysis of contemporary Italian and Serbo-Croatian may shed some light on earlier practices. While Italian and Serbo-Croatian systems of kinship terminology differ somewhat (and while Serbian and Croatian also differ from one another), both are 'mixed' with elements of bifurcate-collateral and lineal systems. Such systems are generally not associated with patrilineal descent groups. They are, however, consistent with paternal joint-families (Hammel 1957: 61–5).[11] In this respect contemporary systems of kinship terminology are consistent with forms of household known to have been present in fifteenth-century Ragusa, Florence, and Venice. But they do not support the view that the *casata* is a lineage of the classic type.[12]

---

[10] On popular schooling of the period, see Grendler (1989).

[11] See also Anderson (1963), Goody (1983: 262–78), and Guerreau-Jalabert (1981: 1043–5).

[12] See Freidenberg (1967) for a discussion of kinship in historic Dalmatia.

Ragusa and Florence: Similarities and Differences

In referring to the *casata*, scholars of present-day Dubrovnik use the term 'family' as well as the more technical terms 'lineage' and 'clan'.[13] 'Family' has a comfortable ambiguity, but it is sometimes not very clear which of several different meanings is intended. Kent has noted that in fifteenth-century Florence the term *famiglia* could be applied to two sorts of units. In his examination of these units, he refers to these two as the domestic group and the patrilineal lineage, respectively. In Florence the latter unit was often referred to by a number of terms (*consortia, domus, casa, schiatta, casato,* and *progenia* among others) and these terms could be used in different senses. Such terms also appear in Ragusa. But although they might be used in different ways, Kent insists that the primary meaning is clear: 'a group of kinsmen tracing descent in the male line from a common ancestor' (1977: 6). He continues, 'In technical language the Florentine *consorteria* was therefore a patrilineal lineage—Florentines themselves sometimes used the words *lignaggio* (lineage) and *agnatio* (agnatic kin group) to describe it.' Kent points out that the Florentine 'lineage' was not like the Genoese *alberghi*, a quasi-familiar association, because the Florentine units 'always claimed to be patrilineal descent groups and in most cases were' (ibid.: 6–7). Some of the lineages did not stem from a single ancestor (their union being founded by treaty) and they could dissolve into separate units later on the grounds that they were not of the same blood. Lineages might also admit outsiders, as the Borromei did in 1457 (ibid.: 7).

Kent's elegant account has become the touchstone for further work on the Florentine household and lineage. Viewed from an anthropological perspective, this book exhibits a familiar form of organization. It is divided into two parts. Part One concentrates on the developmental cycle of households within three Florentine 'lineages'—the Capponi, Ginori, and Rucellai—and shows how ties and sentiments forged within single domestic units created bonds which later patterned the relationships between the several households which had sprung from the original unit. In Part Two the lineage is considered. This second part contains three further chapters and examines the lineage in economic affairs, in politics, and in neighbourhood and commemorative works. Thus, it resembles an abridged version of Fortes's *Dynamics of Clanship* and *Web of Kinship*, but in reverse order.[14] While it was certainly not the first study to view the Florentine *casata* as a patrilineage, it marked the beginning of a period when historians of late medieval Europe placed their material in a comparative anthropological perspective and explicitly adopted

[13] Krekić refers to them as 'families' in his several English and Serbo-Croatian writings. See, for example, Krekić 1986: 399; 1987a: 193. Stuard refers to 'lineages' (1981: 804). Petrovich and Rheubottom use the term 'clans' (1974: 584 and 1988: 363, respectively). The Serbo-Croatian term '*rodovi*' (= clan) is used in Mahnken (1960: 9).

[14] Fortes's seminal articles on the developmental cycle and unilineal descent groups are referred to and there is also a reference to his *Web of Kinship* (Kent 1977: 6, 39). Fortes, a South African by birth and a British academic by choice, would have taken wry pleasure in being referred to as 'the American anthropologist Meyer Fortes' (Molho 1978: 305).

anthropological ideas and terminology in their analyses.[15] While subsequent studies of Florentine kinship have extended Kent's analysis and developed it in new areas, the basic contention has been accepted that 'In technical language the Florentine *consorteria* was therefore a patrilineal lineage'. For example, while Kuehn may question the degree of 'lineage solidarity' expressed in the self-disciplining pacts amongst Peruzzi agnates (which the Kents had analysed), he does not doubt that the Peruzzi were a lineage. And in considering the case of Leon Battista Alberti's illegitimate birth and his awkward relations with his agnates, he does not doubt that they constituted a patriline within the Alberti lineage (1991: 154–6, 172). As a pathfinding study which both summed up what was known about the Florentine *casata* and mapped out further directions for research, Kent's study commends itself for entering into a dialogue with anthropology. What then, in Kent's view (and in technical language), is a lineage?

Let us consider Kent's definition again. A lineage is, he says, 'a group of kinsmen tracing descent in the male line from a common ancestor' (1977: 6). Was there a common ancestor as a point of focus to the group? A number of the family diaries (*ricordi*) kept by Florentines contained genealogical information. But these, kept by individual men for their own benefit and for the benefit of their sons, contained more information about their own lines than collateral branches. This is understandable, as Kent argues, because the starting point was the writer's household and its immediate ancestors (1977: 272–3). One example, the *Cronica Domestica* of Donato Velluti, sketches his own line of descent, 'by which he meant the group of Velluti descended from his great-grandfather' (ibid.: 274).[16] Even the famous *Zibaldone* of Giovanni Rucellai (begun in 1457), 'one of the most extensive and accurate genealogical accounts of a Florentine lineage which has come down to us', contains information on 'all the important lines' descending from his great-great-grandfather. Other living lines of the Rucellai were mentioned, but apparently not sketched in. While, as Kent notes, there are many other Florentine diaries and genealogies which have not been examined, certain conclusions can be drawn from the materials so far presented.

Genealogical recall, even in carefully researched accounts such as Rucellai's *Zibaldone*, was shallow and uneven. The common ancestor referred to was not the founder of the group, but that section from whom the writer was descended. These smaller sections could also be called the 'house' (cf. Klapisch-Zuber 1985: 299). Of the cases cited by Kent, the most distantly recalled ancestor was only four generations removed from the writer. This would create a span of genealogical

---

[15] The close interest in anthropological perspectives covers a broad range of topics such as ritual, symbolism, and the feud as well as kinship and marriage. The borrowing, however, is not uncritical. For example, while finding stimulation in the work of Geertz, Lévi-Strauss, and V. Turner in his analysis of Venetian civic ritual, Muir points out how little anthropological theory has to say about historical change (1981: 58–9). See also the discussions of anthropology in Biersack (1989) and Lloyd (1993).

[16] A footnote mentions the *cronica* of Buonaccorso Pitti. 'His analysis of this group [of three parts] began with his great-great-grandfather, but he was most concerned with his grandfather and his descendants . . .' (page references in the quotation are omitted).

knowledge extending at its furthest remove only to third cousins. In this respect Florentine genealogical knowledge resembles a kindred system rather than one based upon patrilineages. Although accounts such as *Zibaldone* were for private use, they might occasionally be loaned to agnatic kin. But even if this practice were widespread, it does not follow, as Kent argues, that it 'would have contributed to the creation of a shared tradition among related households' (1977: 278). Those borrowing were presumably more ignorant of genealogical knowledge than the lenders and the knowledge they would have obtained would be largely of the lender's 'lines', not necessarily of their own. Further, as Molho *et al.* have shown (1994), the *Zibaldone* was not solely devoted to agnatic kinsmen. Rucellai's account also contains those sibling sets (including both males and females) of five women who married into the Rucellai: his paternal grandmother, mother, wife, and son's wives.

While comparable evidence is not available for Venice, it is worth noting that the Venetian Council of Ten decreed that 'men who are joined together by any of the following ties of relationship cannot hold office [in a *Scuola*] at one and the same time, viz. father, son, brother, son-in-law, father's brother, son's son, brother's son, nephew, cousin-german' (quoted in Pullan 1971: 113). Another Florentine genealogical document, the *memoriale* of Lorenzo da Lutiano, contains maternal lines and mentions specific women as ancestresses (Klapisch-Zuber 1994). This suggests that genealogical knowledge in Florence may have been assembled for a variety of purposes and in a variety of forms. Knowledge of agnatic kin within the Florentine *casata* appears to be of numerous short 'lines', extending two to four generations above living members.

Distinctive sets of personal names in Florence also tend to mark these lines when, for example, a given name is appended to the father's name, which is appended to the grandfather's, and so on. Hence, one might find an Albizzo d'Ugolino d'Albizzo d'Ugolino d'Albizzo Rucellai (F. Kent 1977: 46). Except in those few cases where personal names might give some clue, it is unlikely that most men would have known how the several lines of the *casata* were linked to one another within an overarching genealogical framework. In other words, while some persons had knowledge of genealogical ties extending 'up' from themselves for several generations, there is no clear evidence that they also had knowledge which extended 'down' from the founding ancestor. In Florence it does not seem to be the case, as Kent has suggested, that people within the *casata* can trace 'descent . . . from a common ancestor'. It does not appear that there was a known common ancestor for all persons in the *casata* or an encompassing framework of genealogical knowledge that could map relationships between agnates.

From an examination of patrician genealogies published by Mahnken, one might conclude that the Ragusan *casate* are elaborately segmented patrilineages. They typically begin with an apical ancestor in the topmost generation, show his sons and daughters (and their spouses) in the next, then the offspring of those sons in the following generation, and so on. In each generation the children of female members are omitted. Thus, to take the case of the Babalio as an illustration, there is one male in the founding generation, his four sons in the following generation, seven more men in the third, eleven in the fourth generation, and twenty-one in the fifth (Mahnken 1960: s.v. 'Babalio'). In appearance the genealogies are remarkably like diagrams of such classic patrilineal people as the Tallensi, but this appearance is misleading. The published genealogies are twentieth-century reconstructions based upon the assemblage and linkage of thousands of pieces of information. The lineage pattern is the display device of a contemporary author. Similarly, the links of successive patrifiliation that have been coded in the computer database of the present study as Hackenberg Numbers are also a contemporary device. None of these can be taken to imply Ragusan cultural usage. There is no evidence that fifteenth-century patricians conceived of relationships between themselves in terms of an overarching patrilineal genealogy.

Among people with 'classic' lineage systems such genealogies are presumed known. These consist of both 'top-down' and 'bottom-up' knowledge, although there may be some ambiguity about how the furthest known descendants of the founding ancestor are linked to the furthest known ancestors of the living. It is this middle area of uncertainty in genealogical knowledge which permits adjustment and telescoping to occur (Peters 1960). Such adjustment is important because genealogical knowledge provides a 'charter' (to use a Malinowskian term) for existing relationships. That is, existing patterns of relationships amongst the living have priority and genealogies are 'remembered' in such a manner as to make sense of (and explain) those patterns. As Fortes has argued, 'a "descent group" implies the precise information that these groups are made up of persons whose genealogical relations with one another are exclusively and exhaustively specifiable both by any member and by an informed outsider. Anyone acquainted with the rules of exclusion and inclusion can predict the descent group location of a given person' (1969: 286). *Casata* affiliation can be exclusively and exhaustively specifiable from the outside—but because of the surname, not by genealogical criteria. Within the *casata* it cannot be so specified.

Perhaps descent group location may be determined by other means. Every patrician Ragusan male bore a *casata* name or surname. These were distinctive and associated with heraldic arms. The names are interesting in that while many appear to be Italianate, they are not surnames commonly found in Italy. A variety of different forms of these surnames survive in our sources. In one source, for example, the surname Georgio (a fairly common Italian surname in this instance) is given as 'Çorçi', 'Zorzi', and 'Georgio' (*Specchio*: fos. 1v, 296, 296v).[17] The name of the *casata* is always recorded as part of the name of every patrician mentioned in government documents. Women's names, however, are different. Women are never designated by the name of either their natal *casate* or the *casate* into which they

[17] A single manuscript page can exhibit several forms. Continuing with the Georgio example, a ballot in 1480 lists three of the candidates as a Zorgio, Zorzi, and Georgio (*Act. Maior.* 14: fo. 183v). Similar ingenuity is found in rendering other surnames.

have married. Instead, they are always identified by their association with a named man, either father or husband, and sometimes both.[18] The significance of women in the *casate* will be examined in detail below.

All *casate* claim their place of origin as outside Ragusa. Two of the oldest, the Bonda and Resti, claim Epidaurus (present-day Cavtat) as their ancestral home. The Poça came from Kotor. Others were said to have foreign origins: the Georgio, Gondola, and Mençe from Rome and the Bona from Germany. Others had their origins in Italy, Dalmatia, and the Balkan interior. Interestingly, however, none came from nearby Bosnia, Hercegovina, or Zeta. Therefore, in addition to the distinctive name and arms, each of the *casate* also had a myth of outside origin.

Following the closing of the Great Council, there were seventy-eight such *casate*. Some were very small and soon died out as no legitimate issue were produced who might perpetuate the group. By the fifteenth century the number of *casate* with members eligible to sit on the Great Council had dwindled to thirty-six. There was a similar thinning in Venice of noble *casate* in the Great Council in the century after its closing. Just over one-fifth of the Venetian patrician *casate* became extinct (Chojnacki 1973: 55). Of the thirty-six Ragusan *casate* that survived to the beginning of the fifteenth century, a further three were to disappear during the course of that century. Marussa, the daughter of Palcho de Baraba (ID 2415), was the last survivor of the Baraba. She died in 1451. The last noble Bodaca, Clemens Franciscus de Bodaca (ID 2972), disappeared from the records around 1430. Although there were no Bodaca among the patriciate, Clemens had an illegitimate son who carried on this name. The Gleda also disappeared about this time. Palcho Maroe de Gleda (ID 2392), the last surviving male, died in 1435. Thus, by the mid-fifteenth century there were only thirty-three patrician *casate* left. Some *populo* branches of defunct noble *casate* still survived and were active in the city even though their members were not eligible to sit on the Great Council.

Given what is known about the expected rate of patriline extinction, it is not too surprising that only twenty-four of these noble *casate* survived in 1666 (see Wachter and Laslett 1978).[19] In that year two new merchant *casate* were introduced into the patriciate to make up for the decline in numbers. A further eight were allowed in the following year after the great earthquake had further devastated the city and the ranks of the patriciate.[20]

The Ragusan *casate* differed greatly in size. While existing records do not enable us to know all the men, women, and children at any single point in time, we can estimate their relative sizes according to the number of members they had sitting on the Great Council. The Goçe were clearly the largest *casata* of the period. They

---

[18] In one dowry contract a party is identified as being the mother of a patrician—d. Fiocha, the mother of Marin de Crose (*Pacta Matrimonialia* (hereafter referrred to as *Pacta*) 2: fo. 18–18v).

[19] I am indebted to Peter Laslett for this reference.

[20] On the earthquake and the introduction of new houses, see Petrovich (1974: 586–7). While Petrovich doubts the drastic decline in patrician houses noted by Mahnken, such a decline is consistent with our understanding of patriline extinction.

TABLE 4. Casata *representation on the Great Council, 1455–1490*

Casata name	Average representation[a]
Goçe	33.3
Bona	29.6
Gondola	23.4
Sorgo	17.4
Georgio	16.6
Zrieva	15.8
Mençe	14.9
Resti	12.4
Lucari	12.1
Poça	11.7
Babalio	10.3
Ragnina	10.1
Zamagna	9.6
Benessa	7.8
Caboga	7.4
Buchia	7.4
Volçe	7.1
Saraca	7.0
Palmota	5.0
Grade	4.8
Bonda	4.1
Martinussio	4.0
Tudisio	3.8
Batalo	3.4
Proculo	3.4
Luca	2.8
Binçola	2.7
Crosio	2.6
Getaldo	2.3
Calich	2.1
Mlaschagna	1.9
Bocinolo	1.6
Prodanello	1.5

[a] Average number of adult males sitting on the Great Council between 1455 and 1490.

had an average of 33.3 members sitting between 1455 and 1490. They could boast of more Great Council members than the combined average strength of all eleven of the smallest *casate*—the Batalo, Binçola, Bocinolo, Calich, Crosio, Getaldo, Luca, Mlaschagna, Proculo, Prodanello, and Tudisio—which stood at 30.8 members (see Table 4).[21] There were only nine *casate* that had a dozen or more members on the council. In considering the politics of this city-state, we will need

[21] The reasons for choosing the period from 1455 to 1490 are explained below. Petrovich's ordering of houses by size for the period 1592–1667 is strikingly similar: Goçe, Bona, Sorgo, Gondola, Mençe, Caboga, Georgio, Poça, Zamagna, Resti, Grade, Getaldo, Tudisio, Palmota, Lucari, Babalio, Ragnina, Batalo, Benessa, Saraca, Buchia, etc. (Petrovich 1974: 798, Table 57).

to recall that the total number of active men which each *casata* had in the Great Council is quite small. This has an important bearing on the next point.

Some *casate* show evidence of internal differentiation. The Goçe (also Goze, Goce, or Gučetić) claim to have first arrived in Ragusa about 1000 from Hum (*di Chelmo di Murlachia*). Apparently originally named Pecurario/Pecorario, the Goçe became internally differentiated into several subdivisions bearing distinctive names. One of these, the Dragojević, bore the name of their ancestor, Clemens (Dragoe) Maroe de Goçe (ID 767, fourteenth century). Two other subdivisions, the Goçe de Platea and Goçe de Pusterna, are distinguished by names of particular locations. Pusterna (*Pustijerna*), where the Goçe de Pusterna presumably lived, was the oldest *sexteria* in the city. Another two Goçe divisions, de Fifa (also known as de Martolo) and Pecurario, consist of the commoner descendants of bastard Goçe. Other sections of the Goçe apparently carried no distinctive names (Mahnken 1960: 233). Clemens de Picorario, an early thirteenth-century figure who is shown in the published genealogies as the putative ancestor of all the Goçe, is only four (reconstructed) generations removed from the most senior living Goçe of our period. The founder of the Dragojević section of the Goçe is only one generation removed. It may be that this section bears a distinctive patronymic because it is the largest of the Goçe.

The elaborate branching shown within the published genealogies and the distinctive names for some of the branches suggest the possibility of a segmentary structure. But this conclusion does not appear to be warranted. The Bona, Gondola, and Sorgo, three of the largest *casate* which also show a richly differentiated genealogical structure, do not have their several branches marked by different names while the Mençe and the Georgio do. There is, therefore, no clear relationship between *casata* size, internal genealogical differentiation, and the naming of particular branches within the *casata*. It is particularly noteworthy that when council records refer to named individuals, only given name, patronymic, and *casata* appear. There is no indication of whether the person comes from one branch or another.

Another possible source of differentiation in the *casata* are personal names. In Ragusa there is detailed evidence in the computer database on the transmission of personal names covering five or six generations. For comparative purposes there are also studies of Florentine naming patterns (Klapisch-Zuber 1985; Herlihy 1988). Klapisch-Zuber has suggested that sets of personal names may constitute part of the Florentine *casata*'s patrimony. By this token, the transmission of sets of names in the male line could mark the presence of patrilineages. On the other hand, Lévi-Strauss suggests that the combinatorial systems of personal names found among the Merovingians, Carolingians, and Kwakiutl suggest house-based societies. Lévi-Strauss also considers personal names to be part of the immaterial wealth of the 'house' (1983: 174–5).

In Ragusa it was common practice to name grandsons after their paternal grandfather. Thus, Junius Give de Georgio (ID 2295) had five sons and each of them in

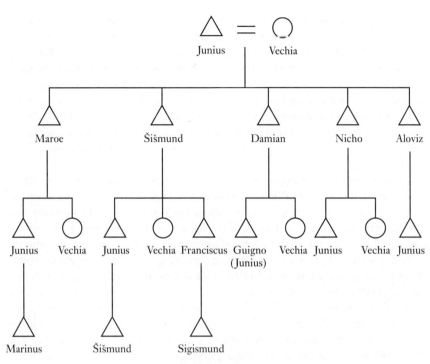

FIG. 1. Naming patterns: the descendants of Junius de Georgio

turn also had a son named Junius: there was Junius Maroe (ID 2298), Junius
Šišmund (ID 2307), Guigno (Junius) Damian (ID 2324), Junius Nicho (ID 2339),
and Junius Aloviz (ID 2342). Junius Maroe, in his turn, had a son Marinus Junius
(ID 2299). Junius Šišmund had a son, Šišmund (ID 2308), and his brother
Franciscus Šišmund (ID 2302) also had a Sigismund (ID 2303) (see Fig. 1). This
tendency to repeat names in alternate generations might indicate patrilineages, but
equally it might be indicative of the kind of 'periodic returns' that Lévi-Strauss
finds in house societies (ibid.: 175).

It is the case that certain names occur in great profusion in parts of a single
casata and are largely absent in other parts. There was, to continue the example
above, only one Junius (ID 2245) elsewhere in the Georgio *casata*. Similarly, elsewhere amongst the Georgio there were a number of Matheuses whereas the name
Matheus did not occur among the descendants of Junius Give. Therefore the very
uneven distribution of given names in various parts of the *casata* could mark off
one patrilineal segment from another. Furthermore, particular combinations of
names might distinguish senior lines from junior ones. Thus, a Georgio with a
combination of Junius and Marinus as given name and patronymic would most
likely be of a senior line whereas someone with the combination of Junius and

Sigismund would be of the next most senior line. Klapisch–Zuber argues that a simple chain of the three names would be 'enough to avoid most of the confusions [of identity] within a lineage, even an extended lineage' (1985: 286). The recording of Ragusan personal names seldom includes more than the given name plus the father's name. Only rarely does a grandfather's name appear. This appears to be identical to Florentine practice (ibid.: 285).[22] Indeed, the notarial practice of extensive abbreviation often makes identification particularly difficult several centuries later. Presumably the clerks (and others with local knowledge) knew who they meant when they wrote 'Ma. Ni. Goçe' even if we cannot be so certain.

There are problems, however, in treating patterns of personal names as evidence of either patrilineages or of 'houses' in house-based societies. As in so many other aspects of patrician life, the giving of names was patterned, yet this pattern contained many variations. In Ragusa there was a tendency to name the eldest son and daughter after the paternal grandfather and grandmother and to name the second son and daughter after the maternal grandparents. Thus the eldest daughter of Šišmund Junius de Georgio (ID 2300) was named after her paternal grandmother, Vechia. This name occurred frequently among the female descendants of Junius de Georgio (see Fig. 1). Yet it was not always given to the eldest daughter. Another brother, Damian Junius de Georgio (ID 2323), gave this name to his youngest daughter. Similarly, the eldest son of Šišmund Junius de Georgio (ID 2300) was not a Junius. He was a Johannes (ID 2301) and he was probably named after his maternal grandfather, Johannes (Givcho) Jacobus de Gondola (ID 1204). While it was common to give children the names of all of their grandparents, the ordering was not necessarily paternal grandparents first, maternal grandparents second.

Through the analysis of Tuscan *ricordanze* Klapisch–Zuber has shown the kinds of sentiments that enter into the naming of children at baptism. While the name was bestowed by godparents in the absence of the parents, it was selected by the child's father or, in rare cases, its mother. Klapisch–Zuber analyses the names given to 266 children, the issue of thirty-three couples. These are cases where 'the author of the *ricordanze* is particularly prolix concerning his reasons for the choice of given names' and where the family's genealogy is fairly well known (1985: 306). Her analysis reveals that most names were those of paternal ascendants. It is in this respect that she can argue that 'given names formed a sort of family patrimony, no part of which should be neglected or lost' (ibid.: 306). She refers to the case of one Tommaso Guidetti who discovered in 1497 that one of his ancestors had the name Mannello. This name had not been used for any Guidetti for several generations. He thus decides to 're-make this ancient name of our house' and bestows this unfashionable name on one of his unfortunate sons (ibid.: 305). As to the reasons,

---

[22] The example of Albizzo d'Ugolino d'Albizzo d'Ugolino d'Albizzo Rucellai referred to above is presumably the scholar's reconstruction, not local usage.

consider the entry in the *ricordanze* of the Florentine Francesco di Tommaso Giovanni made on 26 March 1443: 'The second name that I have had given to him, Giovanni, is in honour of Saint John the Evangelist: the devotion I bear him had made me intend to baptise [one of my children] with his name; but it is also to remake (*rifare*) Giovanni, our brother' (ibid.: 290). This remaking of names, and the retention of a stock of names within the Florentine 'lineage', allows Klapisch-Zuber to argue that such names constitute part of its patrimony. However, it is also the case that about one boy in six and one girl in ten take their names from the maternal line. In addition Klapisch-Zuber could not ascertain the origin of one-quarter of the given names. The problem of names of uncertain origin was most acute for the girls (1985: 291).[23] Some of those names may have come from the maternal line.

Do Ragusan and Florentine naming practices differ? Ragusan patricians recycle the names of ancestors, but these are quite likely to be maternal and affinal kin as well as paternal kin. Therefore, while the pattern of naming contains an agnatic bias, it does not suggest patriliny. The Ragusan evidence suggests the combination of paternal/maternal that Lévi-Strauss finds associated with 'house' societies. Klapisch-Zuber's report on the Florentine material is ambiguous on this point. She argues that both girls and boys 'bear a name taken from the stock of names in the paternal lineage' (ibid.: 291). But the one example given indicates that this name was of the infant's paternal grandmother. If girls' names were drawn from lineage names, this name would come from the paternal grandfather's sister or a comparable female agnate, not the grandfather's wife. Both the Ragusan and Florentine data show great piety towards recently deceased family members. The name of a recently deceased brother or sister would, for example, be bestowed on the next-born child of the appropriate sex. Similarly, the name of the father's first wife is often given to the first daughter born of a second marriage. These practices suggest a piety towards members of the household who have recently died and the close bonds between households linked by marriage. They do not, however, suggest a difference in kinship practice amongst the patricians of Ragusa and Florence with respect to the transmission of personal names. Neither do they suggest that either city had a system of patrilineages.

So far our conclusions are that the *casata* appears as a collection of agnates. Internally agnatic ties are recalled for several generations, but recalled ties are not embraced within an encompassing genealogical framework descending from an apical ancestor who is held to have established the *casata*. While Ragusan genealogies do not exist for our period, those (Florentine) genealogies which have been preserved tend to be 'bottom up' from living persons and terminate, not with the founding ancestor of the *casata*, but with an antecedent about three or four generations removed. Those genealogical ties which are recalled appear to be of cumulative patrifiliation rather than descent and such recalled 'lines' are quite short. It

---

[23] The uncertainty concerned about 34% of the girls and 20% of the boys.

does not seem that members or knowledgeable outsiders can locate *casata* members by genealogical criteria. Furthermore, patterns of personal names mirror ties of complementary filiation: to paternal and maternal grandparents for persons of each sex and to other fondly remembered members of the household. Patterning in the transmission of names does not reflect a pattern of lineage segmentation.

Neither can we say that the use of names of locations, or of other devices, differentiates various part of the *casata*. But so far in this analysis we have examined only one aspect of Kent's definition of a lineage: that is, 'tracing descent in the male line from a common ancestor'. In so far as we can judge from this evidence, the material supports Goody's contention that the *casata* consists of 'descent lines' rather than the more extensive kind of patrilineage that is found in Africa or China (1990: 78–9). We now turn to the question of 'descent' and consider the extent to which the *casata* be considered a descent group.

5

Casata Unity: Size and Political Muscle

The Casata *as Corporation*

Ragusans were fearful of oligarchy and introduced a number of administrative measures to ensure that its constituent *casate* could not subvert the public good. We now turn to consider the role of the *casata* in political affairs. As we have seen, Kent and others regard the Florentine *casata* as a descent group. Most anthropologists would agree with Fortes that 'the most important feature of unilineal descent groups . . . is their corporate organization' (1970: 77–8). What they might disagree about is what constitutes corporacy. One tradition, following Maine, emphasizes perpetuity, collective unity, and universal succession—'the rights and duties of all members present and future in them' (M. Smith 1974: 43). The corporatism of the lineage, as Fortes viewed it, was expressed by structural criteria. The lineage had a single legal personality; it was 'one person' (1970: 78).

In the Fortesian paradigm, the unity of the lineage in its external relationships carried several important structural implications. (1) Relations between units are group-to-group relations and the social order may be said to be constituted by such groups and relations. Evans-Pritchard's analysis of feuding and warfare in *The Nuer* is the classic statement of this principle.[1] Fortes was careful to point out that in a system of unilineal descent groups, lineage membership 'regulates only a part of a person's nexus of statuses, defines only a selection of his rights, duties and capacities and engenders only one sector of his total social identity' (1969: 287).[2] It is 'fundamentally' politico-jural status and capacities that derive from lineage membership. (2) Viewed from the outside, the several members of the lineage (as lineage members) are equivalent to one another. As Fortes put it elsewhere, 'All

---

[1] This case has been frequently misunderstood. Nuer local communities (*cienq*) are open and virtually anyone may take up residence. Co-residence implies joint liability in revenge, defence, and warfare. There are other groups (lineages, *thok dwiel*) which figure in ritual and exogamic relationships. Although local communities and lineages are different kinds of group, there is a systematic relationship between them. Local communities are said to be owned by lineage segments who give them their names and who are 'dominant' in them. Local communities are obliged to ally with or oppose one another according to the position of their 'dominant' lineages in the lineage system. 'Therefore, contrary to Kuper (1982: 92), the lineage structure does order "political activities," in the sense specified by Evans-Pritchard (1940: 5, 211), but it does, as the ethnographer always said it did, between communities associated by name with lineages, rather than between lineages per se' (Scheffler 1986: 345–6).

[2] He also points out the error of regarding unilineal descent as a device for sorting members of society into separate groups, 'like apples in a stack of boxes' (ibid.). Earlier, however, he had not been quite so careful (Fortes 1970 [1953]: 81).

the members of the lineage are equally of it, irrespective of age, sex, or status'
(1945: 135). That is why, when food is divided at Tallensi funerals, it is appor-
tioned according to lineage. Those responsible for the division (that is, the representatives of the lineage) call out and ask if anyone is present from a lineage entitled
to a share. If they are, they are given their appropriate share. It makes no difference whether there is one lineage member present or several. It is the lineage as
'one person' who receives the share (ibid.: 44–5). (3) If the lineage is segmentary
in the manner of the 'classic' African lineage systems, then each segment is also
'one person' with respect to its relationships with co-ordinate segments. And (4)
if lineage segments are counterposed to one another within a segmentary system,
the various segmentary levels cannot be distinguished by morphological criteria
alone. '[T]hey are distinguishable only in functional terms, by the incidence of
jural, ritual, and economic rights, duties, and privileges' (Fortes 1949: 9).

The last point brings up another dimension of corporatism. This view, also
deriving from Maine's comments on the *universitas iuris*, sees corporations as
forming on the basis of common interests—generally on a community of property
relations expressed in productive resources. This second, functionalist, interpretation of corporatism is associated with Goody.

With respect to the issue of the lineage as corporation, the view of Florentine
and Venetian scholars is quite clear. Writing about Venice, Chojnacki argues that
'descent rules are jural constructs that divide society into groups with legal characteristics . . . that bind their members together and distinguish them from other,
similar groups. At bottom, such rules promote orderly relationships . . .' (1985:
241–2).[3] As Klapisch-Zuber has put it with respect to Florence, 'Ultimately, all
members of the lineage of the same sex were interchangeable' (1985: 306). She
cites the renaming of individuals, and the circulation of names, as evidence of
interchangeability. But whether interchangeability implies that the *casata* is also
'one man' in the sense that corporate lineages represent themselves, both internally and to outsiders, is a question that must now be considered.

Perhaps the most compelling piece of evidence concerning Florence is a sworn
pact made between some males of the Peruzzi to keep order amongst themselves.
In their analysis of this pact, the Kents point out that its timing (June 1433) is
highly significant. It occurred towards the end of a period of intense factional
manœuvring from 1426 to 1434 and shows the Peruzzi 'meeting privately and
solemnly to prepare itself for political battle' (D. and F. Kent 1981: 337–8). Such
pacts may have been quite common, although few have survived because 'as secret
documents containing sensitive and even incriminating information, they were
kept hidden away, or were destroyed when a turn in political events made this nec-

---

[3] A footnote makes reference to a range of anthropological writings and points out that this particular formulation does not address a number of the nuances in anthropological treatments of kinship
and descent. One of the references cited is to Goody's discussion of European historical materials where
Goody comments that the *lignages* of Tuscany (and presumably Venice) are quite different from corporate unilineal descent groups (1983: 232).

essary' (ibid.: 338–9). The Kents argue that the pact is 'not an alliance between a number of individuals or families', but 'an agreement within one patrilineage' (ibid.: 340). In this pact certain elders are given authority and power to adminis-ter its provisions. The legalistic form of the document, they suggest, reflects the sense of the Peruzzi as a formally constituted corporation. The subject matter, which could not be known in full to the Kents when they wrote their article, con-cerned a vendetta which, were it not for the pact (and other previous pacts), would have made all Peruzzi possible targets of revenge (Kuehn 1991). It is in this respect that they constitute 'one person'.

This sense of corporateness amongst the Peruzzi is argued with a wealth of detail. They had (as of 1433) their own chapel and one particular neighbourhood was thickly populated with their households. Some of these homesteads showed evidence of a 'unified facade programme' and there was an 'almost self-contained Piazza de' Peruzzi' which was 'literally ringed by tall Peruzzi houses and palaces'. Therein stood the *loggia de' Peruzzi* (ibid.: 345–6). All of this material, carefully and elegantly presented, is very compelling. But does it show that the Peruzzi were a lineage?

In what sense could the Florentine *casata* be considered a corporation? The evi-dence of property ownership is ambiguous. There is, for example, no suggestion that major productive resources were *casata* property. The building of a Rucellai loggia about 1456 required the demolition of a dwelling in which several Rucellai men had portions. One man was incensed that he had not been consulted since he had a share of one-sixth (F. Kent 1977: 242). But in this case it appears that the building in question was owned by several Rucellai in their private capacities.[4] It was not, apparently, jointly held by a Rucellai segment in which each member held a share according to their genealogical position. On the other hand it is also known that the Rucellai maintained a hospital or oratory near Campi in Tuscany which was said to belong to all the Rucellai. When the buildings fell into disrepair, one of the Rucellai appointed a friar to put things right on behalf of 'all his kinsmen and agnates of the house and family of Rucellai' (ibid.: 235). Since Goody places great weight on property-holding, the very shadowy existence of such functions amongst Florentine *casate* may have prompted him to conclude that they were not lineages. They were clearly not 'one man' in terms either of their internal rela-tionships or of their relations to other units within the world of Florentine poli-tics. The pact of 1433 could only bind the signatories to it and other persons under the power of the signatories. The nine signatories came from one-third of the twenty-seven Peruzzi households. The Kents argue that the degree of representa-tion was much higher than this. They suggest that one man, Piero de Giovanni, came from a Peruzzi palace containing five separate households. But does the fact that he was the only one in attendance show that he 'represented' the others? Even if there were evidence to show that some of those attending were representing

[4] This, presumably, is why the disgruntled Nicollò di Vanni mentioned it in his tax report.

others, it remains that the pact was an alliance of particular households. The internal affairs of the Peruzzi as described does not demonstrate corporateness. If the
Peruzzi were a corporate patrilineage, the heads of the various segments could represent all of their agnates, speak on their behalf as if they were 'one person', and
bind them to the conditions reached. They do not appear as corporate units in
their internal relationships. Elsewhere, F. Kent notes that very old or very able men
could exercise wide influence within their *casata*, 'But there was no recognized
system of succession to . . . leadership; it is more proper to say that the *consorteria*
was led, and represented, by a group of elders or heads of households. As Alberti
put it, a lineage was "a republic," a federation of related men and households'
(1977: 246).

Corporateness does not appear to characterize external relationships either. In
the turbulent days of factional fighting between the Medici and their opponents,
the Peruzzi were identified with the anti-Medician faction. When the Medici tri-
umphed in late 1434, 'two small genealogical lines' of Peruzzi were exempted from
the punishment of exile or disqualification from office-holding even though those
lines had three 'representatives' among the signatories to the pact mentioned above.
If the Peruzzi were a lineage, why were they not treated as 'one person' by their
opponents? Why, if the purpose of the pact was to prepare themselves for a political battle, were some of the signatories exempted from the harsh punishment
meted out to the losers in that battle?[5] The answer must be either that a *casato* like
the Peruzzi is not a lineage, or that Florentine lineages did not act in the political
arena.

Turning to Venice, young men became eligible for the Great Council at the age
of 25. However, some as young as 18 could be selected to enter the council at the
age of 20 if they were lucky enough to be chosen in a special lottery. This was held
once every year on the feast day of St Barbara, hence its name of Barbarella
(Chojnacki 1985). Early entry held a number of advantages. Sitting members were
eligible to be elected to paid offices and they swelled the voting ranks of their *casata*.
It might also improve their marriage chances and those of their sisters. It appears
that about half of the young men entered the Great Council through this route.
Those who were unlucky in successive lotteries and had to wait until they were 25
to gain entry felt themselves at a distinct disadvantage. Candidates for the lottery
were put forward by a sponsor and several guarantors, who stood surety for fines
in case the candidate was under 18 or was not a patrician. Most of the sponsors
were the candidate's fathers. But in those cases where the father was absent or
deceased, sponsorship was about equally divided between patrilateral and matri-
lateral kin. In fact mothers and maternal kin provided about one sponsor in every

---

[5] Pacts among the Peruzzi have also been the subject of an elegant and subtle analysis by
Kuehn (1991). While not questioning that the Peruzzi were a lineage, his analysis underlines the
malleability of kinship solidarity. Although he does not state matters in these terms, his interpretation
contains the most convincing evidence for regarding Florentine *casate*, as Goody suggested, as descending kindreds.

five (ibid.: 255). Affines, generally husbands of the candidate's sisters, added to the ranks of non-paternal sponsors (ibid.: 262).

If the Venetian *casata* operated as a corporate unilineal descent group, we might expect a much higher percentage of agnatic representation among the sponsors, especially of notables who might stand in for orphans. Maternal kin and affines might step in if there were no agnates available, such as in small *casate*, but it is surprising not to find more 'lineage' interest in a matter that would so vitally affect *casata* standing and representation.[6] After this brief digression into comparative materials, let us return to Ragusa and examine the role of the *casata* in patrician politics.

We have seen that Ragusan legislation prevented members of a *casata* from jointly holding certain offices. We have also seen that the several members of the Small Council, the executive committee of state with very wide-ranging powers including drawing up slates of nominees for office, had to come from different *casate*. In this respect it is significant that Ragusan statutes make no distinction between persons whose agnatic ties are close and those whose ties are remote. Degrees of agnation are not specified. Neither are large *casate* differentiated from smaller ones. It is common *casata* affiliation, not closeness of agnatic kinship, which is reckoned to be significant. In this respect there is no evidence of internal segmentation on genealogical criteria, but this same material could indicate that legislation regarded the *casata* as 'one person'.

Casata *Size and Domination of the Inner Circle*

In a study covering both the fourteenth and fifteenth centuries, Krekić has examined the frequency with which members of various *casate* held one of the five highest offices constituting the inner circle of government: the Rector, the civil and criminal judges, and the members of the Small Council and Senate (Krekić 1986: 398).[7] He shows that it is the members of the largest *casate* who tend to hold the highest offices. In the fifteenth century, the period that I am concerned with, the top ten *casate* according to Krekić's criteria were (in order): the Goçe, Gondola, Bona, Georgio, Resti, Sorgo, Poça, Zrieva, Mençe, and Zamagno. Of these, the Mençe, Sorgo, Georgio, Gondola, Goçe, Bona, and Zrieva were also among the top seven *casate* in the fourteenth century.[8] Krekić reports that in the fifteenth century, for example, the Goçe held 604 of these positions (or 12 per cent). The Palmota

---

[6] Chojnacki chose a sample of sixteen *casate* for his study, including representatives from small, middling, and large units (1985: 245). Although he does not carry the analysis in this direction, it would be interesting—given the arguments about the genealogical skewing and political mobilization presented below—to find if maternal and other non-agnates were more likely to be sponsors of candidates from small *casate*.

[7] 'knez, sud, Malo vijece i Senat . . .'. Krekić does not specify the judgeships ('sud'), but I assume these to be the *Judici del criminal* and *Consoli de le cause civil*.

[8] Listed in order.

held ninety-four (or 2 per cent). It seems clear therefore, as Krekić argues, that the
Goçe held far more power than the Palmota. Now Krekić does not explain what
the association is between *casata* size and the concentration of power, but it seems
a reasonable implication of his argument to suggest that perhaps the largest ones
use their voting strength in the Great Council to elect their own members into high
office.

Krekić's evidence looks compelling, but how can the argument be tested? In the
period from 1455 to 1490, I have found that there were on average thirty-three
Goçe sitting on the Great Council. In the same period there were (again on average)
five Palmota. Thus for every Palmota sitting on the Great Council and casting
ballots, there were over six times as many Goçe. If agnates tend to vote as a bloc
and support one another in elections to office, then there should be many more
Goçe in high office than Palmota. But, for every Palmota elected to one of the
highest posts, there were exactly six times as many Goçe elected. The proportion
is exactly the same as voting strength. Therefore the numerically much larger Goçe
do not use their absolute size to elect proportionally more of their fellows to high
office. If relative size is taken into consideration, the Palmota were as powerful as
the Goçe.

To what extent, then, is this characteristic of all *casate*? In order to answer this
question, I have counted the number of persons that each *casata* has in the
inner circle for each year from 1455 to 1490. This number was then divided by the
total number of persons in the inner circle (and multiplied by 100). This represents the proportion of inner circle members that a particular *casata* has in a given
year. The same was then done for the number of members each *casata* has sitting
on the Great Council in each year. A similar proportion of Great Council
membership was then calculated. The resultant figure, therefore, represents the
number of agnates in the inner circle for every 100 agnates on the Great
Council. The number of Great Council members includes all males from the *casata*
known to have held office from 1440 to 1490 and who were alive in the particular
year, as well as all males who may not have held office but were known to have
entered the council by that year. This total therefore includes all men who were
eligible to vote. Not all of these men would have been present and voting. Some,
for example, were absent from Ragusa for considerable periods and this would have
precluded their participation in the city's political life. By comparing these pro-
portions, we can see whether a *casata* is over- or under-represented in the inner
circle of high offices. We can also locate particular periods of over- or under-
representation.

A number of interesting results emerge from this analysis. First, there is no
simple association between *casata* size and domination of the highest offices. This
tends to confirm what was observed in the cases of the Goçe and Palmota examined above. The two largest *casate* of the period, for example, tended to be under-
represented in the inner circle. These were the Goçe (with an average of 33.3 Great
Council members) and the Bona (average 29.7). The Bona in particular were

markedly under-represented in the two decades from 1455 to 1474. Yet, it would not be accurate to generalize on the basis of these two largest *casate* and claim that larger *casate*, in general, tend to be under-represented. The third largest *casata*, for example, the Gondola (average 23.4), were over-represented for virtually the entire period from 1455 to 1490. Only at the very beginning and end of the period did their fortunes slip. The next three largest *casate*—the Sorgo (average 17.4), Georgio (average 16.6), and Zrieva (average 15.9)—had periods when they were disproportionally over-represented in the highest offices and other periods when they were under-represented. A similar picture emerges for the smaller *casate*. The six largest *casate* mentioned above constituted an overall majority on the Great Council. They outnumbered the remaining twenty-seven *casate*. Therefore, as Petrovich also observed for the seventeenth century, there is no association between size, *per se*, and the concentration of power. It does not appear that the largest *casate* used their voting strength in the Great Council to elect proportionally more of their own members into the highest offices.

While this result might seem puzzling, it is supported by Chojnacki's study of power within the Venetian patriciate. In an analysis of materials drawn from the late thirteenth century and the mid to late fourteenth century, he found that about one-quarter of the *casate* tended to dominate both Great Council membership and the holding of the more important offices of the state. In a further step which we cannot duplicate with Ragusan materials, he also found that wealth was concentrated in a few *casate*. Further, it tended to be the same ones which were prominent both in political activity and wealth. Over time, however, he found over half of the units did not remain among the leading *casate*.[9] There was mobility within the Venetian patriciate (Chojnacki 1973: 62–7).

Then he makes the most interesting point. In Venice there were fourteen *casate* who were at the centre of the patriciate. They were among the leading *casate* in the Great Council in the 1290s, they held high office in the mid-*trecento*, and they held nearly one-half of the patrician wealth in the *estimo* of 1379. Thus, they were not only powerful and wealthy, but they appeared to remain so over a period of almost ninety years. In asking whether these *casate* were part of an oligarchy, Chojnacki reveals that 'a strikingly close correlation exists between the number of males registered for each family and that family's political and economic prominence' (ibid.: 67).[10] Yet in Venice as in Ragusa, these large and powerful *casate* did not translate their numerical domination of government or their considerable wealth into their own advantage. Chojnacki suggests that 'The reason is not hard to find: they had no single particularist interest' (ibid.: 70). They were found on opposing sides concerning most of the major issues that divided the patriciate. This was also true of the Florentine and Ragusan *casate* as well.

However, there was one major issue where there was unanimity—the honour

---

[9] He uses the term 'families'.
[10] Grubb notes the same association for fifteenth-century Vicenza (1988: 84).

and esteem of the *casata*—as reflected in offices held. Florentines are known to have calculated 'scores' that various *casate* achieved in the scramble for office and tallied both the number of high offices achieved and the antiquity of their reign at the top of the political ladder (F. Kent 1977: 198). They also sought favours on behalf of distant agnates on the grounds that the particular favour was deserved through the esteem which the entire *casata* enjoyed (ibid.: 199). In Venice, too, boys were brought into the Great Council chamber so that they could carry messages to nominators on behalf of agnates eager for office. The clamour of these lads became such a nuisance to proceedings that the council tried (unsuccessfully) to have them banned from council chambers (Queller 1986: 64–5). The great Venetian diarist Sanuto writes often of his disappointments in the quest for offices. After one particularly galling succession of defeats, he attributes these to the lack of support from his brothers and the active opposition of a paternal cousin (Finlay 1980b: 262–3). And when late in life, when he had virtually retired from public life, he is elected to the Zonta (a group of sixty elected to the Senate) he considers it to be 'most likely because he had just become the oldest member of his clan and a certain preeminence was therefore due to him' (ibid.: 273). Other examples could be added to show how office-holding added to the 'symbolic capital' of the *casata*. Why, then, did the large units not make use of their numerical advantage?

A sense of duty to Ragusan civic welfare is the answer provided by Petrovich for material on the seventeenth century. He makes it clear, however, that service to the welfare of the state did not always arise spontaneously from high-minded patrician hearts. A series of inducements and punishments were put into place to ensure this (1974: 717–36). A similar series also existed in the late fifteenth century.

Office-holders were paid salaries. While the remuneration was not large, it could help the more indigent of the patricians or add some useful income to the honour of office. Where certain officials were entitled to expenses, the state did not leave it to the honour of the official to give an honest accounting. Ambassadors were accompanied by non-noble treasurers who kept the accounts and informed upon their masters (*Lib. Vir.*: Caps. 394, 395). Informers were entitled to one-half of the fines levied. It is clear that patricians did not rely on one another's rectitude in financial matters. Nor were they trusting when conduct in office was concerned. Fines were imposed on those who did not attend council meetings. Part of the jus- tification for establishing the *Proveditori de la terra* was to have officials who could undertake judicial review, monitor the conduct of patricians, and supervise elec- tions. To ensure diligence in pursuing these duties, the *Proveditori* were to be awarded one-third of the fines they assessed. There was a need for such measures. Nicola Zupan de Bona (ID 354) apparently misled the Great Council about his age when he was elected *Camerlengi del comone* in 1476. He had not yet achieved the 30 years required of an incumbent. In 1485 there was another scandal when more votes were cast in one ballot than there were patricians in the chamber (*Specchio*, s.v. *Camerlengi del comone*).[11] There was a strong sense of civic duty, but there was also a sense that advancing the interests of one's own did not have to be at the expense of larger civic interests.

Another set of reasons, and one which I believe weighed more heavily than a sense of duty, rested on those administrative devices to which Max Weber referred. The weight of potential electors would count for little if one could not be successful in getting agnates nominated. That required having access to sympathetic persons on the nominating bodies. These were constituted in Ragusa so that large *casate* had only marginal advantage.

It is important to note that agnation alone did not give one the right to sit in Ragusa's Great Council. Only nobles governed. To be noble one had to be the legitimate offspring of both a patrician father and a patrician mother. Thus while Lucas Nicola de Bona (ID 305) was the natural child of Nicola Sarachin de Bona (ID 297) and bore the surname of this important *casata*, he did not have a patrician mother. He was not able, therefore, to join his paternal half-brothers, Jacobus (ID 300) and Stephanus (ID 302), on the Great Council. It is clear that the name 'Bona' is not restricted to nobles. Nor is this an isolated case. There were seven *casate* of this period that included non-nobles. These are, from the published genealogies, the Bodaca, Goçe, Mençe, Palmota, Poça, Sorgo, and Georgio. There may have been more (Mahnken 1960).[12] In the documents of the period, the names of non-noble members (*populo*) of the *casata* are recorded with the surname just like their noble agnates but they lack the honorific '*Ser*'. We cannot say, therefore, that a noble name was a corporate asset of the *casata*. Neither can we claim that it was descent group membership that entitled certain persons to sit on the Great Council. Agnates from the *populo* were also descent group 'members' but they could not participate in the deliberations of the Great Council. That right passed through ties of accumulative patrifiliation. But ties of accumulative patrifiliation through nobles, while necessary for patrician status, were not sufficient entitlement. In this respect it did not matter that one had 'descended' from a patrician ancestor through the male line. What mattered was that one was a legitimate offspring of a patrician father and a patrician mother (cf. Scheffler 1986).

The results of this survey have suggested that Goody is probably correct. The *casata* is not a lineage or a house, but a descending kindred. It was buttressed by an ideology that members of a common household should continue to support one another and show the affection and loyalty necessitated by common residence even when circumstances forced them to separate and establish independent households. It does not appear that the *casata* held structurally significant assets. Assets such as land, the produce from rural estates, or capital goods and the products of

---

[11] Three years later Nicola was properly elected to the same post. On the scandals see Šundrica (1973: 7).
[12] Tracing the non-noble descendants was not one of the objectives of Mahnken's genealogical research.

manufacturing, were owned and managed at the highest level by the household. But while land, capital goods, and other productive assets might form part of the family estate, it appears that more significant assets of the household came from ventures in trade, commerce, and manufacturing. Such assets were built up through a series of *ad hoc* contractual arrangements between partners. Some of these might be other household members, but partners could be commoners or foreigners as well as patricians from outside the *casata*. Such contractual arrangements could have very limited objectives and exist for only a matter of weeks or months, or they might have more general aims and a longer life. But financial success was gradually built up (or lost) through the efforts of individual men. What had been painstakingly won over many years could be easily lost in days. Therefore, given the highly contingent nature of commercial ventures and the high degree of risk involved, it is also understandable that a man would wish to benefit (and have his sons and heirs benefit) from what he had amassed and learned. Documents like the Florentine *ricordanze* may be understood, I suggest, as attempts to archive individual achievements in the hope that these achievements might be preserved and increased by the following generation.

These conclusions of this survey present a mixed picture. The *casata*, like the 'classic' lineage, had hard structural edges. Outsiders were not incorporated as accessory members nor did they act as *casata* members in political affairs. Adoption was not practised and fathers enjoyed considerable power over their offspring (Dinić-Knežević 1972; Čučković 1977).[13] Except for its name and certain other badges of status, the *casata* did not hold structurally significant assets. While civic legislation regarding office-holding tended to view the *casata* as if it were 'one person', it does not appear to have acted as a unit in the one matter where we would expect unity to be most crucial—the advancement of its members in their office-holding careers and the enhancement of the unit's symbolic capital.

The peculiarities of the Florentine political system may have contributed to the importance which has been attached to agnatic kinship. Leading Florentine offices were filled by a process of sortition. While names were drawn at random from purses holding the names of candidates, the crucial step was getting one's name included in the purse. The latter process occurred at the local level where procedures of vetting and selection took place. One needed local, neighbourhood support to be selected. As the Kents suggest, *casate* (they use 'families') made a conscious effort to establish their several households within the same local district (D. and F. Kent 1982: 17–18). Unlike Venice and Ragusa, office-holding was not restricted to patricians. The name of any male citizen who passed scrutiny and who could muster sufficient local strength could be included in the electoral purses. Entry into the world of government and office-holding depended upon success in grass-roots politics. It was not that wealth, or an illustrious name, were unimportant. But they were neither necessary, nor sufficient, for entry into the political

---

[13] For Florence see Kuehn (1981, 1982b, and 1987).

arena. In Venice and Ragusa, in contrast, patrician status was both necessary and sufficient.

The features we have examined are consistent with Goody's interpretation of a descending kindred. They are not, however, consistent with the openness and flexibility that Lévi-Strauss associates with the 'house'. Patricians may have used the metaphor of the house (*casa*) to encourage norms of co-operation and self-sacrifice amongst agnates who no longer dwelt together in a joint household, but the *casata* does not show the diagnostic features associated with units in 'house-based societies'. Therefore, that alternative can be discounted.

There remains one important dimension of the *casata* which has not been examined. We might expect, for example, that the marriages of *casata* members would be important to the *casata*'s symbolic capital. We might also expect that marital alliances among *casate* would be important in understanding patrician politics. Therefore we now turn to consider this important topic.

6

Betrothal Order, Dowry, and the 'Sisters First' Principle

Endogamy Within the Patriciate

Ragusa was very different from both Florence and Venice in one respect. To be considered a patrician and be eligible for office in Ragusa, one must have had both a patrician father and a patrician mother. In Venice, on the other hand, one needed to be the legitimate child of a patrician father. The mother need not be of patrician status. She could be a servant or a free woman of low status so long as she was not a slave (Chojnacki 1990: 167). The picture in Florence is somewhat more complex. There one needed to be a Guelf guildsman who met certain other residential and fiscal requirements. This brings us to the topic of marriage. Marriage, as we shall see, presents us with an unexpected reason why certain *casate* did not dominate Ragusan government. Patrician probity, punitive legislation, and the structure of the nomination system also played a part, but it is aspects of the marriage system which provide a more illuminating explanation.

With respect to the *casata*, women were, as Klapisch-Zuber remarks of Florentine women, like 'passing guests'. 'To contemporary eyes, their movements in relation to the *case* determined their social personality more truly than the lineage group from which they came' (1985: 118). And in Florence as in Ragusa, women were spoken of in relation to their fathers or husbands. In official records they are not referred to by the name of a *casata*. They are the wife or daughter (or widow) of so-and-so. Somewhat paradoxically, however, given this transient character, doctrines of nurturance emphasized the importance of the mother. The mother was believed to nourish her child first with her blood and then with her milk. This nurturance was active and vital in shaping the character of the child. Indeed, doctors recommended that if the mother was not to nurse her own child, the parents should find a wet-nurse who was like the mother. Animal milk was not a suitable alternative. It would make the child brutish. The qualities of the mother were thought to complement the qualities of the father. Yet, in spite of this, the mother did not count. It was the paternal 'blood' that mattered (ibid.: 161).[1]

Despite this ideological imbalance in favour of the father and his 'noble line', we will find that the mother and maternal origin did matter, albeit in circuitous ways. The patterns in the transmission of personal names which we examined in

[1] Cf. Maclean (1980).

the previous chapter are one indication. A man who bears his maternal grand-father's name would be especially drawn towards his maternal kin and would be likely to receive special attention from them in return. A more direct influence would be the necessity of having a patrician mother in order to participate fully in Ragusan civic life.

Because of the requirement of patrician parentage on both sides, the Ragusan patriciate had a very high degree of in-marriage. Diversis states that patricians were forbidden to have non-noble spouses and that during his time there had been no such marriages. The reasons, he suggests, lie in domestic harmony. The most frequent cause of quarrels between spouses is difference in social background, hence the adage 'if you wish to marry, marry your equal' (Diversis 1882: 27).[2] While class endogamy within Europe was common, Stuard has suggested that Ragusa 'produced perhaps the strictest endogamy practised by an elite in medieval Europe' (1981: 798). Molho's examination of the Florentine Dowry Fund has shown, even in Florence's more 'open' marriage market, that homogamy prevailed especially in the propertied classes (1994: 237). Comparative evidence is difficult to find, but the Ragusan materials do provide the means to estimate patrician in-marriage. From an examination of all marriages occurring between 1400 and 1520 and involving at least one patrician spouse, there were 912 first marriages. These involved 772 males and 831 females. Only seventeen males and twenty-six females (2 and 3 per cent, respectively) married persons from outside Ragusa. These outside marriages were with patrician spouses in such nearby cities as Kotor, Zadar, and the like. There are a further twenty-eight spouses who cannot be precisely identified. Even if we assume that every one of these was of non-patrician origin, the percentage of outside marriages would still be less than 5 per cent. It is evident that Stuard's assertion is correct. The amount of in-marriage within this élite was very high.[3]

Stuard has argued that the Ragusan dowry system acted to maintain cohesion within this endogamous patriciate. Since her research into dowry covers the period from the thirteenth to the fifteenth century, the results of our enquiries into the late fifteenth century can neither confirm nor negate her interesting suggestions. But they may at least tell us something about their likelihood. Stuard argues that dowry acted as a means of redistributing wealth. Given the endogamous charac-ter of the patriciate, this redistribution did not work throughout the entire city-state, but only within the patriciate. Indeed, she suggests that this not only helped

---

[2] '*si vis nubere, nube pari.*'
[3] Stuard provides one example of a non-endogamous marriage which occured in 1429 (1981: 798). It was between Nicola Mate de Grade and Caterina, the daughter of Maroe Radiosaglich. I suggest, however, that this is not an exception to patrician endogamy. Stuard appears to have misunderstood the original source. In fact Nicola is not noble. The document begins 'Ego Nicola Ser Matei de grade', which is not the formula which would normally be used by patricians (*Liber Dotium Notariæ*, 5, fo. 60v (hereafter referred to as the *Carta*, after *Carta Dotalis*)). Mahnken correctly records Nicola as of the *populo* but gives the bride's name as 'Catarina' (1960, s.v. 'Grede'). My interpretation of the bride's name, like Stuard's, is 'Caterina'.

to maintain cohesion within the élite, but also helped to promote economic growth. 'Over a generation or two vast individual fortunes were redistributed among the noble families' (1981: 798). She notes, for example, that fathers went to great lengths to give similar dowries to their daughters. In cases where the number of daughters outweighed the number of sons, other kin, neighbours, and friends might step in to help augment the dowry or initiate other measures to help level wealth differences (ibid.).[4]

Stuard suggests that the tutors of orphaned girls also kept a keen eye on the fortunes of their wards so that they, too, would marry with similar dowries to the tutors' own daughters.[5] Remarriage of both widows and widowers also helped to redistribute wealth. The end result of all of these devices, she suggests, was to redistribute wealth and to increase class cohesion. 'The town's total wealth increased, in a sense rewarding such behaviour through the ever-renewing cycle of acquiring new fortunes, which in turn would be redistributed' (1981: 798–9). These are important suggestions and they may shed some light on the apparent lack of solidarity within the *casata*.

Dowry and Class Solidarity

Let us first examine dowry amounts and Stuard's hypothesis about redistribution of wealth. The standard amount for a dowry specified in the betrothal documents (*Pacta Matrimonialia*) in this period was 2,600 *hyperperi*. In this document the potential spouses promise to have one another as husband and wife. If they fall within the prohibited degrees of kinship specified by the Church, the document states this (and occasionally specifies the nature of the impediment) and indicates that a dispensation has been applied for. About one-quarter of all betrothals were dependent upon obtaining a dispensation.[6]

Following the canons of the Fourth Lateran Council of 1215, prospective spouses were required to be at least five degrees of consanguinity removed from one another (cf. Goody 1983: 134–44). The Church followed the Germanico-canonical system of calculating relationships. It embodied a combination of features from the Roman and Germanic systems. Whereas the former counted acts of 'generation' between an Ego and an Alter, the latter was based upon the unity

---

[4] In a footnote Stuard refers to a case where Johannes Blasius de Mençe gives unequal dowries to two daughters. I find no mention of Johannes de Mençe in the document cited (*Carta* 4: fo. 10v). The following document (fo. 11) does mention him, but this latter document is a record of a property sale. I have not been able to trace the dowry record referred to. I know of no case from the late fifteenth century where a neighbour, referred to as such, contributes to a dowry.

[5] Stuard refers to a document concerning the orphaned daughters of Symon de Benessa (1981: 798 n. 9; cf. *Carta* 4: fos. 13, 19). Unfortunately, I can find no reference to the Benessa daughters in the document cited.

[6] This is based upon the betrothal records which survive for the period from 1448 to 1460. Of the 130 records of patrician betrothals, thirty-one mention a dispensation.

of the sibling group who constituted a 'generation' in a second sense. The new Germanico-canonical system was based on links to the closest linking ancestor. The parties constructed a pedigree with the common ancestor at the apex. Degrees were then calculated by starting at the bottom of the pedigree and counting every relationship until the ancestor was reached. For example, brother and sister are related by one degree, a single degree separates the brother (or sister) from their common parent. An uncle and niece were reckoned to be separated by two degrees. Although one degree separates the uncle from his parent—the common ancestor— two degrees separate that ancestor from the niece. After 1215 the Church counted the longest path between two descendants and their common ancestor (cf. Molho 1994: 256–7). Relationships within four degrees were not allowed, or required Church permission. Prohibitions were applied to affines as well as consanguines. It is not surprising that in a small community like the Ragusan patriciate, about one-quarter of prospective marriages required dispensation.

In addition to degrees of relationship, the *Pacta Matrimonialia* may also specify the period within which the bride is to be removed from her father's *casata* and marriage consummated. The names of all the principal parties are given along with much additional information and the contract is dated and notarized.[7] At this point in the proceedings the parties refer to one another by the appropriate affinal kin terms. But of particular importance are the financial details. Ordinarily the bride's father specifies how much money is to be given to the groom and how much of the total is to be used for clothing and ornaments for the bride. The documents often contain penalty clauses should one or the other party default. The longer the period of time between betrothal and consummation, the greater the likelihood that the *Pacta Matrimonialia* would contain penalty clauses.

Most penalty clauses are in favour of the groom should the bride eventually refuse. Occasionally there is a two-way penalty, as in the betrothal between Petroneliza (ID 2062), daughter of Andreas Francho de Sorgo (ID 2601), and Thomas Marin Tomko de Bona (ID 311) (*Pacta* 2: fo. 49–49v). In this case the interval specified between betrothal and consummation is eleven years. This is the largest interval in the records studied and presumably the double guarantee reflects the very young age of the prospective couple. An Addendum to the document added five years later notes that both the bride and groom testified to their agreement. In one document where the betrothal is made in the name of an absent groom, Nicola Çorçi Givchus de Caboga (ID 485), a guarantee of two thousand ducats is promised by the groom's father should the prospective groom refuse marriage upon his return to Ragusa (*Pacta* 2: fos. 96v–97).

Of the standard dotal sum of 2,600 *hyperperi*, 1,000 *hyperperi* was usually designated as being for the bride's clothing and jewellery. A further 1,600 *hyperperi* was for the dotal assign. The groom, or husband, had the use of this money, but the capital was to keep the widow and provide for her heirs. While this amount

---

[7] When the marriage has been consummated, another document is prepared which specifies the amounts. It too bears the names of all principal parties and it is notarized and dated (the *Carta Dotalis*).

might not equal that received by a son as his inheritance, it was still a very substantial sum. It would, for example, be enough to keep the widow in food and necessities for thirty-two years, obtain the leasehold on over fifty shops or houses, or commission thirty-seven boats and the services of 185 sailors for voyages (*Diversa Notariæ* 33: fos. 65, 94, 107: hereafter referred to has *Div. Not.*). This sum represented a very important investment in affinal relationships. If the bride or groom died or there was some other misadventure that prevented the marriage being consummated, the dowry had to be refunded in full. Further, if the period until consummation was of some length, the contract often carried penalty clauses should one party or the other default. One thousand gold ducats was the standard penalty.

The sources themselves do not record any distinctions between the different amounts given in various dowries. Therefore, for purposes of analysis, a crude typology has been devised. While most dowries were 2,600 *hyperperi* (here referred to as 'standard'), some dowries were higher than this. The upper limit for patrician dowries recorded in contracts of the period is about 3,000 *hyperperi*. I shall refer to amounts above the 2,600 *hyperperi* average as a 'lavish' dowry. To place these sums in a comparative perspective, I also examined thirty-three *populo* dowry contracts from 1455 and 1460 which showed a range from a low of 40 to a high of 3,600 *hyperperi*.[8] While most *populo* dowries fell considerably below the patrician standard, there were a few that exceeded the amount of even the most lavish patrician. Some patricians gave less than the 2,600 *hyperperi* standard. These are considered 'paltry' dowries in the discussion below. There is also a fourth category, where those responsible for the dowry committed themselves to paying the standard amount, but might have had to sell property, pay in instalments over a period of time, or make some other arrangements to raise it. Dowries of this type are described as 'marginal'.

If dowry is redistributed as Stuard suggests, we would expect that brides would be somewhat wealthier than their grooms. There should, in other words, be a tendency for women to marry down. We would expect that brothers would tend to give their sisters larger dowries than their own wives received. But comparing the dowries given and received by members of various sibling groups, we find that the standard dowry of 2,600 *hyperperi* was both given and received by brothers in 30 cases. In 43 cases the amounts were different. Of the latter, 22 of the wives brought better dowries, and 21 of the brothers gave better dowries. There is no tendency toward either hypergamy or hypogamy. Marriage within the patriciate is isogamous (see Table 5). In Ragusa of the late fifteenth century, as in other dowry systems, the emphasis is on 'matching like for like' (Goody 1983: 106). There does not appear to be evidence for a redistribution of wealth. But there is evidence for Stuard's suggested equality among sisters. Within particular sibling groups, for example, most sisters are betrothed with equal dowries. Where differences do exist,

---

[8] Mean = 1,140 *hyperperi*, standard deviation = 975.

TABLE 5. *Hypergamy and hypogamy in betrothals*

The table represents the redistributive effects of dowries. The numbers in the cells refer to groups of brothers, and the matrix show what they gave and what they received in dowries in the period studied. For example, 24 groups of brothers gave Category 3 (average) dowries to their sisters, and received dowries of the same category with their wives. The shaded diagonal indicates a broad homogamy: no net redistributive effect in 30 cases. Cases to the right of the diagonal are those in which brothers received less than they gave (22 cases); and to the left those in which they gave less than they received (21 cases).

Give \ Receive	1	2	3	4	5	6	7
1				1			
2	1		2				
3	1		24	4	12	2	
4			9		1		
5	1		4	3	6		
6							
7			2				

Categories of dowries are: (1) substantial; (2) some substantial, some average; (3) average; (4) some average, some marginal; (5) marginal; (6) some marginal, some paltry; (7) paltry.
Source: *Pacta Matrimonialia*: 1–2 (1447–1464).

these are most likely to be found in the larger sibling groups where there are many dowries to be provided. In these larger groups it is the sisters who are betrothed first who benefit from larger dowries. But the greater the number of sisters, the smaller the difference between the dowry provided to the eldest sister and to the others.

If equals marry, as we have seen they do, then wealth would be redistributed, but not throughout the patriciate. On the contrary, the patriciate would tend to sediment by wealth as the rich married the rich and the poor married the poor. This conflicts with Stuard's argument that there was a tendency among Ragusan women to marry down. By marrying down, she contends, wealth was redistributed from wealthier to poorer patricians. 'Social cohesion was the reward of the leveling of individual fortunes' (ibid.: 798). This is an interesting argument about class cohesion, but the data from the second half of the fifteenth century does not support it.

Age at Marriage

Responsibilities of marriage came very early to Ragusan patrician women. Most of the brides were less than 17 years old at betrothal. Within three years they were likely to have consummated their marriages and joined their husbands in the latter's home. The duties of marriage could be heavy. In addition to managing the house and domestic servants, there were also cellars, stables, and garden to be looked after. A comparable set of responsibilities would be attached to a countryside villa if the household had one. We only know the shadowy outlines of domestic life, for studies of household and family life in Ragusa are only beginning to appear.[9] If the average bride was under 17 years old at betrothal, some were much younger. Anucla (ID 2051), the daughter of Çove Francho de Sorgo (ID 2049), was betrothed when she was only 8 years old. Her betrothal contract written on 27 August 1454 made a note of her young age (*Pacta* 2: fo. 21–21v).

The minimum age at marriage, originally 20 for men and 14 for women, was lowered in 1460 to 14 for men and 12 for women. This same piece of legislation further specified that the dotal sum should not exceed 1,600 *hyperperi* nor the sum for the bride's clothing and jewellery exceed 700 *hyperperi* (*Lib. Croc.*: fo. 1v). The recording of age is unusual in these documents, but there is another unusual detail as well in Anucla's betrothal contract. It notes that the groom, Lucianus Lucas de Bona (ID 339), would have the unusually long period of eight years in which to consummate the marriage. This is probably related to Anucla's youth since the average period between betrothal and consummation is about three years (Rheubottom 1988: 363). Like his bride, Lucianus may also have been quite young at betrothal for he does not enter the Great Council until 1457, three years after his betrothal. If he entered the Council in his early twenties, he would have been in his late teens when the betrothal contract was notarized. This contract further specifies that the groom will be paid 1,000 ducats in compensation if Anucla eventually refuses marriage. Such penalty clauses often occur in contracts where there is a long interval between betrothal and consummation.

It is not possible to directly determine the year of birth for most women. Ages of women are only rarely noted. Therefore estimates have been made using information on the year of betrothal, birth order within the group of siblings, and the order of betrothal. From these data it has been possible to compute the interval

---

[9] See, for example, Dinić-Knežević (1974), Čučković (1983), and Stuard (1976, 1983).

between the father's betrothal and the betrothal of his oldest daughter: that inter-val is about twenty years (see Table 6). If we assume that a period of three years elapsed between betrothal, consummation, and the birth of the first child, then it would follow that the 'average' bride was 17 years old at betrothal.

Grooms, however, were much older. Here there is some direct evidence about age because after 1472 the records of the Great Council note the age at which men enter. By comparing the date of entry with the age at entry, it is possible to deter-mine the year of birth. There are 177 men born between 1440 and 1500 whose year of birth and year of (first) betrothal are known. Their average age at first betrothal is 33 years (see Table 7). Therefore, at betrothal the bride was consider-ably younger than the groom. The average difference between their ages exceeded fifteen years. This difference, as we shall see, is critically important in under-standing the political impotence of the *casata*.

The difference, and the absolute ages of bride and groom at betrothal, while striking, is not unusual for the Mediterranean world in the early Renaissance. In Tuscan cities, for example, men were about 28 years old when they married, while their wives were about 19 (Herlihy and Klapisch-Zuber 1985: 205 fig. 7.1). This

TABLE 6. *Betrothal age of brides*

Difference in years between father's and daughter's betrothal	No.	%
Less than 10 years	3	2.6
11–15	24	20.9
16–20	35	30.4
21–25	31	27.0
26–30	15	13.0
31–35	7	6.1
TOTAL	115	100.0

Mean difference = 20.2 years. (Derived from the difference between the year of the father's betrothal and the betrothal year of his oldest, first-born daughter. See the explanation in the text.)

TABLE 7. *Age of grooms at betrothal*

Age at betrothal	No.	%
Less than 20 years	3	1.7
21–25	22	12.4
26–30	45	25.4
31–35	43	24.3
36–40	38	21.4
41–45	15	8.4
46–50	9	5.0
51 and above	2	1.1
TOTAL	177	99.7

Average age at betrothal = 33.2 years.

difference in age between spouses has been taken as one of the distinguishing features of the 'Mediterranean Marriage Pattern'. The other distinguishing feature of the pattern is the presence of a relatively large number of men who never marry. This feature is also present in Ragusa.

To determine the proportion of patrician males who marry, we can examine the sibling groups of those persons who were betrothed in 1455. There are thirty-three such sibling groups from twenty-one *casate* containing a total of 237 persons. If all of these siblings were still alive in 1455, groups that averaged over seven siblings per group would be implied. While this number of siblings appears unusually large, it corresponds to similar evidence from Florence. Klapisch-Zuber found through an analysis of entries in (largely) fifteenth-century *ricordanze* that there were 266 children born to thirty-three couples. This yields an average of eight per sibling group (1985: 291).

Of the 115 males in the Ragusan sibling groups, sixty-nine (60 per cent) survived to marry. It is not possible to determine how many of the unmarried men died before reaching marriageable age or how many were marriageable but unmarried. Of the forty-six unmarried males, six entered religious orders. Thus the two characteristic features of the Mediterranean Marriage Pattern are clearly present in Ragusa. There is late age at marriage for grooms but a much younger age at marriage for their brides, and the presence of a relatively large number of men who never marry. But how is the Mediterranean Marriage Pattern to be explained?

In their account of the Tuscan material, Herlihy and Klapisch-Zuber look to the household and what might be called its functional requisites, an explanation very similar to that suggested earlier by Hajnal (1965: 133). They suggest that in the towns a man needed to achieve economic independence before he could contemplate marriage. A wealthy man 'had to wait even longer than the poor artisan to acquire enough wealth to found a new household suitable for his station in life' (1985: 221–2). They note that substantial dowries had to be transferred. This, plus the high stakes involved in bringing about a delicate marriage alliance, required a long search for a bride and then protracted negotiations.

But most wealthy Tuscan men, like their Ragusan counterparts, did not ensconce their brides in independent households; most brought their brides to join the ongoing household of the groom's father or brothers. Furthermore, the dowry in Tuscany flowed from the bride's family to the groom. It is difficult, therefore, to see how the problem of transferring substantial dowries increases the groom's age at marriage but not the bride's. The argument in terms of capital accumulation and household formation to account for the groom's late age at marriage has a superficial plausibility, but it is not convincing upon closer examination.

When Herlihy and Klapisch-Zuber turn to account for the bride's age at marriage, they shift the focus from economic considerations to demographic ones. For the wealthier classes, they suggest, mortality reduced the number of men who were about the age of 30. Therefore there were relatively more young women between the ages of 15 and 20 than there were potential grooms between the ages of 25 and 30. 'The families of these young girls thus entered a desperate competition for grooms . . . [and this] persuaded many families to offer their daughters in marriage at still more tender ages . . .' (ibid.: 223). When a girl reaches marriageable age, she has potentially available all the unmarried males. The younger the age at which she becomes marriageable, the greater the number of potential husbands. The advantage to those who arrange her marriage is that they have more choice and a longer period of time in which to exercise it.[10] However, in Ragusa as in Florence, the window of opportunity for arranging a marriage was narrow. In Florence 'a father, had at most, three to five years to settle a daughter's future. In reality, he had less' (Molho 1994: 225–6). Molho emphasizes that it was less a matter of numbers than of suitability. 'But suitable husbands, those who met all of a prospective father-in-law's exigent standards, were always difficult to pin down at the moment when a family had decided that a young woman . . . was ready to be placed in marriage' (ibid.: 77).

Marriage Order Within the Sibling Group

In Ragusan sibling groups it was common for sisters to marry before brothers. Consider the case of the eight children of Šišmund de Georgio (ID 2300) who became betrothed in the twenty years between 1450 and 1470 (see Fig. 2). Johannes (ID 2301) was the oldest. Then came Franciscus (ID 2302), Vechia (ID 2303), Junius (ID 2307), Margarita (ID 2305), Maria (ID 2306), and so forth. But when it came to their marriages, Margarita married first even though she was fifth-born. Maria married second, even though she was sixth-born. In fact, Helisabeth (ID 2314), the seventh of these siblings, married before Franciscus, the second. This pattern emerges in group after group. Men tend not to get betrothed until their sisters are betrothed even though this may require a considerable delay.

In the 33 sibling sets studied in detail, 17 adhered to this 'sisters first' pattern, whereas 13 did not.[11] A weak majority of 17 might seem like slender support for an important structural principle, but if we examine the 13 exceptions, they add striking support. The children of Šišmund de Georgio constitute one of these exceptions. Johannes, the eldest, became betrothed in 1459 only after three of his younger sisters had been engaged. Two other sisters, Helisabeth and Antulina (ID 2317), were not yet betrothed but they were the seventh and eighth in this set of

---

[10] Changes over time in the demographic regime can modify this principle in surprising degree, as we shall see later.

[11] Of the further three, two were single-sex sibling groups and one was an only child. It is noteworthy that the 'sisters first' ordering principle does not extend to cousins.

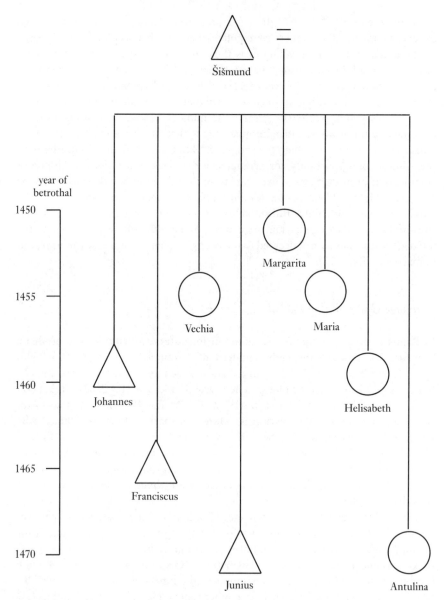

FIG. 2.   Betrothals of the children of Šišmund de Georgio
Source: Mahnken 1960: s.v. 'Georgio'.

married siblings. In cases where the sibling group is very large, the eldest brother may become betrothed before all of his sisters are wed, but most will have been betrothed. There are no sibling sets in which a brother weds before any of his sisters are betrothed.

Other exceptions concern half-sibling sets where the children have a common father but different mothers. Here the principle should be amended to 'full sisters first'. For example, Simon (ID 87), the eldest son (but third child) of Damian Simcho de Benessa (ID 84), did not marry until 1457, by which time four of his full sisters had been betrothed although his much younger half-sister, Johana (ID 100), was still unwed (see Fig. 3). Johana became betrothed in 1460, four years before her much older half-brother Pasqual (ID 92) and seventeen years before her elder full brother, Stefanus (ID 99).

Consider the implications of this for age at betrothal. Other things being equal, an adherence to a principle of 'sisters first' would inflate the age at which men are betrothed. If the sibling group is large and one or two males are born early, the delaying factor could be considerable. This principle would, of course, have little impact in a group where the sisters are born first. The implication is that the 'sisters first' principle could create a significant difference in age at marriage between husbands and wives. Alternatively, it could be argued that the 'sisters first' pattern is an artefact of the differences in age at marriage. According to this second argument, because men marry late, their sisters would have preceded them into wedlock.

The Ragusan evidence supports the first interpretation. First-born Ragusan males with no sisters are betrothed, on average, about two years before those first-born males who have sisters (Rheubottom 1988).[12] It would be difficult to account for this if the delaying effect of sisters was not involved. This reading of the evidence suggests that adherence to a pattern of 'sisters first' does delay the marriage of male siblings. But by how much? An answer to this question can be obtained from a computer simulation.

The units in the simulation are sibling groups which 'experience' demographic events in a random manner. 'Although events occur randomly to individuals they do so at rates appropriate to certain categories of persons and in such a way that the ultimate actual rates of occurrences come as close as possible to the input governing rates' (Hammel and Wachter 1977: 114–15). This simulation examined the effects of three demographic rates and two cultural rules. The first of these rates is sibling group size, which is stochastically determined from a distribution of Ragusan sibling groups. The second rate is birth order, again stochastically determined from a distribution obtained from the Ragusan data. The third rate, sex ratio, is taken from the Florentine *catasto* of 1427 where Herlihy and Klapisch-Zuber found that there were 110 males for every 100 females (1985: 132). The two cultural rules are that sisters are betrothed first in order of age. Each becomes

---

[12] First-born sons without sisters become engaged at an average age of 30.8 years while those with sisters are betrothed at an average age of 32.7 years.

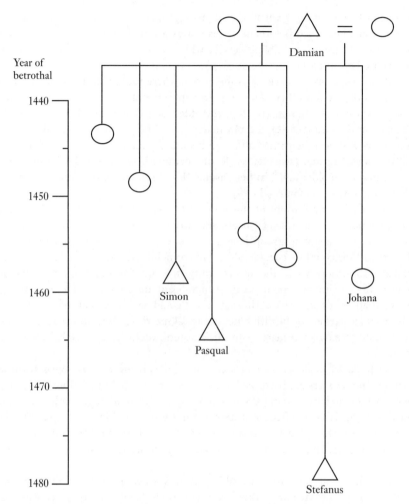

FIG. 3. Betrothals of the children of Damian de Benessa

Source: Mahnken 1960: s.v. 'Benessa'.

betrothed when she reaches the age of 16. Sisters are followed by their brothers—
again in age order. For each run of the simulation, a population of 1,000 individuals was created. The simulation was run 64 times.[13] Computer simulation of
marriage order in a variety of sibling groups suggests that it would delay the
betrothals of brothers by about four years.[14]

[13] The details of the simulation exercise, a sensitivity analysis of the rates, and a pseudocode of the
simulation program are discussed in Rheubottom (1988).
[14] The exact figure for the average delay is 4.1 years. The smallest simulated delay is 3.5 years; the
longest is 6.1.

There is, of course, a considerable difference between the four-year delay brought about by the operation of the 'sisters first' principle and the fifteen-year gap in age between spouses. What is to account for this? There are several possible answers. First, in devising a computer simulation, certain assumptions were made about the size of sibling groups, about intervals between births, and about the sex ratio. Testing the computer simulation systematically by altering these assumptions revealed that changes in the sex ratio have little effect on the delay produced by the 'sisters first' pattern. Changing the intervals between births produces some change in the amount of delay, but the amount is not very significant. It is the size of the sibling group that has the greatest effect. Thus, if the sibling group increased in size, then the size of the gap between the age at marriage for brothers and age of marriage for sisters increases. Such changes might occur in periods that are relatively free of epidemics and plague when average life expectancy increases. In such periods more children are likely to be born and survive. More children means larger sibling groups. The computer simulation reveals that change in sibling group size alone can increase the average gap in siblings' ages at marriage to seven years (Rheubottom 1988: 371–2). The 'sisters first' pattern therefore helps to account for the curious fact that while the age at marriage (betrothal) for women in the Mediterranean Marriage Pattern remains relatively constant, the age at marriage for men can vary (R. Smith 1981).

Another factor which might affect the age at marriage is maternal deaths associated with childbirth or with the associated effects of frequent births. These deaths would tend to create a demographic imbalance by bringing widowers back into the marriage market. Their presence, added to the presence of bachelors, would increase the pool of marriageable men. This could also drive down the age at marriage for women and drive up the age for men.

A more significant factor, however, may be the small size of the endogamous community itself. In relatively closed marriage systems like that of the Ragusan patriciate, only small numbers of women (and men) are available for marriage at any single point in time. The pool of available mates is quite small in absolute terms. Other factors which further restrict its size are the Church's prohibitions on marriage between various categories of kin and affines, as well as a necessity of finding a spouse of comparable wealth and status.

Why should it be important for sisters to become betrothed before brothers? And, why should the order of betrothal be so important? It will be recalled that Herlihy and Klapisch-Zuber stress the importance of becoming economically established before contemplating marriage. If this were true, we would expect that the older, more firmly established men would be more desirable as potential husbands and, following the same rationale, be attracted by those brides with larger dowries. But the Ragusan evidence shows precisely the opposite. It is the brides of the younger men who bring the larger dowries. Indeed, there is a direct—but inverse—relationship between the age of the groom and the amount of the dowry (see Table 8).

TABLE 8. *Age of groom at betrothal and amount of dowry*

Wealth category of dowry received		Age of groom at betrothal				
		25 or less	26–30	31–35	36–40	41+
Standard or	Number	13	14	11	11	7
lavish	%	86.7	66.7	61.1	47.8	38.9
Marginal	Number	2	7	7	12	11
or paltry	%	13.3	33.3	38.9	52.2	61.1
	TOTAL	15	21	18	23	18

If the 'sisters first' pattern cannot be accounted for in terms of economic rationality, it may be that the emphasis contained in the documents on financial details may have led scholars astray. Archival sources do make much of dowry amounts, the sheer quantity of money that had to be raised. The sums were enormous, and in many instances those who had to raise them were well aware of how much wealth the dowry represented and how much trouble and anguish were required to raise it. The *Pacta Matrimonialia* often contain marginalia detailing the problems and delays. For example, the 2,200 *hyperperi* which Maroe Luxa de Bona (ID 270) promised to his son-in-law, Marinus Çorçi de Goçe (ID 806), in July 1448 would be considered paltry.[15] In August that year the first instalment of 1,070 *hyperperi* was paid. A decade was to pass until October 1459 when a further 150 *hyperperi* was paid. This very delayed payment was made by the sons and heirs of Maroe de Bona, who had died in the meantime. A short time later a further 150-*hyperperi* instalment was paid. All of this information is contained in notes added to the original contract. There are marginalia as well. These marginal notes made reference to a decision of the Great Council (on 22 May 1447), to a sale of property notarized on 10 October 1447, and to the dowry contract (*Carta Dotalis*) entered on 6 November 1459 (*Pacta* 1: fo. 18–18v). If payment of the dowry required the sale of part of the family estate to meet expenses, this required official approval. The Small Council had to agree to the request. With their approval the matter could then be brought to the Great Council, where a majority of three-quarters was required (*Lib. Vir.*: Cap. 302). There are not many betrothals where the financial arrangements are straightforward and uncomplicated.

In betrothing his daughter to another man, the bride's father was satisfying his honour obligations to his daughter. Henceforth, her honour would be the concern of her husband and his kin. This transferral of honour obligations from father to husband was very important. Honour meant that she be given as a virgin to her husband. As Kirshner notes, 'Delay [in arranging a marriage] could cost the family

---

[15] The bride, Jelussa (ID 279), was the second of three sisters to be married. All three married before Paladin (ID 272), their oldest brother, and two further brothers.

dearly, since it increased the possibility that a young woman's reputation for virtue would be sullied' (1978: 7, 9). It could also cast a pall over the reputation of the bride's father. If he delayed, could that be interpreted to mean that previous nego-tiations had come to naught? Could other men risk accepting a bride from a family that another might have found wanting?

The honour of one member of the family impinged on the honour of all, as studies in the Mediterranean have shown. Because the bride was very young at the time of betrothal and had been raised in strict seclusion, the best guide to her quality would be the virtue of her family. To ensure that virtue, as Origo notes, 'Her mother should supervise her constantly herself, not allowing her to spend too much time with the servants, with other "silly girls", or even with her own brothers—and her father, too, should keep a perpetually vigilant eye on her' (1963: 190). It is understandable that the father would desire an early betrothal. For even though the young bride might remain under his roof for several more years until her removal, she had become the responsibility of her husband. The betrothal was the public affirmation of this transferral of responsibility. Her father had satisfied his honour obligations with respect to her and had freed his sons of them as well. He had also established his own claims as a man of honour. This reveals another advantage of the early betrothal of daughters. While the expenditure of a dowry might be considered a significant financial loss for the bride's father, it was a gain for the son-in-law. It allowed him an increased measure of financial independence at a time when his own father would probably have died.

Marriage 'Spans' and Direct Exchange

Because of differences in the age at which they marry, sisters tend to marry in a period of time that is different to the period in which their brothers marry. Further, the length of the 'span' of time covering the marriages of sisters is different to that of brothers. As noted above, four daughters of Šišmund de Georgio were betrothed in the period from 1452 to 1460, a span of nine years.[16] Šišmund's three sons were betrothed between 1459 and 1471, a span of thirteen years. The lengths of the two spans in this case are unusual. Typically, the length of the span for sisters is some-what longer than it is for brothers. For example, if there are only two brothers to marry, the (average) interval between their marriages is 5.4 years. For two sisters, the comparable interval is 8.0 years. Between three brothers, the interval is 3.6 years or a total of 7.2 years between the marriage of the first and last brother. For

---

[16] The date of the marriage of Vechia to Simon Damian de Mençe (ID 1437) does not appear in the *Pacta Matrimonialia* or the *Carta Dotalis*. I have placed it between the marriages of Margarita and Maria although it may have occurred earlier. Similarly, Mahnken does not include a date for this betrothal in her genealogies for either the Georgio or Mençe (1960: s.v. 'Georgio' and 'Mençe'). Simon's younger brother married in 1453, therefore Simon's marriage is likely to have been earlier or contemporaneous. The betrothal of Margarita is noted in *Pacta* 1: fo. 74–74v. The betrothals of Maria and Helisabeth are found in *Pacta* 2: fos. 11–11v, 107v, respectively.

three sisters, the interval is 5.0 years, or a total of 10 years. Thus, the Georgio siblings differ from the typical in that the span between the betrothals of brothers is generally shorter than the span for sisters.

This seems a curious result. It might be thought that brothers would have more choice concerning the age at which they marry and, therefore, the span between them would be somewhat longer. But once all their sisters are married, some brothers would be able to marry as early as their mid-twenties, while other men might be delayed until their late thirties or early forties. It would depend upon the number and gender of the siblings, the number of years between them, and so on. Sisters, on the other hand, would be expected to marry when they reached their late teens. Therefore it would seem that the span of years between the first- and last-marrying brother would be longer than that between the first- and last-marrying sister. But, as we have seen, the opposite is the case.

The reasons may be that sisters have little freedom in choosing when they marry. If they marry, they tend to marry in the mid to late teens. Their marriage dates, in other words, are largely determined by the date of their births. But the intervals between these birth dates can be quite varied, not least by being interspersed with the birth dates of brothers. Brothers, on the other hand, do have more freedom in when they may marry, providing that their sisters have married before them. Therefore, once their sisters have married, the brothers can marry in fairly rapid succession. If some brothers have been delayed by having to wait for the betrothal of a younger sister, this might hasten their own marriages when that sister is at last safely betrothed. There is also some pressure from the queue of unmarried siblings behind. Since same-sex siblings tend to marry in order of birth, there will be pressure on older siblings to marry quickly so that they do not unduly delay the marriages of younger siblings. This is why the span between the marriages of the first- and last-married brothers is shorter than the span between sisters. Having examined some of the implications of the 'sisters first' principle for the sibling group, I now turn to consider its implications for marriage arrangements between different sibling groups and the *casata* of which they are a part.

Female siblings tend to marry in different time spans than their brothers. This does not, of course, preclude several sisters from marrying several brothers. But if sisters marry before brothers, we would be unlikely to find many instances of a brother and sister from one sibling group marrying a brother and sister from another. For brevity I refer to such 'brother for sister' marriages as 'direct exchange' marriages. Therefore, if one of the partners to a marriage is from one of the small *casate* which has only one sibling group of marriageable age, then that single marriage is likely to preclude further exchanges. The sisters of the groom are likely to have already married and would be unavailable as mates for the brothers of the bride.

This is borne out by an examination of the marriages occurring between 1440 and 1490. Of the 412 patrician marriages in this period, there are only five apparent cases of direct exchange between pairs of brothers and sisters in different sibling groups. This total includes only those marriages where both husband and wife can be positively identified and where both are patricians. The five exchange marriages involve nine sibling groups. One of these groups is enmeshed in two sets of exchange marriages. While these few cases constitute only 2 per cent of all marriages, their exceptional nature prompts us to examine them in some detail.

The first is a simple case (see Fig. 4). In 1454 Pervula (ID 2236), daughter of the late Leonardo Nixa de Georgio (ID 2235), was betrothed to Orsatus Marin Michael de Bona (ID 200). She was the elder of Leonardo's two children. The betrothal document specified that the marriage was to be consummated within three years. But in April 1457 the groom Orsatus denounces the executors of his father-in-law's estate for not providing the clothing and ornaments promised in the *Pacta Matrimonialia*. In the denunciation he claims that he intended consummating the marriage within six months. In September the same year a further denunciation is registered. What happened after that is not clear, but by 1462 he had married someone else. It may be presumed that Pervula died in the

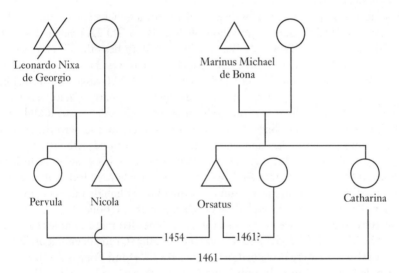

Notes: Only two of the nine Bona siblings are illustrated. Marriages in this and following genealogies are represented by a horizontal line linking the couple from below. Thus:

FIG. 4. Exchange marriages between the Georgio and Bona

Source: Mahnken 1960: s.v. 'Bona' and 'Georgio'.

interval.[17] In 1461, seven years after the original betrothal, Pervula's younger brother Nicola (ID 2237) is betrothed to Catharina de Bona (ID 216), the youngest sister of Orsatus. While this gives the appearance of an exchange marriage, it is more likely to be a reaffirmation of the bond between the Georgio and Bona which was threatened when Pervula and Orsatus did not marry. In this respect it can be argued that this is not a case of direct exchange.

However, there is still the problem of the violation of the 'sisters first' principle in the Bona sibling group. Orsatus Marin de Bona, Pervula's original groom, was the third oldest in a sibling group of nine, and the fifth in the line of seven siblings to marry. A younger sister had already married at the time of his betrothal, as had two of his older brothers and one younger one. There are two other younger sisters in the sibling group who did not marry. They may have died before reaching marriageable age, although this is not known. Catharina, the bride of Nicola Leonardo de Georgio, is the youngest sibling. While Catharina's betrothal violates the 'sisters first' principle, we have seen that it is not unusual for some brothers to marry before sisters if the sibling group is very large or if they must wait for a very much younger sister.

The next example of direct exchange calls forth another explanation. In this case Marussa (ID 227) and Francescho Çohan de Bona (ID 222) married Radula (ID 370) and Andreas Tripho de Bonda (ID 365). Both betrothals took place on 28 October 1453. The dowry amounts were identical as was the interval specified between betrothal and consummation (*Pacta* 2: fos. 1–2).[18] Marussa, the third child but only sister in a sibling group of four, was the first to marry. Therefore it was amongst the Bonda siblings that the problem of marriage order arose. Radula was the fifth of seven Bonda siblings. Andreas was the second, but was betrothed before his two younger sisters, Clara and Maria. He was, however, one of the few remaining male Bonda. His father was the only male Bonda of his generation to have children and this suggests that Andreas's betrothal may have reflected an urgency among the Bonda to ensure the continuity of their line, although it does not explain why this should be done through direct exchange with the Bona.

The third and fourth cases are linked and are somewhat more complex (see Fig. 5). In 1454 Michael (ID 585)[19] and Anucla (ID 587), the son and daughter of Çugno de Zrieva (ID 582), were betrothed to Guigno (ID 2324) and Francischa (ID 2327) Damian de Georgio. Since the only other Georgio sister, Nicoletta (ID 2316), had also become betrothed in the same year, no principle of 'sisters first' was breached on the Georgio side. However, the marriage of Nicoletta was not completed because her intended groom, Polo Tomko de Bona (ID 326), took holy orders. In

[17] The betrothal document has four marginal notes (*Pacta* 1: fo. 22). The first, from May 1454, refers to an entry in the *Carta Venditiones*. The second and third are the denunciations. The fourth, dated 6 February 1459, is unreadable.

[18] Both betrothal documents are incomplete because half of a manuscript page is missing.

[19] Michael does not appear to have been politically active. He holds no offices and does not appear in the listing of Great Council members.

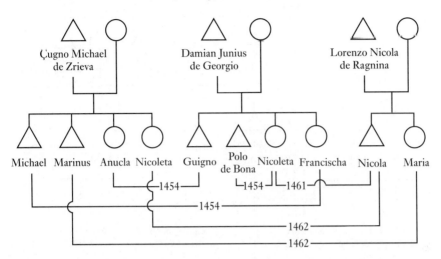

FIG. 5. Exchange marriages between the Zrieva, Georgio, and Ragnina
Source: Mahnken 1960: s.v. 'Georgio', 'Ragnina', and 'Zrieva'.

1461 she became betrothed again, this time to Nicola Lorenzo de Ragnina (ID 1741). Unfortunately Nicoletta died shortly thereafter. Her intended spouse then married Nicoleta Zugno de Zrieva (ID 588) in 1462. She was the youngest sister in the original Zrieva sibling group. Nicola de Ragnina's sister, Maria (ID 1750), then completed this second exchange involving the Zrieva siblings by becoming betrothed to Marinus Zugno de Zrieva (ID 586) the same year.

The fifth case concerns Marussa (ID 834) and Marinus (ID 806), the daughter and son of Çorçi Clemens de Goçe (ID 805). They married Natalis (ID 276) and Jelussa Maroe de Bona (ID 279) in 1448 and 1452, respectively. Amongst the Bona siblings all the sisters married before any of the brothers. Here the exception to the principle of 'sisters first' comes amongst the Goçe siblings. When Marinus married in 1452, four of his five sisters were already married even though he was the oldest sibling. But it seems likely that the fifth sister, Marussa, was a half-sister from his father's second marriage. As we have seen, half-siblings can be exceptions to the 'sisters first' principle.

Thus, only four of the 412 patrician marriages contravene the 'sisters first' principle. One of these involves the marriage of half-siblings, a second concerns a very large sibling group, and the third concerns a sibling group where the marriage appears to have been arranged in order to ensure the continuity of an endangered small *casata*. Only in one case, concerning the marriages of Michael and Anucla Zugno de Zrieva, is a ready explanation lacking. We predicted that one of the implications of the 'sisters first' principle would be that brothers and sisters would marry in different time spans and that there would be few examples of exchange marriage. This has been confirmed.

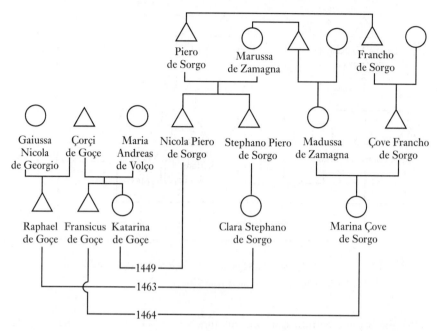

FIG. 6. Delayed marriages between the Goçe and Sorgo

Source: Mahnken 1960: s.v. 'Goçe' and 'Sorgo'.

A further twelve marriages involve a variation on this pattern which we might call deferred exchange. A good example concerns the marriages of three other Goçe siblings in the group just discussed (see Fig. 6). In 1438 Stephano Piero de Sorgo (ID 2068) married. He was the oldest of the siblings and his two younger sisters had already preceded him into wedlock. Eleven years later in 1449 his younger brother Nicola (ID 2084) married Katarina Çorçi de Goçe (ID 832). Katarina was one of twelve children of Çorçi Clemens de Goçe (ID 805). A further fourteen years were to elapse until Raphael (ID 830), Katarina's older brother, married Clara (ID 2072), a daughter of Stephano Piero de Sorgo (ID 2068). This is a case of uncle and niece marrying brother and sister. But this was not the end of the Sorgo/Goçe exchange, for the following year Marina (ID 2056), a cousin once removed from Stephano, married Franciscus Çorçi de Goçe (ID 839). This third marriage completed the exchange between the Goçe and Sorgo, but it also brings to light another exchange. Piero (ID 2067) and Çove de Sorgo (ID 2049), uncle and nephew, had previously married Marussa (ID 2178) and Madussa de Zamagna (ID 2163), aunt and niece, respectively.

While direct marital exchanges might alleviate some of the problems caused by huge dowries while at the same time contributing towards isogamy within the patriciate, direct exchange is made difficult by the 'sisters first' principle. Because sisters marry before brothers, groups of sisters tend to marry in different time spans from their male siblings. And yet, in considering apparent exceptions as well as the example of delayed exchange, there appears to be a tendency within the patriciate to restrict marital alliances within narrow boundaries and to balance one marriage with another. It may be significant that between 1440 and 1490 there were no cases where a pair of brothers married a pair of sisters. The 'sisters' first principle would present no impediments to such unions. The exchanges that we have examined between Sorgo and Goçe on the one hand, and between Sorgo and Zamagna on the other, suggest a tendency towards one marriage between a pair of *casate* being balanced by a second. But this tendency may simply be an artefact of a small number of admittedly exceptional cases. We now turn to directly consider the role of the *casata* as a unit in marriage.

7

The *Casata*, Genealogical Skewing, and Political Support

Marital Alliances Among the Casate

What was the significance of the *casata* for the marriages of its members? If marriages were arranged with a view towards their political usefulness and if the *casata* acted as a unit in political affairs, then we would expect to see evidence of *casata* involvement in arranging marriages. But given the relatively small size of the endogamous patriciate, the shallow depth of the study period and the variations in size of the component *casate*, it is not easy to discern clear patterns. In the half-century from 1440 to 1490, there are too few marriages to permit a meaningful analysis of *casata* alliances. Because of this, it was decided to open the window of observation to include all marriages occurring between 1400 and 1520. If there were patterns of alliance, they would be more likely to emerge in this much larger population of marriages. This is one of the considerable advantages of historical anthropology. It permits one to expand or contract the window of observation to fit the nature of the problem being investigated.

With this much larger number of marriages, let us begin by examining marriages of the largest *casata*, the Goçe. There were 207 Goçe patrician marriages between 1400 and 1520 of which 191 were between the Goçe and twenty-eight other *casate*. Eight were endogamous marriages between Goçe sections.[1] Like most of the larger *casate* within the patriciate, the Goçe spread their marriages widely. This might be expected from the large number of Goçe who married, the patriciate's relatively small size and the Church's restrictions on close kin marriage. But if the *casate* tended to spread their marriages broadly, that did not mean that they spread them evenly or in similar fashion.

To study patterns of marriage alliance, a matrix of all marriages between *casate* was constructed. This information, however, is difficult to interpret because the *casate* differ so considerably in size and in the number of their marriages. One is more likely to marry a Goçe than a Bocinolo, other things being equal, because there are many more Goçe available for marriage than there are Bocinolo. Furthermore, we find that the Goçe did not marry into eight *casate*. Since these were amongst the smallest of the *casate*, it is difficult to know whether

---

[1] Other houses also had endogamous marriages. The significance of such marriages will be considered below. Seven Goçe spouses cannot be identified by *casata* affiliation.

this absence should be taken as an indication of dislike or simply lack of opportunity.

To make allowance for the differences in numbers of persons marrying, the following procedure was adopted. First, it was assumed that if *casata* affiliation were not an important consideration in marital choice, then any individual male would be equally likely to marry any other individual female.[2] On this basis the expected number of marriages between *casate* was calculated.[3] Then the difference between the expected number of marriages and the actual number was calculated. A zero difference would indicate that the number of marriages which occurred between two *casate* was just about what would be expected on the basis of chance. A relatively large positive number would indicate an attraction between *casate* whereas a large negative one would indicate indifference or aversion.

The first observation is that while patterns of preference do not emerge for all *casate*, they do exist for some. These can be displayed in the form of a network of alliances (see Fig. 7). For example, forty-one Grade married in the period and they married into thirteen *casate*. But fifteen of them took Sorgo spouses. Therefore, over one-third of all Grade married into this single *casata*. Here is evidence of strong attachment. Similarly, on the basis of chance we would have expected that some of the 207 Goçe would have found a spouse among the sixteen Buchia who married, yet none did.

If we examine the total number of marriages, it is possible to discern some clustering of allied *casate*. At the centre of one web of intermarrying *casate* are the Sorgo, one of the largest *casate*. They exchange with the Grade and Zamagna in fifteen and twelve marriages, respectively. The Grade and Zamagna also exchange with one another. These three *casate* are strongly interlinked by marriage ties and I shall refer to them as the Sorgo triangle.[4] The Sorgo are also linked to the Caboga through seven marriages, but the Caboga show no special relationship with the other two Sorgo partners, the Grade and Zamagna. The Caboga have two marriages with the Zamagna, less than would be expected by chance, and the nature of their tie with the Grade is very one-sided. All the Caboga/Grade marriages involved Caboga women marrying Grade men.

In addition to marriages within this small cluster, the Sorgo are involved in sixteen marriages with the Bona. There are also thirteen marriages between Sorgo and the Goçe. Both are less than would be expected by chance. These examples show the importance not only of examining marriage links, but of considering the

---

[2] To simplify the calculations, this analysis ignores the fact that some agnates and other kin would not have been possible marriage partners.

[3] In the analysis it was assumed that the pool of all possible marriage partners was made up of all of those who actually married. This omits those who never married. Such an assumption was necessary because it is impossible to tell in many instances if some persons who never married ever reached marriageable age.

[4] Each *casata* disperses its marriages amongst the several sections of its partners. Marriages do not cluster within particular sections.

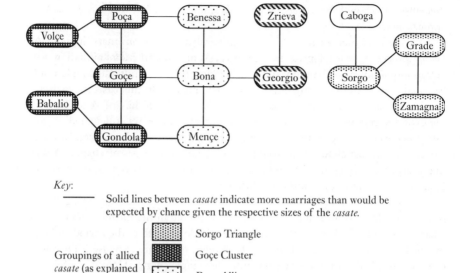

Key:

—————— Solid lines between *casate* indicate more marriages than would be
expected by chance given the respective sizes of the *casate*.

Groupings of allied
casate (as explained
in text)

Sorgo Triangle

Goçe Cluster

Bona Allies

Georgio/Zrieva Dyad

FIG. 7. Marriage connections between large *Casate*, 1400–1520

number of links in relation to the size of the respective *casate* and the likelihood
that marriages are simply due to chance.

The Caboga/Grade marriages mentioned above also indicate that we should not
only consider the number of marriage links between *casate*, but also the degree of
reciprocity. We have seen that the Sorgo/Bona exchange, while involving sixteen
marriages, shows no strong attachment between the two *casate*. The number of
marriages is somewhat less than would be expected by chance. But if we consider
the degree of reciprocity, a new dimension emerges. The Sorgo give thirteen of
their women to the Bona but receive only three Bona women in return. It is noteworthy that in a sixty-year period between 1420 and 1480 the Sorgo received no
Bona brides. Yet in the same period fifty-two Bona women married.

If we look not at marriage attachments, but at marriage avoidances between the
Sorgo allies and others, we find that the Sorgo tend not to intermarry with the
Gondola. The Caboga tend not to intermarry with the Goçe. The Goçe and
Gondola, as we shall see, are two *casate* at the centre of another web of marriages
which I shall refer to as the Goçe cluster.

The Goçe exchange with the Babalio, Benessa, Bona, Gondola, Poça and Volçe.
Unlike the Sorgo/Grade/Zamagna triangle, the *casate* within the Goçe cluster
tend not to marry amongst themselves. Of the Goçe allies only the Babalio and
Gondola intermarry.

The Bona are the centre of another set of intermarrying *casate*. The Bona appear to mediate between the Goçe cluster and the Sorgo/Grade/Zamagna triangle. On the one hand the Bona exchange with both the Sorgo and the Goçe, but tend not to exchange with the allies of either. The Bona are allied with the Benessa, Mençe, and Georgio. The Benessa, in their turn, are linked with the Poça. The Mençe are tied to the Gondola. Both the Poça and Mençe are part of the Goçe cluster. The Bona receive brides from both the Goçe and Sorgo but favour neither with their own women. Yet overall the Bona appear to have a remarkably even-handed marriage policy, giving brides to various *casate* in rough proportion to their size.[5]

The Goçe, Bona, and Sorgo are three of the largest *casate* (see Table 4). They are the first, second, and fourth, respectively—and each is at the centre of a set of intermarrying houses. The third largest *casata*, the Gondola, is one of the Goçe allies and intermarries with the Babalio, another Goçe ally. The fifth and sixth largest houses, the Georgio and Zrieva, constitute an intermarrying dyad although the Georgio also have strong ties with the Bona. The Georgio are also linked by marriage with the Babalio and Poça (among the Goçe allies), and the Zamagna (among the Sorgo triangle). Of the middling-sized houses not previously mentioned, the Resti do not have strong ties with any *casata* although they slightly favour the Zrieva and Poça. The Resti seem to have an aversion to the Bona since there are only two marriages between them when we would have expected about five on the basis of chance. The Lucari favour the Bona and Sorgo, but avoid the Goçe. The Ragnina favour the Poça among the Goçe allies while remaining shy of entanglements with the Gondola (another Goçe ally) and the Bona.

Several points emerge from this. First, patterns of preference and avoidance occur and are quite stable over the period from 1400 to 1520. Over this longer period of time the alliance between the Sorgo and their allies remains intact as does the pattern of ties among the Goçe and theirs. Second, most *casate* give and receive brides from a broad spectrum of other *casate*. Except in the very few cases discussed, patterns of preference and avoidance in marriage are not very strong. The links between the Sorgo and their allies stand out in this respect. Third, the larger the *casata*, the more *casate* it tends to marry into. Most *casate* appear to distribute their marriages roughly according to *casata* size with more marriages being with the larger *casate*, fewer with the smaller. All of this can be taken to indicate a generous marriage policy within the patriciate.

If patterns of marital preference among *casate* are not strongly marked, it may be that the *casata* is not the appropriate unit for the analysis of marriage preference. It might be that smaller sections of the *casata* are more appropriate. It could also be that if there are units of marital alliance, they are not *casata* based. Given the small size of the patriciate as an endogamous unit, it may also be that the absence of strong patterns of alliance and aversion is due to problems of

---

[5] The exceptional nature of the Bona relationship with the Sorgo has been noted above.

availability. Note that two-thirds of the *casate* are quite small. In the 120 years between 1400 and 1520, each of these smaller *casate* had less than fifty people marrying. This would be about (at the generous end) one person available for marriage every three years. Perhaps, to take one case, in those years when forty-five Ragnina were looking for partners, none of the forty-one Benessa were available. In other words, patterns of preference and avoidance may be nothing of the sort. They may simply reflect patterns of availability.

If we examine the 'pool' of brides and grooms available from each *casata* year-by-year, availability is certainly a consideration in possible alliances between *casate*. Even the enormous Goçe did not have one of its 110 marrying women available in the mid-1430s even if someone had wanted to marry one. Yet in the same period the next largest *casata*, the Bona, could provide five brides.

Throughout the period each *casata*'s supply of potential brides waxed and waned. Some of the patterning is general and presumably reflects widespread demographic trends. It seems likely, for example, that the glut of marriages in the early 1450s is a response to the baby boom which followed after the plague years of the 1430s. It seems equally likely that the marriage famines about 1467 and 1482 are associated with the plagues of those years. But there is one conclusion about marriage for which the evidence is clear. There are no data which suggest that the *casata per se* takes an active interest in the marriages of its members.

In a small community such as patrician Ragusa, one might expect to find inter-linking through marriage occurring over time. While there is no evidence that the Ragusans prescribed marriage partners in the sense introduced by Lévi-Strauss, there may be regularities over time in the exchange of partners (1969). In the discussion of *sociétés complexes* elaborated by Héritier, it has been hypothesized that people may be inclined to marry the nearest relative available beyond the prohibited degrees (1981: 163). This suggestion has been the centrepiece of Delille's historical analysis of repeat marriages in the Kingdom of Naples from the fifteenth to the nineteenth centuries and his claim that such marriages constitute an intermediate type between elementary and complex marriage systems (1985). This work is important not merely because it confronts conventional wisdom about South Italian kinship, but because it redirects anthropological attention to the possible linkage between marriage systems and larger kinship groups.

We have seen that the age difference at marriage militates against direct exchange between sibling groups. But the same age differences might have another consequence. According to Héritier's hypothesis, the closest descendants of a common ancestor that might marry would be cases where a groom marries his MMBDD. Given the age differences we have examined, such a marriage would occur when the linking ancestors (the groom's mother's mother and her brother) would be about 69 years old. The next most likely marriage would be between a man and his FMBSD. In this latter case the linking relatives (the groom's father's mother and her brother) would be about 84 years old at the time of the marriage.

Also in this latter case the bride's *casata* and the groom's paternal *casata* would be identical.

Using the genealogical records in the database, it is possible to trace back through the ancestors of both bride and groom to search for common ancestors. Taking the marriages which occurred between 1440 and 1490, I have attempted to trace the ancestry of both bride and groom through five generations. The depth of the genealogical data does not permit fruitful searches much beyond this limit. It was possible to search for linking relatives for the partners in 345 marriages. Looking particularly for possible links in the generations between the second ascending (the grandparental generation) and the fifth generation, the groom potentially has eighty possible ancestors whom he might share with his bride. In practice the number of possible links is much less because of gaps in the genealogical records. This number of gaps increases as one goes back in time.

Of the 345 marriages studied there are only sixty-three (18 per cent) in which there is an identifiable linking relative. It is surprising how few marriages show a linking relative although the small number may be due to lacunae in the genealogical database. The second surprise is that among those who are linked, no dominant pattern emerges. Significantly, given Héritier's hypothesis, where linking relatives exist there are no cases where that relative is either the MMBDD or the FMBSD. The set of linking relatives are a very mixed (genealogical) bag.

Following the conventions established by French studies of consanguine marriages where the numbers refer to ascending links to the common ancestor (the groom being given first), the most common link is between grandchildren of first cousins (4–4, with 27 instances) (Segalen 1991: 102–14). The next is 3–4 with 19 instances followed by 5–4 and 4–5 (with 9 and 8 instances, respectively). These, in turn, are followed by 3–5, 4–3, 5–5, and so on. Since couples are linked in more than one way, the number of links is greater than the number of couples. But this material does not show any evidence of intermediate marriage systems in Ragusa such as those suggested by Delille for the Kingdom of Naples.

Betrothal Arrangements: Fathers and Tutors

In the analysis of marriage, we have assumed that it is the father who arranges the marriages of his children. That assumption must now be examined in greater detail. We found that prospective brides and grooms were about 18 and 33 years old at betrothal, respectively. But the groom did not consummate the marriage and remove the bride to his own home until sometime later. While the length of this interval between betrothal and consummation differed from the mid-1450s to the early 1500s, the average interval was about three years. Thus, on average a wife would be about 21 and her husband 36 at the consummation of their marriage. If the first child of the union were born about two years later, the new mother and

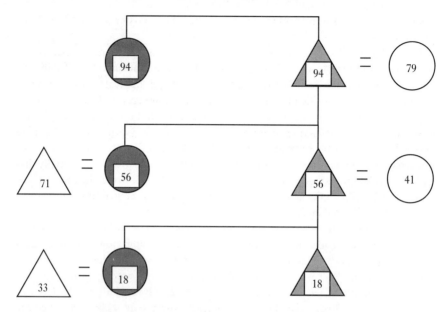

FIG. 8. Relative ages of close (hypothetical) agnates and their spouses

ᵃ Based upon a fifteen-year age difference between husband and wife. All siblings are treated as if they were first-born. Agnates are darkened.

father would then be 23 and 38 years old, respectively.[6] Now, if this first-born child were female and if she were also to become betrothed another eighteen years later, then the mother would be about 41 years of age and the father would be about 56 at her betrothal. Given mortality in early Renaissance Europe, not many men would be alive when their first-born daughters reached betrothal age. Even fewer would survive to arrange the betrothals of their younger daughters.

This discussion has been in terms of a first-born daughter. What if the first-born were a son? If this first-born son became betrothed at 33 years of age, then his mother would be about 56 years of age and his father would be 71 years old. The relative ages of close agnatic kin and their spouses are shown in Figure 8. Not many men live long enough to arrange their daughters' marriages. Even fewer would be alive at the time of their sons' marriages.

In Ragusa the mean age difference between fathers and sons is close to forty years. As Martin has observed, 'where age differences such as these exist and life expectancy at the age of marriage is low, most men will die while their offspring are immature and unable to compete for or manage their estates or offices' (Martin

---

[6] These figures are slightly lower than those noted for Florentine parents of 1427. The average Florentine baby 'was received by a mother 26 years of age, and the average father was nearly 40' (Herlihy 1972: 360).

1981: 402n.).[7] In small *casate*, at the time of the betrothals, there may be no men of a senior generation alive. The relevance of this to the development of political careers will be considered below. Here we will explore some of the implications of this age difference between generations for the arranging of marriage.

Of 335 brides whose betrothal documents survive, 135 (40 per cent) had no living father (*Pacta* 1–5).[8] While these same documents are largely silent about the groom's father, there is other evidence which can be used. After 1472 the records of the Great Council note when a man entered the council and his age at entry. These same records also note the year of death. Comparing these ages and dates with the dates on betrothal documents, it is possible to calculate the number of men who have no father alive at betrothal. Information for 319 males for whom both birth year and year of father's death are known and who also lived long enough to enter the Great Council (*Specchio*: fos. 382–393v) indicates that over 80 per cent of them have no father alive when they are the age to become betrothed.

Thus, at the time of their betrothal, about two-fifths of all maidens have no father alive. In such cases the Small Council appoints a group of tutors to look after their interests. The tutors are responsible for executing the father's will and for arranging his daughter's marriage, which might also include their having to stand pledge for the dotal amount. If part of the estate had to be sold to raise capital for the dowry, the tutors had to petition the Small Council for approval. If approval was forthcoming, then the Small Council put its own recommendation before the Great Council. Betrothals were clearly matters of great consequence. Who, then, were the people making these arrangements?

The Small Council did not recruit tutors from the patriciate at large. Most tutors were kinsfolk of the maiden and as such might be expected to show a special concern for her interests. It is significant that the most commonly occurring relative among the tutors is neither the maiden's father's brother nor her own brother; that is, the agnatic kinsmen most likely to assume the legal mantle of the deceased. Nor is it other agnatic kin who constitute most of the tutors. Indeed, in over 40 per cent of the cases, there is no agnatic kinsman of the bride included among the tutors.

The person most commonly found among the tutors is the mother's brother. The next person most commonly numbered among the tutors is the bride's mother. The father's brother comes third. The relationship between the bride and tutors has been studied in the thirty-seven betrothals of orphaned brides occurring between 1448 and 1462.[9] There are only five brothers numbered among the tutors. Most brothers would have been too young at the time of their sister's betrothal to be assigned this responsibility. The Small Council might also have

---

[7] Similar observations have been made by Goody (1983: 207–9) and Saller (1987: 30).

[8] The series does not begin until 1447 and there is a gap from 1464 to 1495. Prior to 1447 betrothal contracts are found in the *Diversa Notariæ*.

[9] Betrothal documents from this period until 1495 are lost.

believed that the brothers' interests would not necessarily coincide with those of their sisters.

It is noteworthy that agnatic kinsmen of the bride are not the most common tutors, as noted above. If we examine the relationship between each bride and her tutors, we find that the bride's mother's agnates constitute the largest group among tutors, with forty-eight persons. The bride's (father's) agnates come second with thirty-eight. They in turn are followed by a loose collection who are affinally linked to the bride's father such as his sister's husband (six persons), his sister's son (five persons), his mother's brother (five persons), and so on (see Table 9).

The tutors of most maidens are therefore an assortment of kin and affines. This suggests an attempt on the part of the Small Council to support the maiden by choosing a range of (relatively) close kin and affines, but also one which includes several different and potentially competing interests. Significantly, thirteen sets of

TABLE 9. *Relationships between tutees and tutors*

	No.	%
Bride's agnates		
B	5	
FB	17	
FBS	3	
FFBS	6	
Other agnate	7	
Total	38	28
Bride's mother's agnates		
M	20	
MB	21	
MF	3	
MFB	2	
Other maternal agnate	2	
Total	48	35
Affines		
ZH	7	
FZH	6	
FZS	5	
MH	2	
Total	20	14
Others		
Father's maternal kin	8	
Mother's maternal kin	3	
Others	11	
Unknown	10	
Total	32	23
	138	100

tutors contained no agnates of the bride. When distant agnates of the maiden are selected to be tutors, they often turn out to be affinally connected as well. This testifies to the interests involved. It is particularly interesting that no tutorial set contained only agnates. There is one apparent exception, a group of tutors consisting of the bride's agnates and some of their affines which will be examined below.

Tutors are responsible for the dowry's financial arrangements. In this respect fatherless girls differ somewhat from girls whose father is still alive. While only 11 per cent of all maidens marry with a paltry dowry of less than 2,600 *hyperperi*, orphaned brides are more likely to be in this situation than brides whose fathers are still alive. Perhaps men who die young tend to be poorer. But it also seems likely that tutors are somewhat less punctilious about arranging dowries than fathers. They also seem to face greater obstacles or to take more time in overcoming them. This could be because of the number of interested parties and the difficulties in co-ordinating those interests. The dowry arrangements of tutored girls are also more likely to be delayed than those brides whose father is still alive. It is also more likely that the tutors will have to sell some property to finance the dowry. When Nicoleta (ID 298), daughter of the late Nicola Sarachin de Bona (ID 297), was betrothed in October 1448 to Vita Michiel de Zamagna (ID 2186), the *Pacta Matrimonialia* noted that 1,725 *hyperperi* were to be paid within five years. Yet six years later apparently only 372 *hyperperi* had been paid out of the proceeds of a sale. The dotal contract itself was not settled until the next century (*Pacta* 1: fos. 20–1).[10] Although this is not true for Nicoleta, tutored girls whose mother is included among the tutors are generally given higher dowries. It is also the case that when substantial dowries were given, the tutored girls were more likely to receive such a dowry than a girl whose father was still alive.

The grooms of these tutored girls are not distinctive in any way. While there are only a small number of such men for whom age at betrothal is known, their age is very close to the average male age at (first) betrothal.[11] Tutored brides are likely to marry a man who is one of the younger brothers within his sibling group, but there is no evidence to suggest that grooms of tutored girls receive smaller dowries or have to wait longer for their dowries than other grooms. Similarly, such grooms are no more likely to be fatherless at betrothal than the men who marry untutored girls. In all of these respects, therefore, the grooms of fatherless maidens are much like other grooms.

---

[10] This document contains five dated marginalia. Two of these marginal notes refer to arrangements made for payment (including a sale of property) and three are references to other records: the sale (*Venditor Cancell.*, entered 12 December 1455), a minute of the Great Council (*Act. Maior.*, dated 6 March 1484), and the signing of the dotal contract (*Carta*, on 6 December 1500). The extraordinary length of time taken to complete dowry arrangements is unusual although not unique. So, too, is the source of the dowry. Of the total, 1,725 *hyperperi* was to come from Nicoleta's mother and a further 843 *hyperperi* from her mother's mother and namesake, Marussa (ID 2178), daughter of Ursius de Zamagna.

[11] $N = 25$, $\overline{X} = 33.5$ years.

Two important implications follow from this. First, it is clear that the *casata* does not make financial arrangements for the marriages of its orphaned women. The sale of part of a man's estate to finance his daughter's dowry does not depend upon the wishes of his heirs and agnatic descendants. Neither does it require the consent of other agnates within the *casata*. These matters rest with the Small Council and its recommendation to the Great Council. It is the tutors appointed by these bodies who negotiate with the groom and who make the arrangements that are recorded in the *Pacta Matrimonialia*.

It might be that the Small Council tries to subvert marital alliances between *casata*. Could it be a coincidence, for example, that none of the tutored Sorgo brides married a Grade or Zamagna husband? Whatever the outcome of these conjectures, it remains that about 40 per cent of the marriages are unlikely to be alliances between *casate* because these marriages are not arranged by the bride's father. As we have seen, it could not be said that the tutors represent the interests of the *casata* as a corporate group in the marriage. Indeed, it is difficult to see any *casata* interests expressed in marriage arrangements. Yet, if the *casata* were a lineage, it would be most likely to do so. In this respect it is worth quoting Fortes's observation:

In a segmentary lineage system rights over persons are correspondingly segmented and subject to a hierarchy of jural control. They are not so distributed in an unsegmented system of shallow generation depth. This has a direct bearing on the mode of distribution and transfer of marriage rights. In an unsegmented lineage jural authority to receive the critical marriage payment is likely to be held by the lineage head; in a segmented lineage the right may be vested in a woman's father, subject to consent of a superior lineage authority. (1970: 104)

As we have seen, the Ragusan *casata* is not a segmentary lineage; neither is it an unsegmented system of shallow depth. If the *casata* were a lineage, we would expect to see corporate interests clearly represented in the financial arrangements of its members, especially if these concern important patrimonial assets. Marriages in Ragusa did concern such assets. They involved very substantial sums of money and often the sale of valuable immovable property. Yet in the case of the marriages of fatherless maidens, there is no evidence of corporate *casata* interests in the transmission of these patrimonial assets. Furthermore, if the *casata* were a lineage, we would also expect close lineage involvement in the transfer of rights in the persons of its members. Again, they are not. No consent of a *casata* authority is sought for either bride or groom, whether the father is living or dead. This, I believe, is the most compelling evidence that the Ragusan *casata* is not a lineage. Of course it could be argued that the *casata* is a lineage, but that the governing bodies of the state usurped some of its functions. If usurpation occurred, it occurred at least one century before our period. Between 1440 and 1490 the *casata* in Ragusa did not function as a lineage.

To probe the interests that might lie behind the arrangement of marriages, we turn to examine the case of Mirussa (ID 293), daughter of the late Marin Sarachin de Bona (ID 291). When she was betrothed to Paladin Marin de Gondola (ID 1254) in 1458, persons related to her through her father were very prominent among the tutors. This makes this case, referred to earlier, very unusual and worthy of more detailed examination. Amongst her four tutors were her father's brother, Nicola Sarachin de Bona (ID 297), her father's mother, Nicoletta (ID 1191, daughter of Marin Nifficus de Gondola), and her father's sister's husband, Nicola Paulus de Gondola (ID 1260). All three have strong paternal interests. Mirussa's fourth tutor was her stepmother. This woman, Pervola (ID 2233, daughter of Michael Nixa de Georgio), was her father's third wife.

Therefore at the time of the betrothal only two of Mirussa's four mother's brothers (from the Sorgo) were still living. The Small Council did not include either of them among the tutors.[12] Whatever interests her Sorgo maternal kin might have had in Mirussa's betrothal, they appear to have been squeezed out by those with close attachments to her Bona agnates. As we shall see, this is far from being the case.

This was not the first betrothal for the groom. Paladin's first, one of short duration, had been to Maria (ID 504), the daughter of Nicola Maroe de Caboga (ID 503). The second one, to Mirussa, is recorded on 25 November 1458 and it is noted that the marriage is to be consummated by the coming February. This is a very short period of time and it appears that Mirussa is being rapidly bundled into a Bona–Gondola contrived match. Both of Mirussa's non-Bona tutors are also Gondola. Nicola Paulus de Gondola (ID 1260), her FZH, is a first cousin once-removed to the groom.[13] Her paternal grandmother, the second tutor, was also a Gondola.

But matters are not quite so straightforward as this listing of agnatically linked tutors might suggest. Lurking behind this betrothal we can discern the influence of two elderly widows whose own children and brothers' children are tightly intermarried (see Fig. 9). Hidden outside the immediate group of Mirussa's tutors is the first of these widows—Anna (ID 502), the widow of Paulus Give de Gondola (ID 1257) and sister to Nicola Maroe de Caboga (ID 503). Her brother's daughter, Maria, had been first betrothed to Paladino, the current bridegroom. That betrothal, in other words, had united Anna's niece and her husband's grand-nephew. Another niece, Anucla (ID 505), had married into another branch of the Gondola. Thus, this elderly woman and her two nieces (all Cabogas) married three Gondola men.

Turning from the marriages of her brother's children to the marriages of her

[12] The Small Council at that time did not include a Sorgo or Bona. It did, however, include Nicola de Gondola.

[13] Following conventual usage, capital letters represent genealogical positions. Thus 'F' represents father, 'B' represents brother, 'FB' represents the father's brother, and so on. But 'Z' indicates sister and 'S' indicates son. Therefore, 'FZH' is the father's sister's husband. The symbol '>' represents 'older than'.

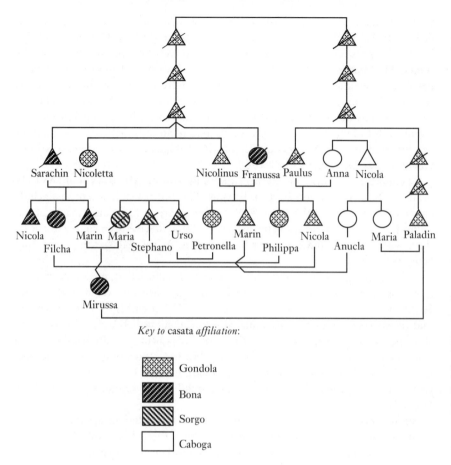

Key to casata *affiliation*:

Gondola

Bona

Sorgo

Caboga

FIG. 9. Partial genealogy of kin and affinal connections at the betrothal of
Mirussa de Bona

Source: Mahnken 1960: s.v. 'Bona', 'Caboga', 'Gondola', and 'Sorgo'.

own, Anna's son, Nicola Paulus de Gondola (ID 1260), had married into the Bona.
As we have seen, he is one of Mirussa's tutors as well as her father's sister's
husband. Anna's daughter, Philippa (ID 1262), is also linked to Mirussa for she is
the widow of Stephano Piero de Sorgo (ID 2068), one of Mirussa's late mother's
brothers. Thus Anna's children are affinally linked to both Mirussa's paternal kin
and to her maternal kin.

A second elderly widow implicated in this betrothal is Nicoletta. She is both
paternal grandmother and tutor. Interestingly, her own marriage had been a case
of brother–sister exchange between the Gondola and Bona. Her brother, Nicolinus
(ID 1145), had married her husband's sister, Franussa (ID 334). Children of both

unions had in turn married into the Sorgos. Nicoletta's son had married Maria de Sorgo and her niece Petronella (ID 1156) had married Urso Piero de Sorgo (ID 2078). This Petronella was now another Sorgo widow. Finally, note that Nicoletta's nephew had married Anna's niece, Anucla (ID 505), and the latter was the sister of Paladino's first wife. Thus while the interests of maternal kin appear to be unrepresented by tutors in this betrothal, there is a thicket of ties between the Bona and Gondola tutors and the (absent) Sorgos.

This material suggests that women, and links through women, may have been very significant in the arranging of marriages. They emerge clearly from the shadows in situations where the bride's father is already deceased, but they may also have played an important behind-the-scenes role in those situations where male relatives are apparently the principal actors. In the very closed domestic worlds of fifteenth-century Ragusa, women would have had access to dwellings and information that would not have been accessible to their husbands. And, because wives were likely to outlive their husbands, they would exert considerable influence upon their sons and daughters.

Generations

To introduce the second implication of the marriage system, let us again return to the age differences between husbands and wives. Herlihy, in a perspicacious article, relates it to the notion of generation. He points out that the historian who wishes to use the 'method of generation' should seek answers to four questions. Three of the four questions concern age cohorts, or what Baxter and Almagor refer to as *social* generations, not *genealogical* generations in *sensu stricto* (1978: 164). As Fortes has argued, 'the process of ranking, reckoning, and grouping individuals by generations is wholly distinct from that of ranking, reckoning, and grouping people by either stages of maturation or the equivalents of age' (1984: 105). He points out that a generation, or a sequence of generations, is a product of kinship and is specified by reference to genealogical connections. This difference is crucial for,

Whereas a generation and a sequence of generations are family-generated, age specification is politico-jurally institutionalized. Generational organization subsumes the ostensible discontinuities between successive generations in a framework of overall continuity. Age selection, by contrast, operates atomistically, with the formally isolated individual as a unit of reference, and leaves the matter of structural continuity or discontinuity in society to the non-familial institutional order. (ibid.: 106)

Since one of Herlihy's questions about age cohorts will also concern us later, we only mention it here in passing. It asks about the relative size of the age cohort in relation to those immediately preceding and following it. We shall examine the relative size of age cohorts in the context of succession to office. But it is Herlihy's third question which poses a crucial issue. 'What', he asks, ' is the mean distance in time separating mothers and fathers from their children?' (1972: 350).

Herlihy suggests that this difference affects the internal structure of families and also the larger society. Within the family he points to the distance and potential antagonism between fathers and sons while the wife and mother has an intermediary position both emotionally and in terms of age. As to the larger societal implications, he directs our attention to the contrast between cohorts of married young women and unmarried young men (ibid.: 360–2). Again, as Fortes would remind us, this is a matter of age, not of generation. But age at marriage does affect generation in an important way.

We recall that husbands tend to be about fifteen years older than their brides. If this age difference at marriage is regular, and if the results are projected onto a genealogy of a hypothetical (male) Ego, the results would be as shown in Figure 10. As this diagram indicates, there would be a considerable discrepancy in the ages of persons who are generally spoken of as being a single (genealogical) generation. Such anomalies are not unusual within the anthropological literature and are often commented upon, particularly in societies where polygyny is common.[14] The significance of age differences has also been intensively studied with reference to marriage systems. There is, in this respect, a very large literature concerning bilateral cross-cousin marriage, sister exchange, and the like.

Here, however, we wish to draw attention to the configuration of kinship relations. If the fifteen-year difference in ages between spouses is systematic, we would find that, in the parents' generation, the father and the father's sisters would be about fifteen years older than the mother and the mother's brother. The father's sister's husband and his sibling are also about fifteen years older than the father and his siblings (FZH > F > MB). The model suggests a systematic skewing or 'tilting' of a single genealogical generation. A similar pattern occurs in Ego's own generation (and in all generations). Ego's father's sister's sons are about fifteen years older than Ego and the mother's brother's sons are about fifteen years younger (FZS > Ego > MBS). Ego would be about the same age as his parallel cousins (FBS = Ego = MZS). To what extent does this model apply to actual generations among the Ragusan patriciate?

It is not possible to measure actual age differences between most members. Not enough birth dates are recorded in these data to analyse the age differences between pairs of persons in different genealogical positions. But there is an alternative, if cruder, method. From 1455 the dates at which men entered the Great Council are known (*Specchio* 1: fos. 386v–394). If we assume that most men entered the council at about the same age, the difference between their dates of entry can be taken as an approximation of their difference in age. Indeed, 75 per cent of all entrants are between 21 and 23 years old at entry. Using this information as an estimate of age,

[14] Fortes's anecdote about Nyaangzum (aged about 50) and his 'son' Teezeen (aged about 70) is typical (1984: 102).

Kin and affines in this genealogy are positioned along the vertical axis in terms of their relative age to show the degree of skewing within the several generations. The three (genealogical) generations are shaded and Ego's agnatic kin are darkened.

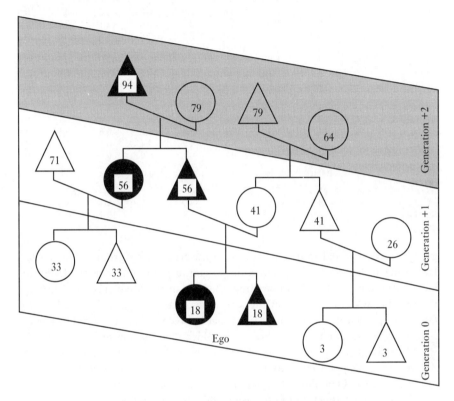

FIG. 10. Relative ages of close (hypothetical) kin

[a] Based upon a fifteen-year age difference between husband and wife. All siblings are represented as if born in the same year.

we find that age differences between various categories of kin do correspond to the pattern predicted by the model (see Table 10).

In the father's generation, for example, Ego's father's sister's husband tends to be about twenty-five years older than Ego. The mother's brother, on the other hand, is only about fifteen years older. Within Ego's own generation, the father's sister's sons tend to be older than Ego. The mother's sister's sons tend to be almost exact contemporaries, while the mother's brother's sons are younger. This confirms the predictions of the model. To summarize, FZH > MZH > MB and in Ego's own generation FZS > MZS > MBS.

One of the features of marriage in the early Renaissance is that wife-receiving

Genealogical Skewing and Support

TABLE 10. *Ego's age in relation to close male kin*

Years Ego younger/older than Alter	FZH	MZH	MB	FZS	MZS	MBS	ZH	WB
31+	0.0	0.0	0.0	0.0	0.0	0.2	0.0	0.0
25 to 30	0.0	0.0	0.6	0.3	0.6	2.1	0.0	1.5
19 to 24	0.0	0.0	1.3	2.3	3.6	5.8	0.0	9.3
13 to 18	0.0	0.0	0.0	3.6	9.0	14.1	0.0	22.2
8 to 12	4.8	0.0	1.9	6.8	11.2	16.0	2.6	21.1
3 to 7	4.8	2.7	4.5	13.4	15.8	19.0	5.8	24.7
−2 to +2	4.8	0.0	8.3	18.9	21.6	18.4	12.7	12.9
−3 to −7	4.8	8.1	16.6	17.9	15.0	14.1	25.4	5.7
−8 to −12	4.8	18.9	14.0	15.4	13.6	5.9	22.8	2.6
−13 to −18	9.5	43.2	26.1	14.0	7.2	3.4	20.1	0.0
−19 to −24	23.8	10.8	17.2	5.6	2.2	0.6	9.5	0.0
−25 to −30	38.1	10.8	8.9	1.7	0.4	0.5	1.1	0.0
less than −30	4.8	5.4	0.6	0.1	0.0	0.0	0.0	0.0
TOTAL (%)	100.0	100.0	100.0	100.0	100.0	100.0	100.0	100.0
No.	21	37	157	694	501	625	189	194
Mean	−18.5	−16.2	−11.9	−3.7	0.5	4.4	−8.3	8.6
Std. Dev.	12.0	7.9	10.4	7.8	8.0	10.4	10.0	10.1

groups were expected to owe deference to the wife-giving groups. The son-in-law/father-in-law relationship was an important one. Not only was the father-in-law a status superior but, as follows from the logic of the Mediterranean Marriage Pattern, he was also older than the son-in-law. But the age difference between father- and son-in-law is not as great as that between father and son. On average a man would be about twenty-three years older than his son-in-law whereas he would be about thirty-eight years older than his eldest son. If the model of age differences is mapped onto affinal relations, then we would expect that Ego's father-in-law would be about the same age as his mother's brother (WF = MB) (but younger than his father), and Ego's sister's husbands would be about the same age as his father's sister's sons (ZH = FZS). These predictions are also confirmed from the Ragusan data on age differences shown in Table 10.

This 'tilting' of genealogical generations, associated with the age difference between husband and wife, has important structural implications. It implies that throughout Ego's life certain paternal kin will be significantly older than 'corresponding' maternal kin. The father and his brothers, for example, will be about a generation older than the mother's brothers. And, since the differing ages and stages of life have associated with them differing opportunities and obligations, the various categories of Ego's kin are likely to be differentially important to Ego in the different phases of Ego's life cycle. We have seen evidence of this already in marriage arrangements where the mother's brother tends to figure prominently among the tutors when the father is deceased. It seems likely that such differing configurations of kin should also be significant in the development of political careers and the success of individuals in obtaining office.

Genealogical Skewing and Political Support

If the age at which husband and wife marry has the structural effects we have outlined, this should be evident in the universe of political support available for their
sons. For purposes of the present analysis, I have examined the kin connections of
all the men who entered the Great Council between the years 1455 and 1490 at
intervals five years apart: at 1460, 1465, 1470, 1475, 1480, 1485, and 1490. Using
this information it is possible to determine the availability of various kinsmen and
affines, and the number of persons who occupy these genealogical positions. The
five-yearly intervals make it possible to chart the changes in both the nature of
these positions and numbers of persons in those positions during various stages in
a political career.

Let us begin by examining those at the very beginning of their political careers.
In their first five years after entering the Great Council, sixty-eight men had
held political office and 315 had not (see Table 11). Surprisingly, those who were
elected to office had *fewer* kinsmen on the Great Council than those who were not
elected. The term 'kinsmen' is used here to refer to two broad categories: 'agnates'
are those who have the same surname as Ego and who belong to the same *casata*;
'other kin' is a very broad category including other consanguines and affines. The
following genealogical positions make up this second category: MB, MBS, MZH,
FZH, FZS, WF, WB, ZH, ZS, DHF, DH, and DS. Of the recent entrants to
the Great Council, those elected to office had an average of 17.0 agnates and 8.4

TABLE 11. *Success in office-holding in relation to kinship support*

	Types of kin			
	Agnates	Other kin	Total	No.
Periods of service	Mean (Std.Dev.)	Mean (Std.Dev.)	Mean (Std.Dev.)	
Less than 5.0 years				
Non-office-holders	19.0 (11.1)	8.0 (5.0)	26.9 (12.0)	315
Office-holders	17.0 (9.9)	8.4 (5.2)	25.4 (10.9)	68
Between 5.0 and 9.9 years				
Non-office-holders	20.7 (10.7)	8.0 (5.0)	28.7 (11.8)	155
Office-holders	17.3 (10.5)	8.9 (5.2)	26.2 (11.8)	131
Between 10.0 and 14.9 years				
Non-office-holders	19.9 (11.0)	7.9 (5.1)	27.8 (12.0)	72
Office-holders				
Office rank 0.0–4.9	18.6 (11.8)	8.2 (4.3)	26.8 (12.7)	71
Office rank 5.0+	19.1 (11.4)	9.3 (5.8)	28.4 (12.4)	70
Between 15.0 and 19.9 years				
Non-office-holders	21.4 (11.9)	9.0 (4.2)	30.4 (11.0)	26
Office-holders				
Office rank 0.0–4.9	20.2 (12.5)	8.3 (4.3)	28.5 (12.7)	32
Office rank 5.0–9.9	18.8 (11.1)	8.7 (5.6)	27.5 (13.2)	69
Office rank 10.0+	21.0 (12.4)	11.1 (4.6)	32.1 (12.7)	23

other kin on the council. Non-office-holders had an average of 19.0 agnates and 8.0 other kin. While the differences are small, they suggest that the number of 'other kin' is more important for achieving an early office than is the number of agnates.

This impression is strengthened by the analysis of data from those who had been in the Great Council more than five years but less than ten years. There were 131 men who had held at least one office in this period and 155 men who had not. Once again, the office-holders had, on average, fewer total kin on the council and those who held office had relatively fewer agnates and relatively more other kin. Office-holders had an average of 17.3 agnates and 9.9 other kin while those who held no office had 20.7 agnates and 8.0 other kin. When men have been in the Great Council for more than ten years (but less than fifteen), a more complex analysis is possible. With this length of service on the council, many men will have held several offices and it is possible to relate kinship support to the importance of the office achieved. All offices have been ranked on a numerical scale which can be taken as a measure of their importance. This scale is based on the point (in terms of years of service in the Great Council) when an office will be held for the first time (see Table 2). Of the men who had been in the council for more than ten years, seventy-two had held no office. A further seventy-one had achieved an office that ranked less than 5.0 on the office-ranking scale, and seventy had held an office that ranked higher than 5.0. Those who held no office had an average of 19.9 agnates and 7.9 other kin on the council. Those who had held one of the lower-ranking offices had an average of 18.6 agnates and 8.2 other kin. Finally, those who held an office ranking higher than 5.0 had 19.1 agnates and 9.3 other kin. A very similar picture emerges for those who have been in the Great Council for more than fifteen years. Those holding an office ranking between 0.0 and 4.9 had an average of 20.2 agnates and 8.3 other kin. Of those holding middling offices between 5.0 and 9.9, the average number of agnates and other kin was 18.8 and 8.7, respectively. Those who achieved an office higher than 10.0 had 21.0 agnates and 11.1 other kin.

There is a clear and striking relationship between success in office-holding and the number of kinsmen on the Great Council. But that relationship is a negative one. Since elections were conducted among the entire membership, we might have expected that those who enjoyed electoral success would have been drawing upon the support of a larger grouping of kinsmen. We might have expected, in other words, that the more kinsmen a person has, the more votes they could expect to receive. But this is not the case. Furthermore, in contrasting agnatic with other kinds of ties, we find a similar pattern. That is, electoral success is inversely related to the number of agnates and positively associated with the number of other kin. Indeed, it is possible to show that in every stage of the political career those who achieve the higher offices have the fewest agnates. Those who gain slightly lower offices have more agnates and those who are elected to no office at all have the most. These results are certainly counter-intuitive.

Within the group of male siblings, we find that the larger the size of the group, the more likely it is that at least one of them will marry. However, there is no simple relationship between the number of brothers in the sibling group, the proportion marrying, or when the marriages occur. On a pure probabilistic basis, one might assume that the more brothers that there are, the greater the likelihood that at least one of them will marry. But this is not the case. For example, it is more likely that at least one brother will marry if there are only two brothers in the group than if there are three. Similarly, one might think that in cases where there is only a single male heir, he would be highly likely to marry in order to carry on the paternal line. But this, too, is not the case. Only sons are less likely to wed than men with brothers. Several interpretations are possible.

On the one hand, it is likely that the fathers of only sons will have died before the son reaches the Great Council. The fathers of two or more sons, on the other hand, tend to die sometime after the oldest son enters the Great Council. Only sons, therefore, may tend to remain unmarried because they have been left with all of the multiple responsibilities of arranging their sisters' weddings, managing the family estate, and participating in trade as well as attending to the affairs of government. The effects of all of these responsibilities might inhibit their political careers. It is the case that when only sons do hold offices, they hold them somewhat later in their careers than oldest sons. However, they still begin their careers somewhat earlier than second or third sons (see Table 12).

Consistent with the above, it may also be the case that obligations to one's sisters and their honourable marriage have higher priority than the obligation to continue the paternal line. We have already seen that Ragusan sibling groups, in contrast to Florentine ones, draw personal names from both the paternal and maternal sides. This may indicate the heightened significance of the sibling group in Ragusa.

What conclusions can be drawn from this? I have suggested that the 'skewing' of genealogical generations has significant structural implications. In the specific context of the Ragusan *casata*, it means that there may be difficulties in co-ordinating the political activities of agnates because successive generations are

TABLE 12. *Sibling position and office-holding*

	Years after entry[a]		
	1st office	2nd office	3rd office
Only sons	6.2 (49)	9.1 (35)	12.6 (29)
Oldest sons	5.6 (109)	8.8 (89)	10.9 (78)
Second sons	6.7 (104)	10.1 (83)	12.4 (71)
Third sons	8.8 (55)	12.7 (46)	15.4 (40)

[a] Numbers in parentheses refer to the number of instances.

unlikely to be co-members of the Great Council. Fathers and paternal uncles are unlikely to be active in the Great Council at the same time as their sons and paternal nephews. I suggested that this might account for the reason that large houses are unable to use their numerical advantage to elect more than their share of members to prestigious offices. Indeed, it has been shown that success in achieving political office is inversely related to the number of agnates that one has on the council.[15]

In addition to the significant age gap between generations of paternal kinsmen, genealogical skewing also has other implications. It implies, for example, that throughout Ego's life certain categories of paternal kin will be significantly older than 'corresponding' categories of maternal kin. Since the differing ages and stages of life have associated with them differing opportunities and obligations, the various categories of Ego's kin are likely to be differentially important to Ego in the different period of the lifecycle. In other words, differing categories of kin and affines are likely to 'phase' in their significance.

The Rise of Junius de Sorgo

These points can be illustrated by referring to one *casata*, the Sorgo, and the development of the political career of one of its members, Junius Pasqual de Sorgo (ID 2007). Junius made one of the most spectacular rises up the ladder of offices into the inner circle of government. He entered the Great Council in 1457 and its inner circle seventeen years later in 1473. To understand his rise to power, we must set his career in the context of his *casata* and his maternal kin and affines.

When Junius entered the Great Council in 1457, only one Sorgo was in the inner circle (see Fig. 13). This was Dragoe Marinus de Sorgo (ID 1949), who had arrived in the inner circle only four years earlier in 1453. Figure 11 also illustrates the problem of political co-ordination. In only one portion of the Sorgo, the descendants of Andruscus, are there two generations represented. This shows the importance of the age difference between successive generations of fathers and sons. While Dragoe Marinus might be said to represent Sorgo interests in the inner circle, his tenure was to be cut short for he died in 1460. A year after Dragoe's death, Çove Francho de Sorgo (ID 2049) reached the inner circle and he

---

[15] In their interpretation of the different élite networks in early fifteenth-century Florence, Padgett and Ansell are forced to treat 'people with a common surname' ('clans') as units of analysis in their understanding of the Medici and opposition parties (1993: 1267), As our analysis has indicated, there are significant reasons for rejecting this assumption—reasons which might also apply to the Florentine material due to the implications of genealogical skewing. However, as we have suggested, the more 'open' nature of the Florentine political area and the importance of mustering local support for inclusion in the electoral purses may have given heightened significance to neighbourhood agnatic ties. Florence, Venice, and Ragusa present an interesting set of structural variations in kinship, marriage, and politics which merit future study.

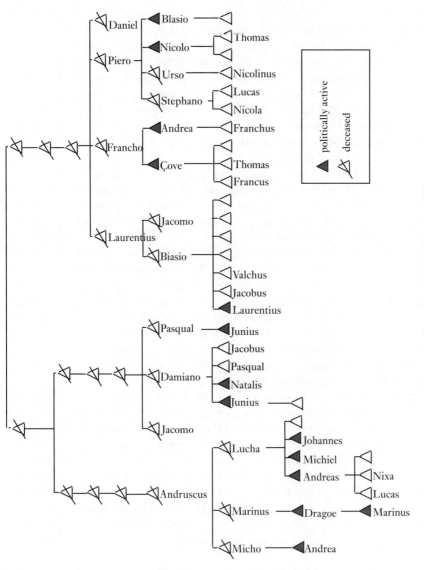

FIG. 11. Genealogy of the Sorgo in 1457

continued to hold inner circle posts until his own death in 1475. Dragoe came from one of the two major sections of the Sorgo, Çove from the other. Thus, in the seventeen-year interval between Junius's entry to the Great Council in 1457 and his ascension to the inner circle in 1473, only one Sorgo was included in the inner circle. This poor representation at the heart of government does not seem to be a reflection of numerical weakness on the part of the Sorgo in the Great Council itself. During the interval from 1455 until 1470, about fourteen Sorgo men sat on the Great Council in any given year.[16] Out of this yearly total about three or four held office. Thus, the voting strength of the Sorgo was not translated into offices or inner circle representation.

The picture of Sorgo fortunes changed dramatically in the following two decades. In 1471 two new Sorgo youths joined the Great Council. A further two entered in 1472. Another four came in 1473, the same year as Junius Pasqual Sorgo entered the inner circle (see Fig. 12). Thus, in five years between 1468 and 1473, Sorgo representation on the Great Council increased dramatically. It may be of significance that the Sorgo in 1473 also contained three two-generation sections: the descendants of Lucha Andruscus, and the descendants of Francho and Piero Vlacussa. Their influence continued to grow slowly throughout the rest of the period and by 1490 there were twenty-six Sorgo on the Great Council. By that time about ten Sorgo were holding office every year and five of these were in the inner circle (see Fig. 13). It would appear that they had achieved a critical mass and were able to translate this into offices. While there is some truth in this simple formula, it belies a much more complex reality. To illustrate this, let us return to the case of Junius Pasqual's career.

Junius's rise was very rapid considering that he did not hold his first office until 1469, twelve years after he entered the council. He had been nominated for *Judicieri del comone* in 1465 but was not elected. Those who were elected in that ballot were much more senior.[17] His own entry into the Great Council, it should be noted, came shortly after the deaths of his father and two uncles: Pasqual (ID 2006), Jacomo (ID 1990), and Damiano (ID 1992) (see Fig. 11). All three of these men had held inner circle posts before their deaths. Within his own generation of the major section of the *casata*, he was in the most junior section and was its only rep-resentative. There were nine politically active men in this section. Perhaps a more telling comparison is with the oldest brothers in the other sibling sets in this part of the *casata*.

Andrea Micho (ID 1940), the first of these oldest brothers, was already a spent force when Junius began his political career. Andrea had held a series of minor

---

[16] This is the average. The low period was from 1466 until 1468 when only twelve Sorgo were on the council (see Fig. 15).

[17] *Act. Maior.* 12: fo. 200v. The most senior of those elected, Paulus Nicola de Saraca (ID 1878), entered the Great Council about 1432. The most junior, Savolin Mathio de Getaldo (ID 748), entered about 1449, eight years before Junius.

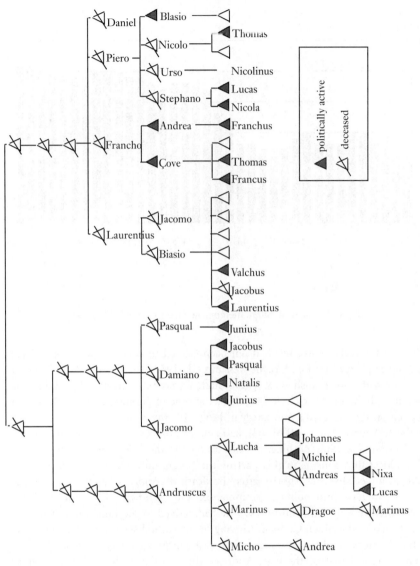

Fig. 12. Genealogy of the Sorgo in 1473

Number of
members

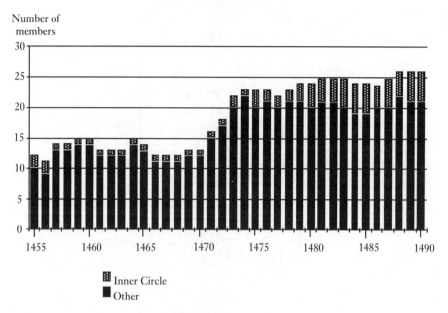

FIG. 13. Number of Sorgo men on the Great Council, 1455–1490

offices in the early 1440s, but had not been elected to anything since 1446.[18] He died in the plague of 1465. Dragoe Marinus (ID 1949), the second of these oldest brothers, had a distinguished career although he was never elected Rector. He was continuously in an inner circle post from the time of Junius's entry to the Great Council until he entered a monastery in 1460. His cousin, the third of these oldest brothers, Andreas Lucha (ID 1962), had held two offices early in the 1460s after a long period of holding nothing, but he also died in the 1465 plague. Thus, of the three oldest first cousins in this part of the Sorgo, only Dragoe Marinus was a political force. However, shortly after the death of Andreas Lucha, his younger brother emerged into political prominence. This brother, Michael Lucha (ID 1969), then rose quickly and by 1479 he had arrived in the inner circle when he was elected to the Small Council. Moving to the second section in this same part of the Sorgo, we find that the story of the last cousin, Junius Damiano (ID 1996), seems to repeat that of the first, Andreas Micho. Like Andreas, Junius's career begins with the holding of three minor offices.[19] But from 1466 until his death in 1491, he is never elected to another office. His younger brother Natalis (ID 2001), although not beginning his political career until he had been in the Great Council for eleven years, did hold a series of middling offices in the decade of the 1470s.

[18] *Officiali lavorieri de pagamento in Ragusi* in 1442 and 1446, *Raxone officiali* in 1443, and *Lane officiali del arte della lana* in 1444 (*Specchio*: s.v.).
[19] *Biscoti officiali* in 1460, *Officiali lavorieri de scritta in Ragusi* in 1462, and *Officiali lavorieri de pagamente in Stagno* in 1466 (*Specchio*: s.v.).

Therefore, of the five oldest brothers in this major segment of the Sorgo, two men appear to have had little ambition or ability. They can scarcely be said to have office-holding careers. The career of the third seems to have been developing very slowly when his sudden death caused the mantle to be passed to a more vigorous and able younger brother. The fourth, Dragoe, had a distinguished career until 1460. This leaves us back at our starting point, Junius Pasqual. When his office-holding career began in 1469, two senior cousins had already died. Two more had proved inept or unwilling. Only he and Michael Lucha survived. Both moved up quickly. At this point it would be tempting to conclude that Michael and Junius were successfully elected to represent the interests of this section of the Sorgo at the centre of government.

Turning to the other part of the Sorgo, it does appear as if each section attempts to achieve representation among the inner circle. Up until his death in 1456, Biasio Laurentius (ID 2027) held inner circle posts. For the next five years until 1461, there was no one from this section elected to any of the most senior offices. In that year Çove Francho (ID 2049) reached this goal. Although at the time of Biasio's death Çove had been on the council for twenty-four years, he had not sufficiently advanced up the ladder of office to be considered a suitable contender.

Thus, from 1457 to 1473 there was only one Sorgo among the total of forty to fifty men who annually held inner circle posts. In this period Sorgo representation constitutes about 6 per cent of the Great Council. They were seriously under-represented in the higher ranks of state offices. By the end of the period the five Sorgo holding inner circle posts constituted about one-tenth of that select category. Proportionally they were then over-represented (see Fig. 15).

Two points emerge from this. First, election to office does not follow from *casata* support, for reasons that we have already discussed concerning the age differences between the generations. Sons tend not to hold high office while their fathers are still alive and younger brothers tend not to advance over senior. But the system of balloting also tends to work against the domination by particular *casate*. Candidates for offices are often selected by the more senior bodies who then present nominees to the Great Council. No single *casata* can dominate nomination proceedings or force their own choices. A range of support is generally necessary for both nomination and then election. Because of the structure of *casata* representation on the Great Council and other electoral bodies, this is beyond the power of any single *casata* no matter how concerted the effort.

This does not mean that *casata* support is unimportant in gaining office. Consider in this respect the endogamous marriages within the Sorgo. In 1428 Junius's FZ, Marussa Juncho (ID 2005), married Piero Vlacussa de Sorgo. This was the second marriage for both partners. While there were apparently no children from this second union, Piero had four sons by his first marriage: Stephano (ID 2068), Urso (ID 2078), Nicola (ID 2084), and Blasio (ID 2092). Marussa became stepmother to these men. There was a further attempt to strengthen the link between these Sorgo sections when Junius's sister, Lignussa (ID 2009), was briefly betrothed to the widower Urso Piero de Sorgo (ID 2078) in 1448. But Urso died and Lignussa was then betrothed to Paulus Nicola de Lucharis (ID 1357) in the following year. Shortly thereafter in 1450 another sister, Katharina (ID 2012), married Laurentius Biasio de Sorgo (ID 2028). These arrangements would have been made by their father, Pasqual Juncho de Sorgo (ID 2006), who lived until Junius's own betrothal year, 1454. Junius thus became brother-in-law of Laurentius as well as his agnate. In this respect he might expect to have close links with Laurentius and his six brothers. And later, when he entered the Great Council, Junius might also support his sister's son, Pasqualis.[20] Through these marriages Junius was linked to two of the three branches in the other major section of the Sorgo. But these were not the only internal links within the Sorgo. Within Junius's own major section another Sorgo–Sorgo marriage took place in 1457. This marriage united Lignussa (ID 1993), the sister of Junius (ID 1996) and Natalis Damiano (ID 2001), with Johannes Lucha de Sorgo (ID 1971). It created an affinal link between the two branches of Junius's own section of the Sorgo. Given the degrees of kinship within which marriage was allowed by the Church, such marriages were at once tokens of increasing (agnatic) distance as well the desire to diminish that distance by creating a new closer link. That closer link, however, could never be an agnatic one and those it joined in new ties would only be a relatively small portion of the major section. The Sorgo were not the only *casata* with endogamous marriages, although they had the most. The Bona, Goçe, Gondola, Lucari, and Poça also had them.

It is not surprising that in a relatively small and highly endogamous population like patrician Ragusa maternal and affinal ties might sometimes carry more political value than distant agnatic ones. The reason is that the small size of the endogamous community is likely to produce dense knots of intermarriages. The density of interaction and mutual involvement is likely to produce a community of interest among those intermarrying that may well outweigh the ties that such persons may have with distant, but otherwise unrelated, agnates. The Sorgo–Sorgo marriages noted here may be an attempt to convert distant agnatic ties into close affinal (and maternal) ones.

These marriages might reaffirm ties between various branches of the Sorgo and constitute a potential basis of support for Junius's political ambitions, but they were not the only source of support. Of his close maternal kin, his MZH Symoneto Piero de Bona (ID 144) and his MZS Antonius Symoneto de Bona (ID 148) were politically active, from 1440 to 1470 and from 1470 to 1490, respectively.[21] Another MZH, Nicolino de Batalo (ID 58), was politically prominent and held inner circle posts from the time of Junius's entry in 1457 until his death in 1475. Junius's MBS, Benedictus Pietro de Gondola (ID 1113), was also active throughout Junius's

---

[20] Pasqualis entered the Great Council in 1482. Two other brothers, Valentinus and Franciscus, entered in 1493 after Junius's death. Junius died in 1491.

[21] As we will see below, Antonius married Nicoleta Andreas Lucha de Sorgo.

career. Two of these cousins, Benedictus de Gondola and Antonius de Bona, were brothers-in-law to one another. But of these four men, only Nicolinus de Batalo had political prominence during Junius's career. Therefore, while close maternal kin may have given support and encouragement, they were not especially powerful or well-placed.

Junius's own wife Gaiussa was a Zamagna. His own marriage, therefore, formed part of the links between the Sorgo, Grade, and Zamagna referred to above. His father-in-law, Michiel Martolus de Zamagna (ID 2182), was in the inner circle before Junius's entry into the Great Council in 1457 and he remained there until his death in 1466. Michiel had two sons and two grandsons who, while not politically prominent themselves, might have given some support to Junius's ambitions with their votes.[22]

Perhaps the most important element behind Junius's rapid rise through the ladder of offices is to be found within Junius's own sibling group. Junius was the only male in a group of seven. All six of his sisters married between 1448 and 1455.[23] Lignussa, the first to marry, married Paulus Nicola de Lucharis (ID 1357) in 1448. Since Paulus was the second son, it was his elder brother, Stephanus (ID 1355), who was very active in politics and served in the inner circle from 1466 until his death in 1479. Paulus himself reached the inner circle shortly afterwards, but he had only served for two years when he also died.

Anucla was the second of Junius's sisters to marry. She was also betrothed in 1448. Her husband, Marco Piero de Bona (ID 160), was the fourth in a large group of brothers. His three elder brothers were successful and very powerful. Symoneto (ID 144), Jacomo (ID 151), and Elia (ID 152) held inner circle posts in 1455–70, 1467–84, and 1463–89, respectively. Marco himself had a very lacklustre officeholding career.

Margussa, the third sister of Junius de Sorgo, married Lampre Illia de Zrieva (ID 651) in 1449. He and his six brothers were all politically active. Andreas Illia (ID 633) held inner circle posts between 1464 and 1466 but died in 1468. Lampre served between 1478 and 1487. Between them the six brothers had eleven sons who sat on the Great Council.

As we have already noted, Katharina, the fourth sister, wed into another branch of the Sorgo in 1450. Francischa, the fifth, married Antonius Nicola de Caboga (ID 512) in 1451. He was one of three politically active brothers. The eldest brother, Blasius Nicola (ID 507), reached the inner circle the same year as Junius. The last sister, Benedicta, became betrothed to Nicolaus Marin de Lucharis (ID

---

[22] Vita Michiel de Zamagna (ID 2186) was active from 1440 to 1482. His sons Michael (ID 2187) and Nicola (ID 2182) entered the Great Council in 1476 and 1480, respectively. Another brother, Paulus (ID 2193), served from 1464 to 1484. None of these men is known to have held any offices.

[23] His father Pasqual died in 1454, just before Benedicta, the youngest sister, was betrothed. She was betrothed with the consent of her mother. Her tutors were her mother, Jelussa; Marcus Piero de Bona, her ZH and MZHB; and Lampriza Elie de Zrieva, her ZH (*Pacta* 2: fos. 35v–36).

1323) in 1455. He did not reach the inner circle until after Junius. Amongst these six families of Sorgo in-laws there were nineteen men who were politically active during Junius's rise to the inner circle, six of whom were in the inner circle themselves.

Junius's affinal connections through his sisters' marriages represent considerable political capital. If we exclude those Sorgo who were also Junius's affines from the count of affines, we still find that the potential support from his sisters' husbands' families equals that which he might have found amongst all of his Sorgo agnates. Moreover, given their distribution amongst the various age cohorts within the Great Council, his affines were in a better position to see that his name was included amongst the nominees for suitable posts. Junius, in turn, was then in a powerful position to offer patronage to his sisters' sons. It is noteworthy that four of his sisters' sons bore Junius's father's name, Pasqual. These were Pasqua Lampre de Zrieva (ID 656), Pasqualis Laurentius de Sorgo (ID 2029), Pasqualis Nicola de Lucari (ID 1325), and Pasqua Antonius de Caboga (ID 514).[24] The potential fount of support from agnates, mother's kin, wife's kin, and sisters' husbands was enormous.

This is not to suggest that other kinds of ties were unimportant. There is considerable evidence from other Mediterranean cities of the period, for example, that ties based upon neighbourhood, age comradeship, or patronage may also have been very important in the formation of political alliances (cf. Klapisch-Zuber 1985: 68–93). It seems likely such ties might also have been important in Ragusan politics.[25] Unfortunately, in the Ragusan case we do not possess sufficient evidence to assess the significance of such ties nor can we compare them with ties of kinship and affinity. This account is therefore unavoidably one-sided.

In the Ragusan case as well as elsewhere in the Mediterranean world of this period, kinship ties are no guarantee of political support. There are many examples of close kin being on different sides of the political fence (cf. Clarke 1991; F. Kent 1977: 214–15). Further, most men were likely to find themselves caught in a web of conflicting loyalties when it came time to choose between the several nominees for an office. Because of the small size of the Ragusan patriciate and its endogamous nature, ties of kinship and affinity within Ragusa formed a very tangled knot.

In considering the rise of Junius into the inner circle, we have noted that Sorgo representation within the Great Council increased between the time of Junius's

---

[24] There is no evidence of the latter Pasqua entering the Great Council.

[25] Ruggiero suggests that a homosexual subculture may have existed in Venice between powerful older men and younger, unmarried men (1985: 159). Krekić (1987b) doubts the presence of homosexual relations in Ragusa. He notes that draconian penalties were adopted by the Senate in 1474 (decapitation, followed by burning of the body) (citing *Lib. Croc.*: fo. 50–50v). This legislation is not easily explained. There are no known prosecutions for sodomy in Ragusa in this period. It may have merely imitated Venetian practice, or perhaps reflected worries about contacts with Ottoman Turks. Krekić thinks it is related to concerns about growing wealth, luxury, and indolence particularly among younger patricians.

entry in 1457 and his election to the *Consoli de le cause civil* in 1473. This increase, however, was not unique to the Sorgo. There was a general increase in the size of the patriciate throughout the period. It is this increase, and its significance for politics among the patriciate, that we consider next.

8

Changes in the Great Council and Political Competition

Growth of the Great Council

Following the plagues of the fourteenth century which had wrought such devastation and misfortune to the city, the fifteenth century brought affluence and population growth. Even though there were serious reoccurrences of plague in 1437, 1465–6, and again in 1482, the Ragusan patriciate grew in size through the fifteenth century. A November entry in the 1432 *Liber Viridis* notes with satisfaction that 'Our city . . . has grown and multiplied, as much in temporal goods and possession, as it has in people and inhabitants' (Krekić 1987a: 197).[1] As Krekić has shown, there are a number of contemporary documents which also comment on this increase in size. Much later in the century, as a result of the continuing growth, the Great Council decided in 1477 that it was prudent to raise the number of Senators required for a quorum from thirty-one to thirty-five. As the legislation noted, 'because by the grace of God the number of noblemen has grown and multiplied' (ibid., quoting *Act. Maior.* 11: fo. 30v).

This 'explosive growth' (Krekić 1987b: 344) is reflected in the number of persons sitting in the Great Council over the period from 1440 to 1490. In 1455, for example, there were about 310 members. By 1490 this number had grown to almost 400. In between these two dates a total of 755 persons are known to have sat on the council. The reasons for the growth are still obscure. Some scholars believe that it might be related to the Ottoman conquest of the Balkans. As the Turkish assault gathered pace, so the argument goes, patrician merchants returned home to Ragusa from trading colonies in the Balkan interior out of fear for their lives and livelihoods. If this did occur, it could have increased Great Council representation. Furthermore, if these returnees married earlier, or if more of them married, this would also have increased the size of the patriciate. Whatever the outcome to these conjectures, the demographic trends over the entire century appear too long-term to reflect short-term movements created by the Ottoman danger. The period of growth in the patriciate began very early in the century and continued almost unabated throughout. The several reoccurrences of the plague

---

[1] The original reads, '*Considerando che la citade notra piu per la gratia del omnipotente dio cha per industri ni merito nostro e acressuta e multiplica, tanto in temporali beni et avere quanto in persone et habitanti . . .*' (*Lib. Vir.*: fo. 137v).

delayed it only slightly. The Ottoman threat was at its height in the 1440s and 1450s, yet the Great Council does not increase markedly in this period, as one would expect if mature patricians were fleeing home. Although the threat could account for an increasing number of patricians residing in Ragusa, it does not explain the prior demographic events which led to their birth, survival, and subsequent dispersal into the Balkan hinterland. Therefore, while the Ottoman invasion of the Balkans may have contributed to the growth of the patriciate, it was not its cause.

With respect to marriage, there is evidence that the age at marriage for men increased from 1450 to 1490. The evidence also suggests that there were two baby booms, one in the late 1420s and a second in the early 1450s. The second of these might have been associated with the return of refugees. There were an unusually large number of marriages in the 1440s and in the first years of the following decade. However, until the demographic regime of the patriciate is more fully analysed, the reasons for this growth will remain unclear. But the growth in the size of the Great Council and the changes in the age at marriage raise a fundamental issue. That issue concerns the passage of time. Heretofore in this analysis of age, marriage, and politics, we have assumed a uniform 'ethnographic present' stretching from 1440 to 1490. We must now consider this assumption and the implications of rejecting it.

The 'Shape' of the Great Council Over Time

While the Great Council grew between 1455 and 1490, that growth was not uniform. Neither was it accomplished through a gradual increase of the youngest segment of the council. It depended both upon the addition of new members and the loss of older ones. For example, in the ten years from 1455 to 1464 the number of new entrants into the council scarcely offset the yearly toll of deaths. As a result the council's membership remained constant. It was only after 1465 that numbers began to increase dramatically. In 1470, for example, nine new members entered. In that same year four members died, a net increase of five members. In 1471 there were fifteen new entrants which more than compensated for the single death which occurred. Again in 1472 there were twenty-three new entrants and two deaths. This pattern continued. Indeed, from 1470 until the end of the period there were only two years in which the number of new entrants did not exceed the number of deaths. One of these was the terrible plague year of 1482 when forty-two died.

These two processes, the entry of new members and the death (or political incapacity) of old ones, were largely independent of one another although not completely so. Since the age at entry into the Great Council varied independently from the age at death, the council's composition changed from year to year. Reflecting these various additions and subtractions to the total membership, we might say that the 'shape' of the council changed significantly throughout the period. In order to examine these changes and their effects in greater detail, I have sampled the Great Council at intervals five years apart from 1455 until the end of the study period in 1490. These have resulted in eight quinquennial 'censuses' (Wrigley 1981: 214). It seemed that intervals five years apart would be close enough to reveal subtle changes in composition, yet not be too numerous to overwhelm the task of analysis especially since each census year would be the subject of further exploration.

For each of these census years, I have examined the internal composition of the council by looking at the entire council in, as it were, cross-section. These cross-sections were derived by considering members' length of service. Members who entered the council within the same five-year period were deemed to constitute a single cohort. Thus, the Great Council in 1455 consisted of several cohorts: those who had less than five years of membership, those who had less than ten years but more than five years, and so on. A cohort, therefore, may be understood as a group of men who have had about the same amount of experience in the Great Council.[2] In any of the various census years, the council would consist of a number of cohorts. The number of cohorts might vary from one census year to the next, and the number of men within a cohort would almost certainly vary. Thus, the composition of the Great Council can be studied along two dimensions: through time from 1455 to 1490 at five-yearly intervals, and cross-sectionally by comparing cohort with cohort. In the analysis which follows, census years are compared with one another as are the cohorts within and between census years.

An example will make the procedure clear. We begin with the quinquennial 'census' of 1455. In this year the Great Council was very heavy with senior men. Over half of the members had been in the council for over twenty years (see Fig. 14). In this year there is also a noticeable dip in the middle of the distribution. This is the cohort of men which had been in council between fifteen and nineteen years. Members of this cohort would have been born around 1437: they were the babies and toddlers who managed to survive the plague of that year. As a result this cohort was unusually small with only twenty members. In 1455 the council was also bottom heavy with large numbers of relatively new entrants. Therefore, we may say that the middle of the distribution of the council was rather squashed in 1455. It does not remain so.

Five years later in 1460 the council had become more top heavy. The most senior cohort of the council, the one with more than thirty years of service, had grown from seventy-two to ninety-six men. This would make the council appear more gerontocratic. Yet the next two cohorts had actually decreased in numbers, from forty-seven to thirty-nine men in the case of those who had served between twenty-five and twenty-nine years, and from forty-three to seventeen for those with

---

[2] Members of a cohort need not be of similar age, although most will be. On cohort analysis, Mason *et al.* (1973) has been particularly useful. See also Rodgers (1982).

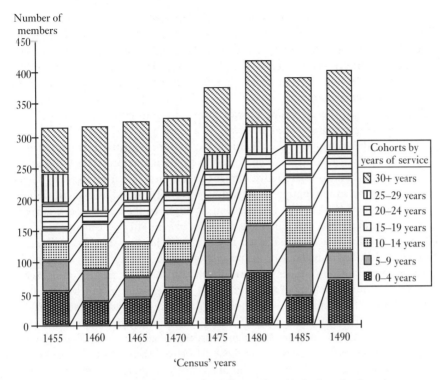

Number of
members

FIG. 14. The Great Council 1455–1490, membership by length of service

between twenty and twenty-four years of service. The last-mentioned cohort is the same small cohort noted in the 1455 council, but it has now shifted upward in the distribution as its members have aged. Therefore in the interval between 1455 and 1460, the overall shape of the council has altered.

In 1465 the shape of the council has continued to change. With the passage of another five years, the 'dip' noted earlier is now found among those with between twenty-five and twenty-nine years of service whereas the most senior sections have continued to grow. The senior cohorts with over thirty years of service now contain 110 men. The council in this period is at its most gerontocratic both in terms of absolute size and in terms of the proportion of the total membership. Five years later in 1470, and indeed every five years thereafter, the Great Council continues to present a shifting appearance. Figure 14 summarizes all of this data showing changes in the size both of the total council at the various census years and of the several cohorts within each census year.

Therefore, examined sequentially from 1455 to 1490, we can see that the proportion of junior members increases, as we would expect from the overall growth of the council, but this increase is not very uniform and the distribution of Great

Council members by years of service reveals some striking peculiarities. First, the proportion of junior members increased throughout the period, peaking in the early 1480s. By 1480, for example, over half the members had been in the council for less than fifteen years whereas in 1455 only a quarter of the membership had held seats for less than fifteen years. Therefore, we might say that the council was at its most 'senior' around the year 1455 and at its most 'junior' around 1480. Clearly, however, the increasing growth in membership between 1455 and 1490 cannot be simply characterized as leading to a more 'youthful' council.

How are these changes to be regarded? Or, to put the matter in a more ortho-dox anthropological context, when does the 'ethnographic present' of this study begin and end? However attractive it might have appeared during the early stages of analysis, the simple option of regarding the entire period as a single 'ethno-graphic present' must be open to question. It might be the case that one govern-mental year in Ragusa was much like the next. In year after year members of the Rector's Small Council were elected in December/January. The Rector himself was elected at the last meeting of the preceding month. There was an almost clock-like regularity in the routines of government. But however similar one govern-mental year might appear to the next, small changes were in process. We have already noted, for example, how elections for the *Conte de Stagno* drifted from May in 1480 to November in 1485. By 1488 this drifting had brought the month of elec-tion back to May once again. Other processes were also at work. The changing shape of the Great Council is one of them. Moreover, these processes carried sig-nificant structural implications. We do not know how aware the patricians might have been of these processes and their implications. In many respects the Great Council of 1440 was very similar to the Great Council of 1490. It is likely that patricians thought that they were virtually identical. There are, and were, good reasons for thinking so. But if we must query the notion of a single 'ethnographic present' extending over half a century, we can not simply substitute a series of intervals, each five years in length, as a succession of 'ethnographic presents'. These intervals of five years have been devised to facilitate analysis and to provide a framework for systematic comparison. They permit the insertion of temporality into our account, but they do not define its parameters.

The changing shape of the Great Council has significant structural implications. Note has already been made of the 'dip' in the middle of the 1455 Great Council. Following through the changes in the council's composition, there is also a 'crest' of young entrants in the council of 1480, that is the cohort of men who have served four years or less. As the use of terms like 'dips', 'troughs', and 'crests' implies, there appear to be regular changes which move wave-like through the com-position of the Great Council. These have a periodicity of approximately a quarter-century. This is very similar to a phenomenon first noted in nineteenth-century Norwegian marriage data by Eilert Sundt (1980) and which now bears his name, Sundt's Law.

In the Norwegian case, the crests were understood as the result of an unusually large number of births within a short period of time. Such baby booms occurred in the aftermath of epidemics which decimated large sections of the population. During the course of such epidemics, as Sundt noted, weddings tend to be postponed only to occur in great profusion when the epidemic is past. In the aftermath of the disaster the total number of weddings not only includes young couples getting married for the first time, but it is augmented by those who have postponed wedding plans as well as widows and widowers finding new unions. An unusual number of births then follows this unusual number of weddings. A generation later the offspring from these unions themselves marry. A second flurry of marriages and a second baby boom then follows, but this time the numbers of marriages and births are not quite as large as before. After another generation passes there will be yet another round. But once again the effects will be diminished. Sundt argued that the effects of unusual demographic events can thus progress through a population over time in wave-like fashion. However, more recent demographic research has shown that quasi-cycles of about thirty years are characteristic of pre-industrial populations and that such cycles do not depend, as Sundt suggested, on catastrophic shock for their occurrence (Lee 1978: 195).[3] I suggest that the 'crests' and 'dips' represent quasi-cycles moving through the Great Council from 1455 to 1490.

Ragusan quasi-cycles are also the results of an unusual number of weddings and subsequent births. This can be shown by analysing kinship ties between members of leading and following crests (or dips). There is a characteristic kinship tie between men of the senior cohort and its associated cohort of the quasi-cycle, but it is not one of fathers and sons (or father's brothers and brother's sons). Consider, for example, the 'crest' noticed in the cohort with less than four years of service in the 1455 Great Council. Of the eighty-six men in the 1480 junior cohort, only three had fathers in the corresponding 1455 cohort (there were two fathers, one of whom had two sons). This certainly does not show strong father–son connections between these two cohorts. Given what we have shown about the age gap between fathers and sons due to the late age at marriage, this would be expected. The sons of the 1455 cohort did not begin to enter the Great Council until sometime after 1480. Furthermore, many men of the youthful 'crest' of the 1480 council (that is, those with four years or less of service) had no living fathers when they first began to enter the Great Council in 1476. Therefore the successive crests and dips moving wave-like at approximately quarter-century intervals through the Great Council are not associated with one another as containing successive generations of 'fathers' and 'sons'.

However, as Sundt's interpretation of the Norwegian data might suggest, successive peaks and dips could be associated as 'mother' and 'son', or, considering the all-male nature of the Great Council, as between 'mother's brother' and 'sister's son'. Using the youngest cohort of the 1455 council as an illustration, we find that

---

[3] I am grateful to Roger Schofield for drawing Lee's work to my attention.

a man is most likely to have a MB in the cohort with between twenty-five and twenty-nine years of service and a ZH in the cohort with twenty to twenty-four years' service.[4] Therefore, the most likely close 'genealogical' tie between men of successive peaks (or dips) is that between MB/ZS and ZH/WB. This interpretation is consistent with the two baby booms of 1420 and 1450 noted earlier. The changing shape of the council, with its waves of successive 'crests' and 'dips', has significant implications for Ragusan politics.

Competition for Office

While the increase in numbers was seen as a boon for the city, it also led to increasing competition for office amongst the patriciate. More men were available to compete for about the same number of offices. Throughout the period a number of measures were enacted which reflect this increasing pressure for office. Some new offices were created, some existing ones were expanded, and there were also changes in the regulations concerning office-holding which made it possible for more men to hold office. All these measures point to a concern about the effects which competition for office was having as well as deliberations about measures which might alleviate it. In October 1469 the Great Council decided that members of the Senate could not concurrently hold another office.[5] Prior to this date Senators might also hold certain other offices. Therefore, this measure increased the number of offices available in a single year, albeit by a relatively small amount. Another way of reducing competition was by adding new offices. The creation of the *Proveditori de la terra* in November 1477 might have been partially prompted by such a consideration. This new post was to be a very senior one. The five incumbents were to be at least 50 years of age and would also sit on the Senate as a matter of right. The establishing ordinance stipulated that these men should be drawn from five different houses (*Lib. Croc.*: fos. 60–9).[6] Another measure increased the length of the interval before the incumbents of certain offices could be re-elected to those same offices (ibid.: fos. 83, 86v, 92v).

Two major changes were introduced at the very end of this period which should have led to important alterations in the pattern of office-holding. In June 1490 the Great Council increased the size of the Senate by adding ten new seats. A week later it established a completely new council, the *Collegio de la Appellatione*, and elected twenty-one men to sit on it (ibid.: fos. 95–96v).[7] The new councillors were

---

[4] $\overline{X} = 27.1$ and $\overline{X} = 20.2$ years for MB and ZH, respectively.

[5] There were a few exceptions: the *Cazamorti* and Procurators like the *Procuratori de San Blasio in Ragusa* who held office for life (*Lib. Croc.*: fo. 37v).

[6] The wording is simply 'de v casate'. The ordinance establishing this important post is very comprehensive with 45 major clauses. A number of additions and amendments were made to the ordinance in the months which followed.

[7] Measures establishing the additional Senators and members of the *Collegio* are found in *Act. Maior.* 15: fos. 250–251v, 257–8.

to be men of 35 years or older. These two changes show the attempts being taken to increase the number of offices and to broaden the extent of office holding. But since the consequences of these changes would only have been felt beyond our period, we cannot tell how effective these remedies were.

In addition to changes in the number of offices and in the nature of office-holding, there is further evidence of increasing competition in the outcomes of the elections themselves. As the period progressed from 1455 to 1490, the size of the majorities of winning candidates decreased. For example, the *Doanieri* were elected with majorities of 64 per cent in 1455. By 1480 the size of the winning majority had decreased to 59 per cent. At the end of the period that majority had been reduced to little more than 50 per cent. Furthermore, the majorities decrease across the full spectrum of offices from the humble *Biscoti officiali* and *Officiali lavorieri de scritta in Ragusi* to such exalted posts as that of Rector and *Consoli de le cause civil*.[8]

Perhaps the extent of competition can best be gauged by the regular monthly elections for Rector. As council attendance increased through the period, the size of Rectorial majorities decreased. In 1455, for example, an average of 135 men cast ballots in Rectorial elections and the average majority was 67 per cent. By 1490 the number of men voting had increased to an average of 176 while the size of the winning majority had shrunk to 57 per cent.[9]

These average figures conceal great variations. In 1460, for example, persons are elected to the office of Rector with majorities which average 65 per cent. Yet in that same year Johannes Andreas de Volçe (ID 2110) was elected to be Rector for February by a vote of 111 in favour and only 13 opposed—a majority of 90 per cent. In November of that same year Andreas Micocius de Resti (ID 1800) was elected in a very close vote with 72 in favour and 66 opposed—a majority of only 52 per cent.[10] Therefore not only were there differences throughout the years, there were also sharp variations within a single year. It seems likely that the very large turnout in February and the large majorities which resulted may be related to the feast day of S Blaise (Sv. Vlaho), the patron saint of Ragusa, which falls in this month. The most worthy and venerable men were put forward to hold the Rectorship in February. But whatever variations there may have been within particular years, there was a very distinctive trend throughout the period. The Great Council grew in size and there was increasing competition for office.

Nominees for office were usually of similar experience and length of service. Therefore it follows that the more men that there are of similar experience, the

---

[8] This conclusion is based upon election results for the years 1455, 1460, 1465, 1470, 1480, 1485, and 1490. Fifteen offices were examined. Records of the Great Council for the period 1472–77 are lost. This is why the election results for the year 1475 are missing.

[9] Only the number of men casting pro or con votes are counted. This omits those abstaining. While pro and con votes are always recorded, abstentions were only intermittently noted in Great Council records. The plague year of 1465 is unusual in that no elections for Rector were held during June and July and attendance at council sessions was sharply reduced.

[10] Andreas de Resti also had 10 abstentions (*Act. Maior.* 11: fos. 159v, 206).

less likely it is that they will hold office. The converse is also true. But there are some important exceptions. One exception is the gerontocratic domination of government by the most senior men. The second exception concerns the uneven distribution of men within the Great Council in terms of length of service.

The Inner Circle

So far as gerontocracy is concerned, senior men tend to monopolize the more senior and prestigious offices. Therefore the likelihood of holding office is not only inversely related to the number of similarly aged competitors, but it is also inversely related to the number of more senior men. The number of offices held by the more senior cohorts (that is, those with over thirty years' service in the Great Council) is not related to their proportion of the total Great Council membership, but to the absolute size of the cohort itself. In periods when there were many more of these senior men, they simply held more offices. Moreover, they also tended to monopolize the most prestigious ones.

After a man had been in the Great Council for about thirty years and had served in a number of different offices, he would have gained sufficient stature to be elected to one of these key positions of government as Rector, a member of the Senate, one of the Small Council, or as one of the judges of the Criminal or Civil Courts (*Judici del criminal* or *Consoli de le cause civil*).[11] I have referred to these posts, and the men occupying them, as the inner circle of government. The links between these different offices and councils were close. For example, a judge of the Criminal Court would also advise the Rector as a member of the Rector's Small Council and, as a Small Council member, he would also be entitled to a seat on the Senate. Furthermore, at particular times individuals and incumbents of particular offices were co-opted to join *ad hoc* deliberative and consultative bodies. Thus, while members of government were prohibited from succeeding themselves in particular offices, and while they circulated quite quickly from office to office, those in the topmost offices constituted a relatively closed circle. The term 'inner circle' is not a translation of a local term, but neither is it an analytical fabrication. The rather loose collection of persons who constitute this inner circle are referred to in documents as *sapiens*, the wise (ones).

Movement into this inner circle came slowly and only after a man had served in many elected offices. For example, Franciscus Stephanus de Benessa (ID 113) was directly elected to the Senate by the Great Council in 1487. This was his first position at the centre of power, but he had already served in ten previous posts, all of them different, and he had been in the Great Council for twenty-three years. His rise, even so, was fairly spectacular. Most men who were elected to one of the inner circle posts had served in about fifteen previous offices before they were elected.

---

[11] These are the same offices considered by Krekić in his analysis of the concentration of power (1986).

In any single year there were approximately fifty-six persons in the inner circle although the number fluctuated somewhat from year to year. But once elected into the world of the *sapiens*, a man was seldom out. The career of Bartholo Çuan de Goçe (ID 972) is a good illustration. In 1448 he had been directly elected into the Senate and this was the first of his inner circle positions. He then became Rector in 1452, a judge of the Criminal Court in 1453, a judge of the Civil Court in 1455, Rector again in 1457, and so on. From 1450 until 1490 he was never out of the inner circle. He was Rector twelve times, on the Small Council and Civil Court ten times each, and directly elected to the Senate on five occasions.

Such an unbroken record of inner circle office-holding is unusual, particularly over a period of several decades. Most men who finally achieve one inner circle position will thereafter occasionally hold other offices. When they do it is most likely to be as one of the *Procuratori* of a church or monastery; or to be *Advocati del proprio*, *Advocati del comone*, *Conte de Slano*, *Cazamorti*, or *Conte de Stagno*. These latter five posts account for over 80 per cent of the posts outside the inner circle held by the *sapiens*. They are all senior, prestigious offices. This suggests a degree of differentiation within the ranks of the inner circle.

If we examine the inner circle during the decade from 1481 to 1490, we find that it consists of a 'core' of about forty men like Bartholo de Goçe.[12] Such men are routinely elected to the Senate or to another of the posts that carry Senate membership. There is only an occasional year when they are not in the Senate. In any given year about thirty-five men, or seven-eighths of all core members, would hold an inner circle post. They are the mainstay of government, its ruling élite. In addition to them, there are about another twenty men who might hold an inner circle post for a year or two, but who then hold no office or else are elected to some other, non-inner-circle, offices. After an absence from the inner circle for a year or two, they might be once again elected. I refer to such men as 'adjuncts'.

The filling of inner circle posts required about forty patricians per year, about one-quarter of all the office-holders in a year. The qualification is necessary because some men moved in and out of several posts in rapid succession or held positions concurrently. For example, one of the Civil Judges might be elected Rector for a month and then return to being a Civil Judge when his tenure as Rector was over.

A person's rate of advancement up through the office hierarchy into the inner circle might reflect his experience and growing expertise. But this movement also depended in part upon the numbers and types of men within the inner circle itself. Because of the nature and number of posts at the top of government, there was an upper limit on the number of men who could be routinely elected. This limit could be increased if the most senior men held office less frequently, or if the

[12] For convenience I occasionally write about the 'inner circle' as if it were a bounded group and refer to various patricians as being its 'members'. Neither term is appropriate, but they may serve in place of more accurate, if more cumbersome, phrases.

number of top offices increased. While these alternatives will be considered separately, they should not be thought of as excluding one another.

A senior man might have held office less frequently if his personal affairs took
him away from Ragusa or if he became ill. Unfortunately, while there is some evidence about illness and travel concerning a few men, such information is much too
fragmentary to assess the effects of absences on patterns of office-holding. Archival
sources are much more forthcoming concerning the effect of death upon the ranks
of the inner circle. Between 1455 and 1490, there were an average of fifty-six inner
circle members but this bland figure conceals a trend over the period towards an
ever larger inner circle. Early in the period, for example, the average was about
forty-seven. By the end it had reached sixty-six. As this pattern of growth suggests, losses through deaths tended to be more than offset by newcomers being
incorporated into the ranks of the select. In only one year was there no death within
the inner circle. That exceptional year was 1490. But the process of replacement
of deceased members by new 'cadets' was not uniform. In the middle of the decade
between 1455 and 1464 there was a net loss created by the deaths of seven members
in 1457. By 1465 those losses had been redressed through the introduction of new
cadet members and there were then about fifty men regularly holding inner circle
posts. The years 1465 and 1466 were plague years and a drop might have been
expected, but the eleven inner circle members who did die were more than compensated through the addition of thirteen newcomers. In the following year there
were eleven additions and only two deaths. This increased the number of men
holding inner circle posts to sixty.

During the next fifteen years the number of men holding the top posts dropped
slightly and then began to rise. The number rose to sixty-five in 1481 when there
was another setback with the plague of 1482. In this plague year twelve of the élite
died. But, as in the case of the earlier plague, there was a larger than normal intake
of newcomers. In 1482, eight new men were elected into the Senate and related
offices. This left the total size of the élite at sixty-one. Here it remained until 1486
when it began to rise again. In 1490 there were sixty-eight men who regularly held
an inner circle post.

From the information available about periods of plague, it appears that deliber-
ate efforts were made to replace losses among the inner circle and maintain
numbers. Indeed, the picture which emerges in plague years suggests that there
was an over-compensation at times of high mortality. The size of the inner circle
increased sharply in the aftermath of the 1465–6 plague, for example. But there
was clearly no one-for-one pattern of replacement.

As has been noted, long-standing members of the inner circle tended to hold
one office after another with scarcely a break. Mathio Tomko de Bona (ID 320), a
member of the cohort of eleven who entered the inner circle in 1467 in the aftermath of the plague, did likewise. He was elected to the Small Council in 1467, the
Senate in 1469, the Small Council again in 1470, and the Civil Court in 1472, and
so on. From his first election in 1467, therefore, he was never out of the inner

circle. But he was somewhat unusual. Most men who were elected to an inner circle post for the first time were not re-elected to another such post until several years had elapsed. A continuous unbroken run of such posts from entry was not the usual pattern. Yet among the cohort of men who were elected into the inner circle in the aftermath of the plague, Mathio Tomko de Bona was not the only one to have almost continuous inner circle service. Nicho Junius de Georgio (ID 2333), Marinus Benedetto de Gondola (ID 1181), Paladinus Petrus de Lucari (ID 1314), and Nicola Biasio de Ragnina (ID 1727) did as well.

An 'in and out' pattern of inner circle office-holding was more typical of the adjuncts. But gradually, the longer a person served in high office, the greater the time spent 'in' the inner circle and the less time spent 'out'. Therefore, while there was no strict one-for-one replacement of inner circle members, one consequence of adding proportionally more newcomers might have been to keep the number of office-holding members relatively constant. Newcomers would hold office less frequently than the more senior men, therefore as mortality took its toll among newcomers and senior men alike, there would be a fairly steady replenishment of the inner circle. Senior men would hold an office almost every year and surviving newcomers would gradually hold top offices more frequently as some of the senior men died off. However, political life among the élite is more complex than this.

Even though the number of senior offices increased over time, this increase and natural mortality among the élite did not alleviate competition. As the number of inner circle members increased, so did competition. Even though there were more offices, there were also many more men seeking them. As the number of inner circle members grew, the proportion of men being able to hold such posts for four or five years (in a five-year period) decreased. In other words, there was more sharing of the top posts. For example, in the five years from 1456 to 1460, there were about thirty men who were continually holding the top posts. Much later, from 1486 to 1490, there were also about thirty. Yet the total number of men in the inner circle averages fifty-three for the earlier period and sixty-six for the latter.

Considering this, is it possible that relatively few men monopolize the highest offices because they are the only ones to survive to sufficient age? In other words, is concentration of power largely a matter of longevity? In order to see if those who made it into the inner circle did so merely because they happened to live long enough, we can examine those men who entered the Great Council prior to 1472, yet who also survived into the decade from 1481 to 1490.[13] The youngest of them would have had about twenty-five years of service in the Great Council by 1481. They would also have been at least 47 years old by that year, an age by which one might have expected to reach the inner circle. Of the total of 220 such men, there were ninety-six inner circle members and 124 who were not. A comparison reveals

[13] The most junior inner circle member serving in the decade 1481–90 had entered the Great Council in 1471. This is the reason that 1472 was taken as the threshold year.

that the inner circle tends to include the oldest of these men, as would be expected, but it does not appear that longevity accounts for inner circle membership. There are, for example, 106 men who entered the Great Council before 1454. Of these seventy-seven (72 per cent) had reached inner circle posts and twenty-nine (27 per cent) had not. This suggests that while one had to live to a good age to be elected to an inner circle post, success in reaching the top is not merely a matter of living long enough.

Inner circle posts carried both power and prestige, but the number of such posts available each year was (relatively) fixed. The number of senior men, however, was not. In periods when there more senior men, more of them held inner circle posts. In such periods, more of them were also holding the occasional junior post outside of the inner circle. Assuming that senior men held an advantage in ballots containing a mixture of senior and junior nominees, then, when they were not serving in an inner circle post, senior men would also tend to monopolize other high posts. The juniors, now being deprived of their customary offices, would assume posts normally occupied by their juniors. Since the total number of government posts available in a year was fairly constant, this effect would tend to 'cascade down' from the most prestigious and senior posts to the most junior. The impact of this cascading effect would depend, in the first instance, on the number of men in the inner circle and also on the number of those who were their immediate juniors. Further effects would depend upon the relative numbers of those juniors and those who were, in turn, their juniors, and so on.

For example, in 1455 there were seventy-two very senior men in the Great Council with over thirty years of service. Of these sixty-two (86 per cent) held at least one office during the interval from 1455 to 1459. Of those holding office, eighteen (25 per cent) did not hold an inner circle post. By 1460 the number of very senior men had grown from seventy-two to ninety-six, and of these eighty-one (84 per cent) held office in the period 1460–4. Reflecting this increase in numbers and, presumably, the greater competition for high office, thirty-six of these most senior men (38 per cent) did not hold an inner circle post in the period. But what is particularly interesting is the effect that the size of the most senior cohort had upon the chances of men in the following cohort to hold high office.

While the number of very senior men grew from 1455 to 1460 (from seventy-two to ninety-two), about the same number of men held inner circle offices in the periods 1455–9 and 1460–4 (forty-four and forty-five, respectively). Of the forty-five very senior men serving in the inner circle from 1460 to 1464, thirty-eight had also held inner circle posts in the previous period. The seven incoming men who had not, had held other important offices. In addition there were a further seven very senior men who held no office at all in the entire period from 1455 to 1464. The increase in the number of the most senior men in this period resulted in more men holding a non-inner-circle office (an increase from eighteen to thirty-six) or in holding no office at all (an increase from ten to fifteen). In many instances, these men simply held more posts such as that of *Advocati del proprio* (increasing from twelve to sixteen) or *Advocati del comone* (increasing from twenty to twenty-nine) which were often held by experienced men. But they also, and this is the significant point, held other posts that more junior men might have expected to occupy. In 1460–4, for example, some of these additional offices were *Camerlengi del comone* (four instances), *Gatti officiali* (three instances), *Conte de Isola de Mezo et de Calamota* (three instances), and *Conte de la Gosta* (three instances).

Thus, in periods when there were many senior men, they tended to hold more inner circle offices. The same holds true for the next most senior cohort, the one after that, and so on down the ranks of the Great Council. Therefore, while there was an approximately constant 'volume' of offices to be filled, in periods when there were relatively more senior men, there were consequently relatively fewer offices left for the more junior men to hold. Competition for offices, therefore, can be understood in term of pressures emanating from the top down. But this is only one part of a complex picture. One element concerns the numbers of senior men and the numbers of juniors. Another is the distribution of offices and councils. For while there were many inner circle offices, there were relatively few offices which served as stepping stones to them.

The most common route into this select world of the inner circle was through the offices of *Advocati del proprio* and *Cazamorti*. Both of these were held about one year prior to election into the inner circle. Other common routes were through the offices of *Massari de le biave*, *Advocati del comone*, and *Doanieri*. These latter posts were held on average about four years prior to elevation into the world of the *sapiens*.[14] Table 13 shows an ordering of the offices with an indication of the number available to various segments of the Great Council.[15] It is clear that there were relatively few posts available at a level just below that of the inner circle. This paucity of posts created a serious bottleneck in the route to high office. While there were many offices available to (say) those with fifteen to nineteen years of service in the Great Council, there were fewer for those with twenty to twenty-four years' service, and still fewer for those with twenty-five to twenty-nine years.

In this respect it is interesting to find that the members of the newly established *Collegio de la Appellatione* in 1490 were men who had not yet reached the inner circle. Three were from the cohort which had between twenty-five and twenty-nine years of service in the Great Council, five were from the next most senior cohort, and six were from the third. In addition there were a few men like Orsatus Marin Michiel de Bona (ID 200) and Laurentius Biasio de Sorgo (ID 2028) who had many more years of service (forty-two and thirty-eight years, respectively) but who had not quite scaled the heights into the inner circle. Thus the establishment

[14] These offices were the ones held immediately prior to being elected to an inner circle post (for the first time) as shown through an analysis of the careers of sixty-eight men. These are men who entered the Great Council after 1440, who held at least one inner circle post, and whose office-holding careers are known in their entirety.

[15] The representation of availability is only approximate. As the following discussion makes clear, the relative positions of the various offices, as well as the numbers of men seeking them, exist in a dynamic relationship and change over time.

TABLE 13. *Availability of offices to various segments of the Great Council*

Offices	Incumbents	
Proveditori de la terra	5	
Conte de Stagno	2	
Rector	12	
Consereri del menor conselo	6	Inner Circle
Pregato (Senate)	15	
Judici del criminal	5	
Consoli de le cause civil (d. stabili)	6	
Cazamorti	5	25–29 years
Conte Slano	1	
Lane officiali del arte della lana	3	
Conte de Canale	2	20–24 years
Advocati del comone	3	
Salinari	3	
Consilium causa civilium (d. mobili)	6	
Advocati del proprio	6	
Conte de Zupana	1	
Doanieri	4	
Off. Hospedal de Misericordia, Scripta	2	
Off. lavorieri de pagamente in Stagno	2	
Off. Hospedal de Misericordia, Pagamento	2	
Aqueducto de la fontana officiali	3	
Massari de le biave	3	15–19 years
Castellan de Sochol	1	
Justicieri del comone	5	
Vicario del rector	1	
Camerlengi del comone	4	
Off. lavorieri de scritta in Stagno	2	
Gatti officiali	3	
Raxone officiali	5	
Conte de Isola de Mezo et de Calamota	1	
Castellan de quelmar, Castello de sotto	1	
Castellan de quelmar, Castello de sopra	1	
Capitanio de la ponta	1	
Advocati alla camara del arte della lana	2	
Stime officiali	4	10–14 years
Fontigieri	3	
Armamento officiali, pagamento	3	
Salezo officiali	3	
Off. lavorieri de pagamento in Ragusi	3	
Off. lavorieri de scritta in Ragusi	3	
Off. de scritta de armamento	2	5–9 years
Castellan de Stagno	1	
Cechieri	4	
Conte Lagoste	1	
Biscoti officiali	3	0–4 years
Scrivari over garcon dela dohane grande	1	

Note: As explained in the text, the positioning of offices and councils is approximate as are the years after entry into the Great Council when the posts are held for the first time.

of the *Collegio de la Appellatione* appears to have added offices to that portion of the office hierarchy where there had been relatively few previously and thereby removed some of the pressure of competition.

The bottleneck effect, however, had another restricting dimension. Offices like that of *Cazamorti* which served as stepping stones into the inner circle were precisely the same offices which were most likely to be held by a member of the inner circle at those times when he was not holding an inner circle post. This heightened the bottleneck effect and made it particularly difficult for men to break into the ranks of the inner circle. In this respect it is interesting to contrast two intervals: one (1455–9) with a very low number of men entering the ranks of the inner circle and another (1475–9) with a very high number. The period 1455–9, when only nine men began holding inner circle posts for the first time, was also the period when serving inner circle members were most likely to be holding the posts of *Cazamorti* and *Massari de le biave*. But 1475–9, when twenty-one began holding inner circle posts, was the period which had the fewest inner circle members serving as *Advocati del proprio*, *Cazamorti*, or *Advocati del comone*.

Gerontocratic domination did not penetrate through all offices. Some were simply thought too junior and demeaning for a senior man to hold. None of the most senior men was ever elected to be *Scrivari over garcon dela dohane grande*, for example. Other junior posts, such as that of *Biscoti officiali* or *Cechieri*, were also inappropriate for the elderly grandees. Thus, there were 'floors' associated with particular age and status cohorts, and these established thresholds below which it was unseemly to seek, or accept, office.

Therefore, in the competition for office, senior men took the most powerful and prestigious posts. In periods when there were more of them, they took posts which in other times might have gone to more junior men. This, as we have seen, had a cascading effect down the hierarchy of office. The question of who a man's competitors for political office are most likely to be does not, therefore, yield a simple answer. They are, other things being equal, his contemporaries. The more near contemporaries he has, the less likely it is that he will hold office. Similarly, their relative scarcity will increase his chances. But his chances do not only depend upon his contemporaries, but also upon the numbers and relative seniority of more experienced men. They depend, in other words, on his place in the distribution of Great Council members and on the shape of that distribution at particular moments in time.

It is likely, therefore, that differing cohorts, entering the Great Council at differing periods, will experience differing amounts of competition over their political careers. Let us, in this regard, compare two cohorts from different periods who have reached the same stage in their political careers; that is, the period in which the men will have been in the Great Council between ten and fourteen years. This is a crucial point in the development of their political careers in two respects. First, it is the stage in which the truly significant offices begin to be held. Election to a good office at this time can help launch a political career. Second, and a point we will examine in more detail shortly, it is also the stage when a man is most likely to marry. While members of both cohorts have the same length of service in the Great Council, these two cohorts have been chosen for closer analysis because they differ greatly in size. The cohort which had reached this stage in the census year of 1465 is the smallest cohort, with only thirty-five men, whereas the cohort from the 1485 census year is the largest, with seventy-seven. The more men that there are in the cohort, the less likely it is that any one of them will hold office. For example, in the smallest cohort, nineteen men held office (almost 60 per cent) whereas amongst the largest only twenty-five held office (33 per cent). As the cohorts increase in size, the percentage of men holding office tends to decrease. In this respect, men who enter the Great Council at differing periods will experience differing amounts of competition, and this depends upon the numbers of their contemporaries.

The experience of various cohorts depends not only upon their own size, but also on the size of the next most senior cohort. This is a result of the 'cascading' effect noted earlier. It is brought about by the advantages of seniority as well as by the shape of the council at particular periods. For example, the thirty-five men with between ten and fourteen years' service at the 1465 census year had a much larger cohort (with fifty-one men) immediately senior to them. In that census year, men of the junior cohort were nominated for office fifteen times whereas the men of the next most senior cohort were nominated forty-five times. The difference between them indicates the age inferiority, as well as the smaller size, of the younger cohort. Compare this with the seventy-seven men from the comparable cohort in the 1485 census year. This cohort was larger than the next most senior cohort, which had sixty men. Consequently, they were nominated twenty-eight times for office in 1485 whereas the more senior cohort was nominated thirty-three times. The difference between these two adjacent cohorts again indicates the inferior status of the younger cohort, but in this case it is partially offset by the relatively larger size of the younger cohort as well as the overall effects of the very much larger Great Council.

In addition, not only are the members of larger cohorts less likely to hold office, but those who do are also more likely to hold a lower office. For example, the post most frequently held by members of the smaller cohorts is one of the four *Stime officiali*, an office held generally after an average of 11.5 years of service. In the larger cohorts, however, the posts most frequently held are *Officiali lavorieri de scritta in Ragusi* or *Officiali lavorieri de pagamento in Ragusi*. Both of the latter are more junior posts held after 7.9 and 8.3 years' service, respectively.[16]

As we might expect, men tend not to contest for offices for which their length of service would be inappropriate even though they might receive a nomination

---

[16] This is based on an analysis of offices held in five of the seven census years. The two census years 1480 and 1485 were omitted because there were significant changes in the offices available in the decade of the 1480s. For example, no *Cechieri* were elected between 1485 and 1490, and no *Armamento officiali* between 1481 and 1488 (*Specchio*: s.v. *Cechieri* and *Armamento officiali*).

for such offices from time to time. For example, in 1465 both Simon Junius de Calich (ID 533) and Junius Giovane de Tudisio (ID 2100) were nominated for *Biscoti officiali* on separate occasions, yet neither contested this very junior post. It was men from yet more junior cohorts who contested it (*Act. Maior.* 12: fos. 202v and 212). Similarly, men do not contest more senior posts for which they might have been honoured with a nomination. Junius Pasqual de Sorgo (ID 2007) and Franciscus Šišmund de Georgio (ID 2302) were nominated for *Judicieri del comone* and *Advocati del proprio* in the same year. In both instances the posts were contested by men who were very much more senior (ibid.: fos. 200 and 232). Junius, as we have seen, had a large pool of kin and affines who might have supported him, but he had been in the Great Council only eight years. Both he and Franciscus were part of a relatively small cohort. They were, therefore, advantaged in the quest for office and this may be the reason why they were nominated for *Judicieri* and *Advocati*. But the posts for which men such as Simon and Junius were more usually nominated, and which they contested and sometimes won, were offices such as *Armamento officiali*, *Fontigieri*, and *Raxone officiali* (ibid.: fos. 201v, 202v, 223v, 234v). Their opponents for these offices were from their own cohort, or ones immediately adjacent to it. Therefore, in both the likelihood of holding office and in the standing of the office held, members of larger cohorts are disadvantaged. Furthermore, the 'shape' of the Great Council at various times affects the likelihood of holding office and the type of office held.

The period from 1455 to 1490 was therefore not only a period of growth for the patriciate but one that shows a continually changing dynamic within the ranks of its politically active members. Growth brought with it important changes in the distribution of Great Council members—in the 'shape' of the council, as we have termed it. The continually changing shape also affected the likelihood of holding office and in the amount of competition for office. While we have examined this primarily from the vantage point of the top of the office hierarchy, those offices associated with the inner circle, its effects were felt in all sections of the hierarchy, as we have seen with reference to 'cascading' and the 'bottleneck' effect. But if our vantage point has been largely from the top down, it has been distorted in another manner as well.

In this analysis we have only examined competition from one perspective. We have been largely concerned with the numbers of men. We have examined the size of the several cohorts and seen how their size changed over time. We have also compared several cohorts at several differing points in time. This perspective was concerned with the relative size of masses of men. But there is also another dimension, one which is still related to the numbers of men, yet which is separate from it. This is the arrangement of the several offices and councils—the question of hierarchy itself and the stability of that hierarchy over time.

9

Bureaucracy and Office

Bureaucracy and Office

Within anthropology the notion of office is associated with the writings of Max Weber and particularly with his classic discussion of bureaucracy.[1] Parsons summarizes Weber's position as follows:

It [bureaucracy] involves an organization devoted to what is from the point of view of the participants an impersonal end. It is based on a type of division of labor which involves specialization in terms of clearly differentiated functions, divided according to technical criteria, with a corresponding division of authority hierarchically organized, heading up to a central organ, and specialized technical qualifications on the part of the participants. The role of each participant is conceived as an 'office' where he acts by virtue of the authority vested in the office and not of his personal influence. (1949: 506)

Anthropological treatments of office have tended to concentrate on the last feature—the separation between offices and their holders (Gluckman 1955: 198). There have been particularly telling analyses of rituals of investiture. Accounts of divine kingship are probably the best-known example.[2] But anthropological accounts of other aspects of bureaucracy are much less developed. This in itself may also be a legacy of Weberian influence.

The features of bureaucracy Weber draws attention to are characteristic of *modern* bureaucracy. While he traces their beginnings to the Middle Ages, his discussion of Venice and of collegiality and of administration by notables shows that he regarded Venetian government as pre-bureaucratic (Weber 1949: 271–82, 290–2, and 1268–72). In Venice jurisdictional areas were not clearly demarcated. Indeed, Weber suggests that there were overlapping jurisdictions which forced officials to compete with one another for administrative and jurisdictional power (ibid.: 1271).

Weber associates the lack of clarity in administrative demarcation with the characteristics of notables. Government was in the hands of a monopoly association, *die Geschlechter*—literally 'the families' (ibid.: 1267). The preservation of the advantages of this association rested on 'the very strict mutual control of the noble families over each other', and the *administrative techniques* through which this was

---

[1] See, among others, Fortes 1962, M. Smith 1960.
[2] See Feeley-Harnik (1985). Anthropological accounts, in turn, have influenced historical analyses. With respect to rituals surrounding Venice's Doge, see Muir 1981, Boholm 1992.

accomplished such as the competitive separation of powers, short terms of offices, and so on (ibid.: 1271, my emphasis). As we have seen, these are characteristic of Ragusan government as well.

Central to Weber's notion of the modern bureaucracy is the principle of clear official *jurisdictional areas* within the bureaucratic framework. This is related to 'the principles of *office hierarchy*' with 'a clearly established system of super- and sub-ordination in which there is a supervision of the lower offices by the higher ones' (1968: 956–7, both emphases in original). Weber points out that the system of monocratic hierarchy is necessary for the supervision of subordinates as well as to facilitate procedures of appeal. But if jurisdictional areas within Ragusan government are not always clearly defined, and if its councils and offices are not arranged in a clearly articulated system of super- and sub-ordination, that does not mean that there is an absence of hierarchy. Jurisdictional clarity and well-defined lines of authority may help to sharpen the outlines of hierarchy and to facilitate procedures of control and appeal, but they are not preconditions for its existence.

In our account of Ragusa we have been able to isolate a provisional hierarchical arrangement of offices by examining when they are held in the careers of their incumbents. And just as we have been able to discern a 'shape' to the distribution of Great Council members which alters over time, so we might also speak of a 'shape' to the arrangement of offices. The material in Table 13 and the discussion of the 'bottleneck effect' have implied this. We have also seen that some offices are only available to the most senior men while others carry age or other qualifications. That shape would depend upon the arrangement of offices *vis-à-vis* one another. But in outlining the structure of Ragusan government it was noted that while offices could be ordered in a hierarchy, there was also considerable variation in the points where a single office was held for the first time. This raises the question of how much hierarchy there was and the extent to which that hierarchy remained stable over time.

First, how much hierarchy was there? One answer to this question has already been given. In the process of analysing the career patterns of patrician office-holders, the various councils and offices were given a number which corresponded to their position in a rank order. These ordinal numbers were based upon the mean number of years which had elapsed between entry into the Great Council and the first time that a particular office was held. However, since these are ordinal and not cardinal numbers, it would be a mistake to read significance into differences between them. The position of *Gatti officiali*, for example, ranks nineteenth in that listing while that of *Advocati del proprio* ranks thirty-fourth, yet the difference between them is much less marked than the difference in rank order suggests. The position of *Gatti officiali* is held, on average, 16.4 years after entering the Great Council whereas that of the *Advocati* is held 20.2 years after entering. Not only is the difference between these averages small, but the averages themselves belie considerable variation. The standard deviations about these mean values are quite large

(6.9 and 6.4, respectively). In the face of such variation, to what extent can we say that such offices were actually ranked *vis-à-vis* one another?

One way of answering this question is to examine whether particular pairs of offices tend to be held in a fixed order—Office 'A' is always held before Office 'B'. In some cases there might be the appearance of ordering, but this ordering might merely be an artefact of when the post happens to be held in a career of office-holding and where election depends upon patterns of availability, rivalry between persons and factions, and a host of other adventitious factors. Those nominating and electing may have had no particular expectation that one of these posts should be held before another. The alternative would be that nominators and electors were operating on the expectation that Post 'A' should be held prior to Post 'B'.

If the ordering observed between particular pairs of offices were a product of sequencing (but not of a set of cultural expectations), then where a considerable number of years has elapsed between the holding of one office of a pair and the holding of the second in the same pair, we would predict that it is always one of the pair which is held early and the other held late. Similarly, when the two offices of a pair are held fairly close together, then we would predict that in some instances one of the pair would be held first, and in other instances the other. These situations would arise if there were no determinant relationship between particular pairs of offices and the only significant variable were when they were held in an office-holding career. Indeed, this is what we find. In cases where one office of a pair regularly precedes another, there is usually a considerable number of years between the holding of the first office and the holding of the second. Indeed, we can say that the greater the difference in years, the more determinant the appearance of ordering. Similarly, when two offices are held at about the same time in political careers, there appears to be no preference about whether Post 'A' should be held first or Post 'B'.

But determinant relationships do exist between particular pairs of offices where such preferential ordering occurs. A determinant relationship is here understood to be one in which there are at least ten careers in which both offices are held and where one of the offices precedes the other in at least 90 per cent of the pairings.

Determinant relationships exist between the following pairs of offices: *Scrivari over garcon dela dohane grande* and *Biscoti officiali* (held early), *Biscoti officiali* and *Cechieri* (also held early), *Biscoti officiali* and *Armamento officiali* (early), *Cechieri* and *Advocati alla camara del arte* (held towards the beginning of the middle range), *Raxone officiali* and *Doanieri* (middle), *Officiali lavorieri de scritta in Stagno* and *Massari de le biave* (also middle), *Justicieri de comone* and *Advocati del proprio* (towards the end of the middle range), and *Advocati del comone* and *Consoli de le cause civil* (held late). There may be other determinant relationships as well. Some combinations do not appear frequently enough in the sample of careers to be included in the analysis. For example, only two individuals whose careers were studied, Jacomo Martolo de Zrieva (ID 565) and Nicolinus Marin de Gondola (ID 1147), held both the posts of *Gatti officiali* and *Advocati del proprio*.[3]

These cases, and others like them, clearly indicate that a hierarchical relationship existed between particular pairs of offices which could be held at about the same point in a career. Furthermore, such pairings were to be found in various parts of the office hierarchy from the most junior posts to the most senior. The hierarchy itself had a characteristic shape which remained (relatively) stable throughout the period. This reinforces the orthodox anthropological and Weberian view that offices are positions through which persons pass as they become more powerful and experienced in the affairs of government (Goody 1966: 2). For example, in M. Smith's sophisticated Weberian analysis of government in Zazzau, offices are seen as corporations sole whose persistence in the face of change is due to its 'ultimately ideological character, as a corporate unit, a perpetual status especially appropriate for the organization of a governmental system' (1960: 58). This is a view which is fully consistent with the structural-functionalism current in anthropology when Smith was writing. In such views the structure of offices is the stable ground against which transient figures of office-holders move. Where the positioning of offices is considered as an empirical problem, the answer tends to be found in the whims of the ruler and/or the functional importance of the office. It is not often made clear how, or by whom, that functional importance is determined. But the procedures of nomination and election in Ragusa suggest another possibility for interpreting office.

Elections and Social Value

We have noted that Ragusan offices change hands frequently. Most of them change hands at least every year. The allocation of persons to these posts requires procedures of nomination to ensure that there is a degree of fit between the duties and stature of the post and the calibre of persons who occupy them. Ballots then ratify this selection while making a further selection amongst the nominees. The ballots, held in open session of the Great Council, aggregate the views of all sitting patricians into a single view of the body politic. The results are expressed in terms of votes for, against, or abstaining. These votes for and against, like the kula valuables or pearl shells in Melanesian ceremonial exchange systems, may be regarded as tokens of esteem which represent the relative 'value' of the nominees at a point in time. Now Ragusan offices, as tokens, circulate rapidly. Most can only be held for a year or less, and an office-token cannot be exchanged for itself. Indeed, if a person is not bestowed with another office-token in the meantime, two years must ordinarily elapse before the same token can be bestowed again. A person may

---

[3] *Specchio*, s.v. *Gatti officiali* and *Advocati del proprio*. This assumes that any two posts might be held during a political career. A further possibility (which has not been examined) may be that certain combinations of posts should not occur.

TABLE 14. *Results of Rectorial ballots in 1490*

Candidate [month of incumbency][a]	Majority (%)	Cumulative score[b]
Orsolin Nicola de Mençe (ID 1421) [January]	69.4	958.7
Paladino Givcho de Gondola (ID 1216) [March]	57.7	832.8
Naocho Nicola de Saraca (ID 1917) [November]	57.1	700.2
Nicolinus Martolo de Zrieva (ID 569) [September]	53.3	683.8
Maroe Martholo de Georgio (ID 2218) [October]	54.6	502.8
Nicola Ruschus de Poça (ID 1596) [December]	51.0	490.5
Orsatus Marin de Bona (ID 200) [July]	52.6	301.8
Nicola Marin de Lucari (ID 1323) [June]	50.3	242.1

Notes:

[a] *Act. Maior.* 15: fos. 242, 252, 258v, 263v, 265, 267, and 270. Michael Nicolaus de Poça (ID 1562), Nicho Junius de Georgio (ID 2333), Dragoe Aloisius de Goçe (ID 773), and Climento Marin de Goçe (ID 1024), also elected Rector in 1490, have been excluded from this table. They entered the Great Council at an unknown date making impossible the calculation of a comparable cumulated score.

[b] The sum total (of the rank) of all offices held between entry into the Great Council and 1489. The rank values refer to mean years after entry.

therefore be regarded as accumulating value according to the number of office-tokens they have held and the period in which they have held them. A person accumulates a line of value through the succession of offices held.

If we examine the size of the majority received in a ballot as one metric of value, we find that this is directly associated with the number of offices held. For example, in the Rectorial elections of 1490, Orsolin Nicola Vlachussa de Mençe (ID 1421) received the greatest majority with almost 70 per cent of the votes cast.[4] He had also accumulated the largest score of previous offices held. This score is the sum total (of the mean years after entry) of all offices he had held between his entry into the Great Council and 1489. That score was 959. In contrast, Nicola Marin Michael de Lucari, elected Rector for June 1490, only had a majority of 50 per cent. He also had the lowest score of previous offices held, with 242 (see Table 14). The association between the majority received and the cumulative score is very close. The same association is also found in elections to the Senate and Small Council. Amongst the somewhat younger and more inexperienced men elected to the newly founded *Collegio de la Appellatione* this association is also found, although it is not as clearly stamped as in the case of the Rector.

The orthodox view of office, which has dominated classical anthropological accounts, treats offices as an array of positions which serve particular (governmental) functions. An alternative view, and the one which has characterized this study, looks not to the rights and duties which define particular positions, but rather at the movement of office-holders through a series of posts. This is a prosopographical view (Stone 1987). It also totalizes in that it attempts to discern general patterns in what is a collection of individual careers. This perspective, while unconventional in terms of the analysis of politics in nation-states, is nevertheless

[4] Orsolin was elected in December of that year to be the Rector in January 1491.

classically anthropological. Offices, in this view, are tokens of esteem. Persons accumulate value as they move through a succession of ranked offices. But if persons accumulate value by passing through offices, might it also be the case that offices in turn are valued by the calibre of persons who pass through them?

This is an issue of stability in the positioning of offices, but it is also an issue of the meaning of office rank. Given the variation we have seen around the mean values of the office-holding hierarchy, the question of stability might be thought unanswerable. However, it appears that throughout the period from 1440 to 1490, most of the offices and councils maintained their position in the hierarchical order. For example, if we plot the number of years after entry into the Great Council that each incumbent holds an office, the resultant trend is essentially flat or slightly negative, as indicated by the slope of the regression line. The office of *Armamento officiali* can be taken as illustrative (see Fig. 15). While there is variation in when this post is held, it tends to be held about fourteen years after entry both in the early part of the period and later. The slight negative tendency noticed here may be related to the more youthful nature of the Great Council in the later decades.

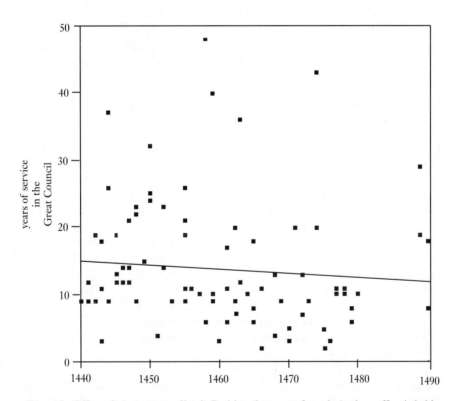

FIG. 15. Office of *Armamento officiali*. Position (in years of service) when office is held for the first time

Bureaucracy and Office

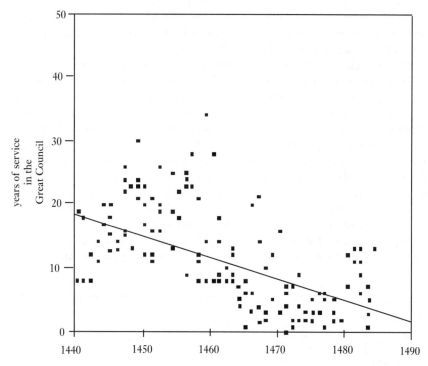

FIG. 16. Office of *Cechieri*. Position (in years of service) when office is held for the first time

Like the *Armamento officiali*, most offices maintain their relative position of the order of office. But not all do so.

If we examine a similar plot for the office of *Cechieri*, it shows a very marked drop over time (Fig. 16). In the early part of the period it was held (for the first time) about twenty years after entry. But by the end of the period, it was being held about ten years after entry. Relative to other offices, therefore, it dropped down the office hierarchy. The post of *Conte de Canali* also shifted its position (Fig. 17). Here the movement was in the opposite direction. As time progressed, it was held later and later. Therefore, it could be said to have moved up the office hierarchy. The net effect of these changes over time was to slightly reduce the number of middle-range offices while increasing the availability of both junior and senior posts. The effect was more pronounced amongst the senior posts, not because of shifts in position such as that noted for the *Conte de Canali*, but because of the addition of new posts.

A more detailed analysis of the case of the *Cechieri* indicates that the decline in the position of this post between 1455 and 1480 is not linked to particular *casate*. Members of 26 different *casate* hold this post during the decline, with the larger *casate* having the more incumbents, as we might expect. Furthermore, members

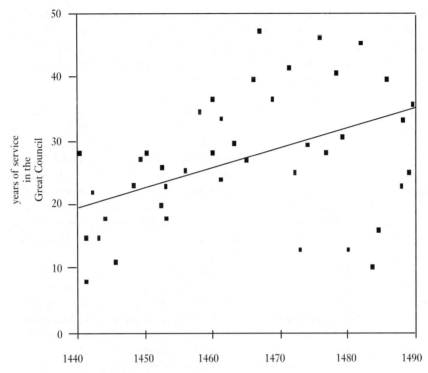

F IG. 17. Office of *Conte de Canali*. Position (in years of service) when office is held for the first time

of almost all of these *casate* are to be found amongst those who appear to be leading the decline as well as those who defy it. For example, consider the case of three Goçe brothers, the sons of Çorçi de Goçe. While Nicola (ID 822) and Dragoe (ID 828) first hold the post eighteen and thirteen years after entry, in 1461 and 1463, respectively, their younger brother Franciscus (ID 839) has only been in the Great Council for two years when he first becomes one of the *Cechieri* in 1467. But this does not indicate that Franciscus is politically precocious or that Nicola and Dragoe are lacking in potential. Both of the latter continue with distinguished political careers. Nicola is elected to the Senate shortly before his death in 1477 while Dragoe goes on to become the Rector in 1481.

In this work I have examined the governing of a historical city-state. The work not only refers to a particular *period* of a half-century, but attempts to chart the significance of the *passage* of time. The point of this can be simply stated. Although it was buffeted by major events, throughout the period from 1440 to 1490 the government of Ragusa appears remarkably stable. Year after year, and at about the same time every year, ballots are held to elect the same number of incumbents to the same offices. This tedious repetition would seem to be ample proof, if proof were needed, that Ragusa enjoyed a remarkably stable government throughout the period. However, proof is not needed. The same pattern of balloting for the same offices and councils pre-dates our chosen period by at least one century and follows it for several more. But routine and stability are not the same thing. As we have seen, there were significant changes occurring.

The appearance of stability is a mirage. It is clearly a mirage for the observer of the late twentieth century. While we do not know in any detail what patricians of the period thought, we presume that it was a mirage for them as well. Let me begin by suggesting reasons why it was a mirage and then, secondly, why patricians may have been unaware of it. Since some of these reasons have been discussed at length in the previous chapter, I only enumerate them here. They are (1) the shifting numbers of men available to serve in particular offices at particular times, (2) the changing shape of the Great Council, (3) the movement of dips and crests of men through it, (4) the changing amount of competition at differing points in time and for differing sections of the Great Council, and (5) the movement of offices within the hierarchy of offices throughout the period.

If these alterations can be discerned in the mass of data analysed in this study, why might the patricians of the period have been unaware of them? I suggest three reasons. First, the experience of men was vastly different even for those age mates who entered the Great Council at the same time. A cohort, a set of men entering the Great Council within a five-year interval, is a useful analytical simplification. It does not necessarily have much sociological significance. Not all the members of a cohort, for example, would have been of the same age and experience. Georgius Polo de Poça (ID 1624) and Marcus Andreas de Zrieva (ID 637) both began their political careers in June 1474. Georgius, however, was 31 years old while Marcus was just 20 (*Specchio*: fo. 389v). Georgius began to hold office almost immediately. Marcus, however, waited six years for his first post, by which time Georgius had already held four offices. Therefore, while cohort members may have similar length of experience in the Great Council, the nature of that experience can be very different. Some cohort members may have the experience of holding many offices, others may have held none. Further, and what is probably the more telling point, some cohort members may become rapidly differentiated from one another. Certain men rapidly move up through the offices of government so that after the passage of a few years they are competing with men who have much longer service. In terms of their political standing, such men will have left their entrance cohort and become *de facto* members of more senior ones. There are great differences between men in their rate of rise through the offices and councils of government.

Secondly, the variations in office-holding are highly significant. There is no single road or path up through the offices. Indeed, it is not even possible to speak in the plural of 'paths'. Men who have reached the top have done so in quite different ways. Some held dozens of different offices. Others, while holding office dozens of times, will have served in relatively few offices on multiple occasions.

Still others may have combined both, moving rapidly for a time through a succession of offices and then apparently stagnating in only a few which are held repeatedly. Not only this. We found that some offices shift position in the hierarchy over time. Therefore two men may have held the same post at about the same point in their careers, but when one man held it the post may have been regarded as quite senior and his holding it an indication of great potential. At a different time, holding the same post might be regarded as mundane. While these variations in cohort and office-holding have been discussed separately, they are not so much different as additive. What they reveal is great variation in the experience of patrician men rising through the offices. But in the midst of all of this, there were also forces at work which maintained a fiction of continuity and constancy in government.

Crucial ones were the broad pattern of order we have already discussed, such as the undoubted seniority of such offices as that of *Proveditori* or the juniority of the *Biscoti officiali*. We have also noted the ordering within particular pairs of offices. This would have been enforced by the framework of legislation which imposed an ordering on some offices, such as that which set out age criteria for the holding of particular offices. All of these devices would have added conviction to an ideology of stability in government. There is another, less obvious, feature to which I wish to draw attention. This is the authoritative voice of the more senior men in representing the nature of government and the experience of office-holding to their juniors.

There was great deference paid to the views of the most senior and experienced. The elderly were living embodiments of a glorious past. They could testify to what they had heard and observed, particularly from those who were already very elderly when they themselves were young, inexperienced, and highly impressionable. They could also speak from great personal experience. Few younger men would be in a position to gainsay their views. Even fewer would be inclined to give public voice to such views, given the great veneration for age.

Two points need to be made about the authoritative opinions of seniors. The first is that they were likely to support and buttress one another in the very unlikely event of a challenge from below. It is in their common interest that the primacy of age be maintained and that they defer to one another in terms of broad principles. Second, in points where they might disagree, such disagreement might be interpreted as the irascibility of age and personal rivalry, with no doubt being cast on the authoritativeness of gerontocratic opinion. Furthermore, within each household and set of close kinsfolk, the personal experience of the most senior men was likely to inform the views of younger men. While domestically transmitted views might gainsay the publicly stated views of the most gerontocratic and respected men, self-interest and deference were unlikely to let such family views intrude into public discourse in governmental councils. Further, the very great range of personal experience even within a small group of kinsmen would present sufficient ambiguity about the nature of the cultural world of government to disguise its ongoing changes while at the same time preserving the fiction of stability and continuity. With the sources available to us on Ragusa, these must remain as conjectures. They are, however, consistent with what is know about the political culture in other late medieval city-states like Venice and Florence.

The analysis of office-holding and its connections with bureaucracy represents a marked departure from traditional forms of analysis within political anthropology with its emphasis on structure and form. That earlier literature highlighted the essential features of what was thought to be a normative order. Further, the attempt to discover such order was linked to quite different views about the goals of the anthropological enterprise. Those goals, now largely abandoned, were to discover and catalogue the range and variation of social forms and to find the conditions which were necessary or sufficient for their continuance. That enterprise floundered under the twin weight of the taxonomic morass which had been created, and by new, sharply critical, theoretical assessments such as 'practice theory' (Bourdieu 1977). Political anthropology turned elsewhere, tempted by the insights offered by such developments as Foucaultian notions of power, by the feminist critique, and by a renewed Marxism. The analysis presented in this chapter may suggest one means of studying the relationship between practice and form without privileging the latter.

10

Conclusion

As the fifteenth century drew to a close, Ragusa was rapidly moving into her Golden Age. This was to become a period of territorial consolidation, of growth in her mercantile strength and maritime power, and of relative peace at home. This was to provide the basis for the development of civic splendour, cultural achievement, and great material prosperity.[1] While she may have been dwarfed by the power and splendour of Venice and Istanbul, part of her historical significance derives from her pivotal and mediating position on the great historical divide between the Ottoman East and Christian West. In the context of the great sweep of the 'long' sixteenth century documented so magisterially by Braudel, one might fairly ask: What is the significance of a limited, specialized study of the patrician class of a small, marginal city-state?

While her patrician class was the principal architect of her diplomacy and economic policy, and while individual members of that class were leading figures in both commerce and government, neither Ragusa itself nor its patrician class constituted a 'closed' world. There were, for example, other leading merchants within Ragusa who, although not patrician, had great wealth and important commercial interests both in the Balkan interior and on the Mediterranean seaboard. They may have exerted some influence on Ragusan government even though they could not sit on governing councils or hold state office. Nor were they the only voices that may have been listened to. One cannot discount the influence of 'outsiders', both those residing in Ragusa and the myriad others that resident Ragusans encountered in their frequent travels. These comments serve as reminders, if reminders are needed, that the world of Ragusa's patricians was in no sense closed. Yet in the course of analysis I have treated patrician marriage and politics as if they were a 'closed' system. This requires further comment.

If the patrician world was not 'closed', it is possible to demonstrate that in several respects the Ragusan patrician class falls near the end of a open–closed continuum. By examining all marriages and other unions for which there is evidence, it is possible to show that almost all marriages were with other Ragusan patricians. There were other unions between patricians and commoners which were not regarded as marriages and the offspring of these were never accorded patrician status. The apparent unity and unanimity of this class is very striking. It is remark-

---

[1] A number of these achievements are beautifully documented in the published catalogue to the museum exhibition of 'Dubrovnik's Golden Age' (Zlatno doba dubrovnika, 1987).

able that the state in this period commissioned no statues or portraits of its heroes and titans even though we can discern some figures of great ability and power within it.[2] The city-state was presented as a single entity, managed by a single corporate body.

A number of important points have emerged during the course of this analysis, arguably each of these being but a hint and a suggestion. While they appear to concern a specialized and narrow interest—the dynamics of the ruling class in a small city-state in late-medieval/early-Renaissance Europe—they may have some relevance outside of that place and time. They may also have something to say about the relationship between history and anthropology, at least about the practice of particular kinds of history and a certain type of social anthropology.

At an early stage of the enquiry it was necessary to extend the 'window of observation' from the initially planned two decades to one covering a half-century. This extension was required in order to capture the full development of some political careers. But even a period of that length is not a panacea. It only permits the examination of the complete careers of a few men. Moreover, since the period of observation is arbitrarily chosen, it does not permit the study of those careers starting before 1440 whose trajectories might shape the events and structures in our chosen period. Similarly, a half-century cannot capture the significance of father–son ties or of other relationships which may have a significant political legacy lasting more than a half-century. These points are elementary. In making them I am not making a plea for longer periods of observation. Long periods may be highly important for particular lines of enquiry, but some types of enquiries require shorter, more focused, periods of observation. The plague years are obvious candidates. The significance of these years and their consequences for political and marital alliances have escaped our attention. Yet those short periods of disturbance might have provided valuable insights into the seemingly boring routines of other years. These remarks should remind us, if we need reminding, that no period of observation can be—like that famous porridge—'just right'.

As the *rapprochement* between history and social anthropology has gathered pace, much anthropological attention has been directed to the very difficult conceptual issues involved in the enterprise. Prompted both by culture theory and by deconstructionist theories of literature, categories of description and analysis like 'open' and 'closed', 'internal' and 'external', and 'long term' and 'short term' have come under scrutiny, So have seemingly more basic terms like 'event', 'the past', or 'memory'. To many anthropologists a searching examination and exposure of such shibboleths and dichotomies within its own conceptual repertoire was overdue. In addition to these conceptual issues, there may also have been several different forms of historiography within anthropology masquerading as a single

---

[2] The only monument erected by the Republic to honour one of its citizens, the bust of Miho Pracat in the atrium of the Rector's Palace, dates from 1637. The dedication of squares to the poet Ivan Gundulić and the scientist Rudjer Bošković were much later developments.

form, each with its attendant potentialities and problems (Comaroff and Comaroff 1992: 20). The literature is now rich in works which discuss the problems of 'doing' history.

Yet there is a curious discrepancy within anthropology concerning its relationship with history. In the midst of the burgeoning critical literature within anthropology, there are strikingly few studies about the chain of events concerning particular persons in particular places through particular times. This is curious given that the defining methodological characteristic of the historical enterprise is its time metric. This is the dimension which anthropology has been least successful in addressing. Surprisingly, in view of the considerable discussion concerning categories of analysis, the notion of 'process' is mentioned, highlighted even, but it is seldom 'theorized' or 'operationalized'. If anthropological history (or historical anthropology) is to develop beyond an autocritique of its own vocabulary and agenda, it must incorporate this time metric and account for changes/transformations through time.

The relationship between history and anthropology has implications for both disciplines. The previous chapters of this book have been able to show some of the ways that an essentially anthropological analysis can contribute to a classic historical problem. It is one of the hallmarks—indeed, a cliché—of anthropology's comparative approach to posit that the several features of social and cultural life constitute an interrelated 'whole'. In this context we have explored the 'structural implications'—to resurrect Leach's term—of marriage arrangements and kinship forms and linked these to office-holding. It is important to stress that structural implications can only point to working hypotheses. Interconnections cannot be assumed. These must be sought and tested.

In the particular case of the Ragusan patriciate, our analysis was prompted by comparative studies of marriage systems elsewhere and in such an unlikely setting as some islands off the northern Australian coastline. While the Australian context and material is very different, it clearly showed that age differentials between spouses have significant implications for the availability of mates and for local politics. Following the findings of Herlihy and Klapisch-Zuber for Florence and drawing upon the insights provided by the Australian Aboriginal material, we were able to demonstrate not only that the Mediterranean Marriage Pattern also existed in Ragusa, but that it constituted a *pattern* in a much more elaborate sense than the Florentine scholars had suggested. While anthropology's pioneering dream of being a generalizing social science may have been misconceived, the impetus towards comparative analysis and generalization has resulted in a rich armoury of examples and middle-range theories about the interrelationships between social institutions. It has also yielded a series of arguments about the reasons for them.

If Ragusa falls towards the end of the 'closed' patriciate continuum, future research might examine the implications of 'closed' and 'open' marriage systems, and 'closed' and 'open' political orders in the range presented by Ragusa, Venice, and Florence in the late-medieval period. While a direct comparative analysis is probably not feasible because of the differences in size of the three city-states and because of the huge data requirements, these differences could be modelled using techniques of computer simulation. The simulation exercise undertaken as part of our analysis of the 'sisters first' effect gives only a crude indication of the power of this mode of exploratory analysis. There is now, for example, an interesting body of literature on the Medici of Florence which argues that the Medici manipulated the marriages of their supporters to build a network of alliances to further and consolidate their rise to power (D. Kent 1978; Padgett and Ansell 1993). This argument could also be examined using simulation techniques and its findings explored in the context of Ragusa and Venice. The rich literature on these three city-states presents an excellent laboratory for a controlled comparison which explores the parameters of élite formation and control.

While comparison may be facilitated by conditions such as a shared cultural milieu, it does not depend upon them. In a similar vein to the Mediterranean Marriage Pattern, it was the interconnected features of lineage systems found in such differing forms and in such disparate parts of the world as sub-Saharan Africa and China which had led Goody to suggest that the kind of features found in Tuscan society were characteristic of descending kindreds, not patrilineages. Through a detailed investigation of the Ragusan *casata*, and by comparing it with what is known about similar institutions in Florence and Venice, we have been able to confirm Goody's insight and to give it substance. This was made possible, as was suggested above, by following through, as a working hypothesis, the implications of structural arrangements. The purpose of that analysis was not to show the fit between Florentine and Ragusan institutions and anthropological typologies of types of descent groups. It was, rather, to map the outlines of the Ragusan *casata* and to compare it with what is known about similarly named institutions in Florence and Venice. This shows, I believe, the difference that essentially anthropological analysis can make to the understanding of a classic historical problem. But what about the reverse? What contribution can history make to anthropology?

There are several answers to this question. Here I wish to consider two inter-related ones. The first contribution which history can make—as a source of materials and practice for anthropological analysis—may seem at first glance to be rather banal and even demeaning. I argue that it is not. In our examination of Ragusan kinship, marriage, and politics, it has been extremely important to have had access to extensive material on the entire patrician class. For example, if we had only used the Sorgo as a representative case study, we might have concluded that marriages within the *casata* were common and, because of the unusually large number of marriages between the Sorgo, Zamagno, and Grade, that marriage exchanges between clusters of *casate* were important. Yet neither statement is true, as we have seen. Further, however emotionally important *casata* affiliation may have been to the patricians, we could find little evidence of that importance in either marriage or political support. This conclusion came from examining, in the Ragusan context, what is known about the characteristics of lineage systems.

I have drawn particular attention to the ways in which the present account has depended upon an unusual and privileged data set. By building upon the foundations laid by Mahnken's genealogical research, we have been able to compile a complete genealogical record of the entire patrician class. As a result of this we have been able to examine the internal structure of all thirty-three *casate* as well as all known marriages between them. Judged by the standards of kinship studies within anthropology, this data set is highly unusual. In the course of traditional 'dirt' anthropological fieldwork, it would be extremely difficult to collect and verify genealogical and marriage information on an entire population the size of the Ragusan patriciate. It would be impossible to do so for a period extending over half a century. In the present case our analysis has been made possible by the 'closed' nature of the patriciate, by the relatively small size of that class, by the remarkable industry of Ragusa's notaries extending over several centuries, and finally by the care and diligence which which all of their labours have been preserved in Dubrovnik's archives.[3]

This highly unusual and complete set of genealogies have enabled us to show that Ragusan *casate*, or segments of *casate*, do not act as units in marital alliances. While there are some interesting exceptions such as the Sorgo and their congeries which merit further study, marriages between *casate* appear remarkably even-handed. The extensiveness and completeness of this genealogical data permitted the investigation of a number of interconnected enquiries concerning the marriage regime: age at marriage and the ordering of marriages, dowry provisions, the significance of various kinfolk and affines in the making of wedding arrangements, and so on. While these might appear as a series of separate and discrete enquiries, we were able to show how they were interrelated and how each of them was also related to Ragusan politics and the competition for office.

The data set concerning elections and office-holding that we have compiled is also unusually large and privileged. And, as with the genealogical material, its privileged nature also depends upon the same set of factors. Because most anthropological fieldwork is conducted by a single investigator, and because of the limited amount of time that can be spent in the field, it would be very difficult to collect a comparable body of material during fieldwork—even one specifically devoted to politics and office-holding.

But the sheer size of the data sets used in this account, as well as the numerical summaries of that material, is important in other ways. Because the material considered in the present study has been, as it were, 'pre-collected' in historical archives, it permits the anthropologist to investigate problems that would be incon-

---

[3] While the resources of the Venetian and Florentine archives are potentially much richer in genealogical and marriage data, the much greater size of the Venetian patriciate and the 'open' nature of the Florentine marriage system would make it extremely difficult to compile a comparable data set. I offer some speculative comments on how these difficulties may be circumvented below.

ceivable using highly labour-intensive hunting-and-gathering fieldwork.[4] If political anthropology has concentrated on the micro-politics of particular settings
or on very ornate rituals of succession and investiture rather than office-holding
or administrative structures, it is not because the latter are less important than the
former. It is, rather, because of the overhead costs of fieldwork—time and labour.
From the anthropological side, one of the appreciable benefits of enquiries using
archival sources is that it makes possible some lines of enquiry which would be
impractical to research using conventional anthropological techniques. This advantage has, of course, to be balanced against the several problems involved in using
archival sources.[5] It is not just the type of material held in archives which is important, although this should not be minimized, but also its quantity.

Here we encounter the second contribution that history can make to anthropology. Within social anthropology the study of the interrelationship between patterns of kinship and marriage on the one hand, and of political relationships on
the other, constitutes one of the classic genres. Much of this genre takes the form
of virtuosic statements of dazzling (and seemingly unlikely) hypotheses rather than
convincing demonstrations with detailed supporting evidence. Evans-Pritchard's
'brilliant simplification' of Nuer politics—the phrase comes from Leach—as well
as Leach's own treatment of the Kachin political system are famous examples from
an earlier era. These two studies, and others like them, have generated a very large
secondary literature of exegesis and disputation. It is not only the brilliance of the
hypotheses that has raised doubt and controversy, but also the scantiness of material which would enable others to test them. For example, Evans-Pritchard's discussion of feuding amongst the Nuer is couched in generalized terms. No names
or locations are given and there are no references to specific instances. It is unlikely
that he ever witnessed the unfolding of a feud. Similarly, and for the same reason,
in his discussion of warfare we only learn about the pattern of alliances—the
famous discussion of fission and fusion amongst segments in the political system.
We are not presented with the details of how warring parties are recruited, of mobilization, of the size and composition of the forces involved, of how engagements
occur, or even about their frequency.[6] This is not intended as a criticism of the
exemplary quality of Evans-Pritchard's field research or analysis. Yet it remains
the case that his account should be regarded as a set of brilliant hypotheses. The
testing of these hypotheses would require both different material and more detailed

---

[4] Much fieldwork data is also 'pre-collected' in the sense that it is encapsulated in the experience of
informants and the anthropologist elicits and collects it. In the case of both archives and informants,
the problem is the same one of locating and gaining access to sources. Archival sources, however, have
the advantage of being better stored and catalogued.

[5] I estimate that the present study has required three years of archival research, about another two
years of data preparation, and about four years of analysis. This does not include the time acquiring
skills in languages, palaeography, programming, and in coding and debugging programs.

[6] He records that he has seen camps and tribal sections massed for war and 'on the verge of fighting', but no further details are mentioned (Evans-Pritchard 1940: 152). This is particularly interesting
in view of his analysis of the Nuer political system. In that analysis it is villages, not camps, that are
treated as political units.

material than Evans-Pritchard presents about the processes involved in both feuding and warfare.

This introduces the problem of time and process. The difficulty is that anthropologists often do not have access to evidence about process, but can only make inferences about it. The limited amount of time that can be spent in the field, even if that fieldwork is 'extended' into the past using the memory and recall of informants (to create a very extended 'ethnographic present'), may still only reveal enough evidence to suggest, rather than document, the presence of shadowy patterns. As this study has shown, archival sources may provide a possible solution to the problem of shallow time depth. The continuous run of source material stretching over decades or centuries may permit the examination of processes and the testing of hypotheses about them. We have been particularly fortunate in having access to the rich sources of the Dubrovnik archives that provide this kind of depth.

The very large amount of evidence stretching over a half-century concerning office-holding enabled us to show, first, that the Great Council increased markedly in size over the period albeit not uniformly. Second, it also showed how the changing 'shape' of the council affected competition for office and the structure of the office hierarchy.

Our account of the council and of Ragusan government falls within that type of historiography which the Comaroffs refer to as the 'historical study of social institutions' (1992: 21). In this respect it may be helpful to outline their comments about it. One of the difficulties with this type of study, as they point out, is its problematic transition 'from data to generalization, even to structure, history to form' (ibid.). Their objection is to the rigidity of an earlier type of structural-functional analysis and its insensitivity to the negotiated, labile character of practice. They then point out that while this kind of history may be suggestive, when clothed in statistical garb and framed in terms of 'principles' and ascriptive norms, appearances may be quite misleading. Worse, when arguments are buttressed with numerically based generalizations, they 'may manufacture misinformation' (ibid.: 22). In the particular case of the Zulu succession struggles they refer to, it is the logic of practice which gives these struggles form. But how do we show that such struggles have a logic and a form unless we can show that there is a pattern to the similarities and differences? There are, I suggest, several different issues involved.

First, is it the case that numerically based conclusions, drawn from this information, manufacture misinformation because of their persuasive form and the 'enchantment' of statistical treatment (ibid.)? They may do so. Any form of representation may conceal, enchant, or misinform. It may also reveal, disenchant, or inform. No form of representation—words, pictures, tables of statistics—is privileged in either respect. If statistics are more likely to enchant than words, it is because anthropologists are much less sophisticated in the use and understanding of the former.

I would argue that numerical summaries can draw attention the possibility of form. They may also draw attention to range, variation, and the very provisional and problematic nature of analytical categories.[7] It was, for example, the range in dowry quantities that enabled us to test the suggestion that dowries were associated with the levelling of income inequalities amongst the patriciate. Similarly, it was the variation in Great Council representation amongst the several *casate* that led to the very detailed analysis of *casata* size, their political clout in council elections, and the problems of mobilizing agnates in political affairs. Finally, and most important, while the analysis of the hierarchy of office depended upon detailed numerical analysis, that analysis rested upon the logic of practice. Indeed, the argument about office contested the notion that incumbents passed a series of offices that were arranged according to a normative order.

This book has not attempted a demographic analysis of the conditions that led to Great Council growth. That kind of analysis would require kinds of information which the Dubrovnik archives do not possess for our period. But while fertility schedules and similar materials are not available, it does not mean that this avenue of enquiry is closed. It may be possible to 'reverse engineer' Ragusa's demographic regime using computer simulation by working from what is known about Ragusa and interpolating missing material from comparable sites such as Florence. As mentioned above, the potential significance of computer simulations for both anthropology and history is very great. In contrast to the usual direction of scientific explanation, which is from complexity to simplicity, simulation starts with simplicity and gradually introduces complexity to more closely mirror the reality of the phenomena we are attempting to understand.

Turning to the changing shape of the Great Council and its significance for competition for office, what might be considered a single process is here actually the intersection of several. One of these is the yearly round of elections and another is the entry, ageing, and death of council members. Both of these are complex, as is the interaction between them. For example, it might have been assumed that the calendar of elections is relatively simple since the dates for elections to particular offices tend to be fixed to particular parts of the year in an annual cycle. Yet, in the case of one office at least, we were able to show that over the period of a decade the date of election (to the office of *Conte de Stagno*) tended to drift later and later in the round of elections. The demonstration of this process depended upon annual election results stretching over a decade.

The analysis underlying the changing shape of the Great Council was rather different. Here a succession of 'census' years were chosen which were taken to represent the state of affairs on the council at five-yearly intervals. The series could be likened to a succession of 'ethnographic presents' each with a depth of one

---

[7] The work of the Manchester school contains well-known examples. Turner's detailed analysis of 'Social Dramas' in Ndembu villages is widely admired, but the persuasiveness of this material depends upon Turner's careful prior analysis of quantitative data in the opening chapters (1957: xviii; see also Mitchell 1967).

calendar year. The period of a calendar year is arbitrary. While it may help to reveal trends across a spread of years, it also conceals. We know, for example, that individuals were generally unavailable as candidates for office when they held an incumbency. Thus, in the January elections of one of our 'census' years, only certain men would be available to be nominated and contest a post. As the election year developed, other men would become available as their terms of office expired, and still others would become ineligible to contest posts if they had been elected to an office in the meantime. The succession of periods of availability and unavailability would be different for different men. More importantly for purposes of analysing competition, these successions of periods would bring some men into direct competition yet prevent competition between others. The presence and significance of such patterns, if patterns there be, are hidden in the view we obtain through the series of census years. To examine them we would need more material stretching over a continuous span of years.

Similarly, series of census years may be said to show a process of growth stretching over a number of years, but it is important to note the senses in which this rendering of 'process' is misleading. The fairly uniform development in numbers shown by the succession of five-yearly censuses disguises a period of no growth in the early part of our half-century. This was indicated but not explained. It also hides any disturbances created by the two periods of plague and makes the 'process' of growth and replacement appear to be much smoother than it probably was. The occasional plagues created obvious disturbances. In this analysis we have not examined the plagues and their consequences for competition and office-holding. That examination might consider the succession of elections, marriages, and the like for a continuous period of years leading up to the onset of the plague, during the time of the plague itself, and then again for a comparable continuous period after the plague—three 'ethnographic presents', back-to-back. The episodic quality of these plagues suggests that any effects they may have set in train are also likely to be episodic, but we have not developed on this topic in our analysis except tangentially with reference to marriage and kinship.

We were able, however, to show how the changing size of the inner circle affected the ability of more junior men to hold office. In times when there were more senior men, their control cascaded down the hierarchy of offices. We were also able to explore with the same materials the effects that this would have on differently sized cohorts at different times. This is an examination of 'process' in a limited sense and only in a narrow area, but it has given both hope and substance to my conviction that if the collaboration between history and anthropology is to be fruitful, both disciplines must attempt to theorize and operationalize this notion.

Anthropological analysis works within a frame of an 'ethnographic present', an arbitrary period with indefinite boundaries. Time disappears within the parameters of that frame. It is made to disappear in order to permit the study of interconnections. It is not that anthropology, or anthropologists, are insensitive to the passage of time or to the significance of particular 'times' or historical movements, as contemporary concern with issues such as globalization or the information age clearly indicate. Rather, their working heuristic forces its temporary suspension. But then how is it to be reintroduced? How can process be studied? These are important questions which are likely to provoke multiple answers. One possible answer, suggested by our analysis, is to join with historians in examining the historical record. In instances such as the rich sources concerning Ragusa/Dubrovnik, this record enables the anthropologist to transcend some of the limitations of both time and place.

APPENDIX A

Surnames/*Casata* Names

Forms used in this study	Alternative forms
Babalio*	Bobali
	Bobalević (Sl.)
Baraba*	
Batalo*	Baseglio
	Basero
	Basilio
	Batal (Sl.)
Benessa*	Benesa
	Benešić (Sl.)
Binçola	Binzola*
	Binčulić (Sl.)
Bocinolo	Bucignolo*
	Bučinčić (Sl.)
Bodaça	Bodaza*
	Bodacia
	Bodačić (Sl.)
Bona*	Bunić (Sl.)
Bonda*	Bunda
	Bundić (Sl.)
Buchia*	Bucha
	Buča (Sl.)
Caboga*	Chaboga
	Kabušić (Sl.)
Calich*	Kaličić (Sl.)
Crosio*	Crose
	Crosi
	Crusi
	Krusić (Sl.)
Georgio	Zorzi*
	Çorçi
	Šurgović (Sl.)
Getaldo*	Ghetaldo
	Getaldić (Sl.)
Gleda*	Gleya
	Gledić (Sl.)
Goçe	Goze*
	Gozze

Forms used in this study	Alternative forms
	Gučetić (Sl.)
Gondola*	Gundula
	Gondula
	Gundulić (Sl.)
Grade	Gradi*
	Grede
	Gradić (Sl.)
Luca	Lucha*
	Lučić (Sl.)
Lucari	Luchari*
	Lucaro
	Lukarević (Sl.)
Martinussio	Martinus*
	Martinušić (Sl.)
Mençe	Menze*
	Menčetić (Sl.)
Mlaschagna	Mlaschogna*
	Mlasković (Sl.)
Palmota*	Palmotić (Sl.)
Poça	Poza*
	Pucić (Sl.)
Proculo*	Pruglović (Sl.)
Prodanello	Prodanelo*
	Prodančić (Sl.)
Ragnina*	Ranina
	Ranenić (Sl.)
Resti*	Ristis
	Rastić (Sl.)
Saraca	Saracha*
	Saračić (Sl.)
Sorgo*	Surgo
	Sorkočević (Sl.)
Tudisio*	Tudišević (Sl.)
Volçe	Volzo*
	Volcio
Zamagna	Zamagno*
	Šamanović (Sl.)
Zrieva	Çrieva*
	Cerva
	Crijević (Sl.)

Notes:

* designates the form most often encountered in the archival sources of this period

(Sl) Slavic form

APPENDIX B

Sources, Data, and the Database

The material for this study derives from several sources. One important source is the so-called *Specchio* or Chancellor's Handbook (*Manuali Practici del Cancelliere*, 1). Two major parts of this handbook have been used. The first part lists all of the offices filled from the ranks of the patriciate and, under each office, its incumbents and the date of the office. There is also some additional information on who replaced whom in office and the reasons why the person was replaced. All of this information has been entered into a file of the database called 'Offhold'. This file consists of over 7,500 records. The second part of the *Specchio* lists all of the members of the Great Council from about 1449 to 1499. From 1455 it also records the date of entry and, from 1472, the age of the entrant. For some men it includes the year of death and (very occasionally) the place and cause of death.

All of the information from the *Specchio* concerning Great Council membership, including the order in which the names are listed, has been entered into another file in the database called 'Specchio'. In both files personal names have been replaced with identification numbers. Names which appear in the documents are usually abbreviated. While the given name may appear in full, the father's and grandfather's names, when they are included, seldom do. The deciphering of names is both a science and an art. It depends upon a long familiarity with the handwriting of the clerk and his system of abbreviations. It also depends upon knowing in advance what he might have intended to write. Clerks were not overly concerned about maintaining consistency in the way names were rendered. The computer database is invaluable here. As a document is added to a file in the database, the computer checks the name against the list of persons with similar names or against all persons known to have been alive at that date. Computer programs have been written to identify persons and to spot anomalous or problematic cases for more detailed checking. Additional programs have been written to check names and dates for consistency.

The (several) forms of personal names are contained in a third file called 'Names'. Similarly, the (several) names for the various offices in 'Offhold' have also been replaced with another set of identification numbers which are linked to another file called 'Offices'. In addition to the office name and identification number, the 'Offices' file contains information concerning the number of incumbents, age restrictions concerning the office, salary, term of office, references to legislation concerning the office, and so on. Since these separate files are linked through identification numbers and dates, complex linkages and searches are possible. The diagram indicates some of the links.

A second source of information concerning offices comes from the minutes of the Great Council (*Act. Maior.*). For every fifth year between 1440 and 1490, I recorded the outcomes of the various elections to office. There are over a thousand such elections. This information has been entered into two further files. One file called 'Ballots' includes the ballot (with a unique identification number), office identification number, date, agenda item, number of

persons voting, and so on. Another called 'Candidates' includes ballot number, name identification number, votes for, votes against, votes abstaining, and so on.

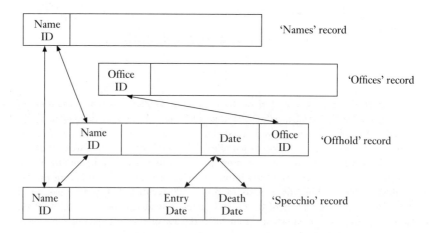

Other files contain information on kinship and marriage. The most important of these
is 'Genealogy'. In addition to the name identification number, it includes information on
genealogical position (the 'Hackenberg Number': see Appendix C) within the *casata*, gender,
year of birth, death year, status, and other matters concerning personal history. For purposes of tracing kinship links, it also includes the mother's identification number. Further
files on marriage contain husband's and wife's identification numbers and information about
marriage contracts and dowry bequests.

The Ragusan database is evolving and expanding. New files are added and older files and
records are amended and corrected. Therefore, it is misleading to speak of the database as
if it were a single, finished entity. As the analysis and writing of this study proceeded, the
database was being continually refined and expanded. That process continues.

APPENDIX C

Politically Active Men, 1440–1490

Following is a list of the 813 men presumed to have been politically active sometime between 1440 and 1490. They are listed alphabetically by surname, name, father's name, and then grandfather's name. The form adopted here is that found in Mahnken's published genealogies (1960). This ('standard') form often differs from the several forms found in manuscript sources. I have adopted Mahnken's forms to assist those who might wish compare this account with her text. The identification number in the first column is given to help distinguish between individuals with identical names. It is also intended to facilitate those who wish to consult the Ragusan Database where the 'Names' file contains the 'standard' Mahnken forms as well as various forms found in the Dubrovnik archives. The 'Names' file also contains references to archival sources for the several forms.

Column 6 contains the Hackenberg Number. It is named after Robert Hackenberg who first outlined the system (1967). This series of two-digit numbers encodes an individual's '*casata*' affiliation and genealogical location in Mahnken's genealogies (as amended). The first two digits of the Hackenberg Number identify the *casata*. The following pairs of digits indicate the generation level and the birth order position of the person in the sibling group. Thus, in the Hackenberg Number of Andreas Volçius Babalio (01-040102), '01-' indicates that Andreas is from the Babalio *casata*. To locate Andreas we follow the pairs of digits from the founding ancestor. Thus, Andreas is a descendant of Blasius, the fourth sibling in the founding generation (04). Andreas's ancestor in the next generation is Volçius, the oldest sibling (01). Andreas himself is the second sibling (02).

Column 7 shows the year when the person entered the Great Council. From 1454 onwards the year of entry is known. Years prior to 1454 have been estimated using marriage data, materials on office-holding, and the person's relative position in the listing of Great Council members (*Specchio*: fos. 382–392v). If the source of the entry year is taken from a ballot ('Ballot'), a nomination for office ('lstNom'), or from a list of office-holders ('lstOff'), this is indicated in the next column (8). Column 9 is the last known year of political activity. Usually this is the year of death unless indicated otherwise in the next column (10). In most cases the year of death is that recorded in Mahnken. Otherwise the year may be given as the end of the period 1440–90 ('Period'), the year of the last known office or nomination for office ('LastOff' or 'LastNom'), or the year the person entered a religious order ('EntRel'). In instances where my information differs from that contained in Mahnken, this is indicated in the notes.

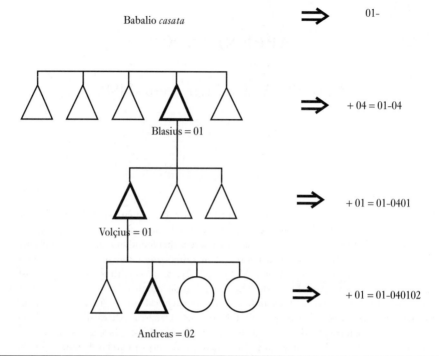

Babalio *casata*   ⟹   01-

⟹   + 04 = 01-04

Blasius = 01

Volçius = 01

⟹   + 01 = 01-0401

⟹   + 01 = 01-040102

Andreas = 02

ID (1)	Surname (2)	Name (3)	Father (4)	Grandfather (5)	Hackenberg Number (6)	Entry year (7) (8)	End year (9) (10)
18	Babalio	Andreas	Volçius		01-040102	1421	1473
38	"	Benedetto	Savinus		01-040404	1433	1454[1]
23	"	Blasius	Andreas	Volçius	01-04010203	1460	1490 Period
51	"	Blasius	Nicola	Savinus	01-04041002	1488	1518
32	"	Blasius	Savinus		01-040402	1420	1476
16	"	Blasius	Volço	Blasius	01-0401010301	1473	1482
26	"	Franciscus	Andreas	Volçius	01-04010206	1464	1490 LastOff
43	"	Givcho	Savinus		01-040406	1419	1469
46	"	Hieronymus	Givcho	Savinus	01-04040603	1472	1489 LastOff
35	"	Johannes	Blasius	Savinus	01-04040203	1471	1490 LastOff
20	"	Junius	Andreas	Volçius	01-04010202	1455	1507
47	"	Marinus	Givcho	Savinus	01-04040604	1476	1493
3	"	Michael	Volçe		01-030103	1425	1456
50	"	Nicola	Savinus		01-040410	1427	1482
6	"	Paulus	Michiel	Volçe	01-03010303	1468	1524
24	"	Petrus	Andreas	Volçius	01-04010204	1464	1490 Period
48	"	Raphael	Givcho	Savinus	01-04040605	1485	1493
33	"	Savinus	Blasius	Savinus	01-04040201	1467	1524
7	"	Savinus	Michiel	Volçe	01-03010304	1474	1522
2451	"	Savinus	Nicola	Savinus	01-04041001	1479	1489 LastOff

This listing omits the neighbouring notables Ivaniš Vlatković, Vladislav (the son of Herceg Stefan Tomašević), and Žarko Vlatoković (*Specchio*: fo. 386) and Radinoj Vlatković (ibid.: fo. 386v), who were given seats on the Great Council but who held no offices.

[1] Mahnken's entry for the death year of 1460 is incorrect. He was holding office as late as April 1453 (*Specchio*: s.v. *Lavorieri de pagamento in Stagno*) but had died by the time his daughter was betrothed in November 1454 (*Pacta* 2: fo. 27).

ID (1)	Surname (2)	Name (3)	Father (4)	Grandfather (5)	Hackenberg Number (6)	Entry year (7)	(8)	End year (9)	(10)
34	Babalio	Simon	Blasius	Savinus	01-04040202	1467		1499	
4	"	Volçius	Michiel	Volçe	01-03010301	1457		1465	
15	"	Volço	Blasius	Volçius	01-04010103	?		1457	
71	Batalo	Basilius	Marcho		03-010104010602	1465		1478	
69	"	Marcho	Basellus		03-0101040106	1430		1465	
81	"	Matcho	Basellus		03-0101040107	1437		1444	
58	"	Nicolino	Francho		03-0101010205	1419		1475	
74	"	Paulus	Marcho		03-010104010603	1465		1514	
57	"	Stephanus	Francho		03-0101010204	1431		1472	
108	Benessa	Andreas	Franciscus	Marghus	04-0501010103	1465		1490	Period
84	"	Damian	Simcho	Dymcus	04-01030202	1437		1482	
88	"	Damian	Simon	Damian	04-010302020301	1488		1500	
109	"	Franciscus	Andreas	Franciscus	04-050101010301	1488		1530	
105	"	Franciscus	Marghus		04-05010101	1432		1469	
113	"	Franciscus	Stephanus	Marghus	04-0501010302	1464		1517	
112	"	Johannes	Stephanus	Marghus	04-0501010301	1464		1469	
120	"	Marinus	Stephanus	Marghus	04-0501010310	1473		1485	
2933	"	Nicola	Damian	Simcho	04-0103020213	1473		1495	
119	"	Pancratius	Stephanus	Marghus	04-0501010309	1470		1494	
92	"	Pasqual	Damian	Simcho	04-0103020204	1446		1476	
87	"	Simon	Damian	Simcho	04-0103020203	1445		1490	Period
99	"	Stefanus	Damian	Simcho	04-0103020209	1465		1490	LastOff
111	"	Stephanus	Marghus		04-05010103	1425		1461	
2932	"	Ziprian	Damian	Simcho	04-0103020212	1476		1493	
131	Binçola	Antonio	Dobre		05-0103	?		1446	
134	"	Franciscus	Çovan	Dobre	05-010401	1473		1482	
136	"	Marinus	Çovan	Dobre	05-010403	1487		1518	
140	"	Martholus	Andreas		05-03	1416		1445	
127	"	Nicola	Dobre		05-0101	1433		1470	
135	"	Nicola	Çovan	Dobre	05-010402	1477		1482	
133	"	Çovan	Dobre		05-0104	1419		1482	
424	Bocinolo	Marinus	Micho	Marinus	06-010601	1477		1490	Period
423	"	Micho	Marinus		06-0106	1414		1466	
203	Bona	Aloisius	Nicola	Marin	08-02030205020401	1483		1490	Period
233	"	Andreas	Nicola	Vlachussa	08-030301020602	1476		1504	
256	"	Antonio	Luca	Zugno	08-030301040107	1471		1490	LastOff
148	"	Antonius	Symoneto	Piero	08-02030201010103	1470		1512	
258	"	Bartholo	Luca	Zugno	08-030301040109	1489		1525	
281	"	Bartolus	Maroe	Luxa	08-0303010907	1460		1494	
175	"	Bernardo	Nicola	Symcus	08-02030201020607	1482		1490	Period
328	"	Bernardus	Tomko	Marinus	08-0303020207	1454	1stOff	1505	
238	"	Blasius	Marinus	Vlachussa	08-030301020801	1467		1482	
234	"	Blasius	Nicola	Vlachussa	08-030301020603	1480		1489	
2453	"	Damianus	Simon	Martinus	08-02030201040201[2]	1480		1517	
152	"	Elia	Piero	Symcus	08-02030201010203	1436		1489	
222	"	Francescho	Çohan	Vlachussa	08-030301020301	1452	1stOff	1501	
2466	"	Franciscus	Simon	Martinus	08-02030201040202[3]	1488		1539	
252	"	Georgius	Luca	Zugno	08-030301040103	1460		1495	
277	"	Georgius	Natalis	Maroe	08-030301090401	1482		1524	
318	"	Giovanni	Tomko	Marinus	08-0303020202	1437		1489	
170	"	Hieronymus	Nicola	Symcus	08-020302010602	1459		1479	
158	"	Jacobus	Elia	Piero	08-0203020101306	1489		1534	
300	"	Jacobus	Nicola	Sarachin	08-030302010203	1477		1507	
151	"	Jacomo	Piero	Symcus	08-020302010102	1428		1484	
337	"	Jeronimus	Lucas	Marinus	08-0303020701	1454		1459	EntRel
153	"	Johannes	Elia	Piero	08-02030201010301	1476		1503	
235	"	Johannes	Nicola	Vlachussa	08-030301020604	1488		1490	Period
249	"	Junius	Luca	Zugno	08-030301040101	1460		1518	

[2] *Specchio*: fo. 391. Not recorded in Mahnken's genealogies.
[3] *Specchio*: fo. 392. Not recorded in Mahnken's genealogies.

ID (1)	Surname (2)	Name (3)	Father (4)	Grandfather (5)	Hackenberg Number (6)	Entry year (7)	(8)	End year (9)	(10)
271	Bona	Luca	Maroe	Luxa	08-0303010901	1424		1445	
248	"	Luca	Çugno	Luxa	08-0303010401	1433		1484	
228	"	Lucas	Çohan	Vlachussa	08-0303010020304	1466		1473	
339	"	Lucianus	Lucas	Marinus	08-0303020703	1457		1482	
160	"	Marco	Piero	Symcus	08-020302010105	1442		1481	
191	"	Marin	Michiel		08-0203020502	1411		1461	
291	"	Marin	Sarachin	Marinus	08-0303020101	1434		1457	
310	"	Marin	Tomko	Marinus	08-0303020201	1430		1465	
352	"	Marin	Zupan	Marinus	08-0303020805	1464		1483	
193	"	Marinus	Michiel	Marin	08-02030205020101	1471		1510	
273	"	Marinus	Paladin	Maroe	08-0303010090201	1478		1500	
2446	"	Marinus	Si(?)	Mich(?)	08-[4]	1477		1501	
182	"	Marinus	Stephano	Symcus	08-020302010704	1472		1490	LastOff
183	"	Marinus	Symcus		08-0203020108	1430		1466	
237	"	Marinus	Vlachussa	Luxa	08-0303010208	1429		1465	
270	"	Maroe	Luxa		08-03030109	1426		1449	
2447	"	Martholiza	Ma(?)		08-[5]	1477		1490	Period
215	"	Martin	Marin	Michiel	08-020302050208	1454	Ballot	1505	
226	"	Matheus	Çohan	Vlachussa	08-030301020302	1460		1490	
320	"	Mathio	Tomko	Marinus	08-0303020204	1443	1stOff	1493	
260	"	Mathio	Çugno	Luxa	08-0303010402	1451	1stOff	1454	LastOff
254	"	Michael	Luca	Zugno	08-030301040105	1468	1stOff	1496	
241	"	Michael	Marinus	Vlachussa	08-030301020803	1481		1487	
232	"	Michael	Nicola	Vlachussa	08-030301020601	1470		1523	
359	"	Michael	Zupan	Marinus	08-0303020811	1476		1479	
192	"	Michiel	Marin	Michiel	08-0203020501	1448	1stOff	1468	LastOff
171	"	Michiel	Nicola	Symcus	08-020302010603	1460		1498[6]	
265	"	Micho	Luxa		08-0303020105	1467		1478	LastOff
276	"	Natalis	Maroe	Luxa	08-0303010904	1430		1499	
202	"	Nicola	Marin	Michiel	08-020302050204	1443		1482	
297	"	Nicola	Sarachin	Marinus	08-0303020102	1425		1479	
168	"	Nicola	Symcus		08-0203020106	1421		1465	
231	"	Nicola	Vlachussa		08-0303010206	1433		1476	
354	"	Nicola	Zupan	Marinus	08-0303020807	1467		1482	
239	"	Nicolaus	Marinus	Vlachussa	08-030301020802	1471		1523	
257	"	Nicolo	Luca	Zugno	08-030301040108	1483		1500	
200	"	Orsatus	Marin	Michiel	08-020302050203	1447	Ballot	1492	
272	"	Paladin	Maroe	Luxa	08-0303010902	1450	1stOff	1463	LastOff
154	"	Petrus	Elia	Piero	08-02030201010302	1480		1490	Period
143	"	Piero	Symcus		08-0203020101	1418		1454	
326	"	Polo	Tomko	Marinus	08-0303020205	1450		1460	EntRel.
327	"	Sarachinus	Tomko	Marinus	08-0303020206	1457		1460	
157	"	Simon	Elia	Piero	08-02030201010305	1488		1519	
198	"	Simon	Marin	Michiel	08-020302050202	1447	1stOff	1458	LastOff
166	"	Simon	Martinus	Symcus	08-020302010402	1444		1490	Period
204	"	Simon	Nicola	Marin	08-02030205020402	1489		1493	
179	"	Simon	Stephano	Symcus	08-020302010701	1467		1474	LastOff
178	"	Stephano	Symcus		08-0203020107	1421		1454	LastOff
312	"	Stephanus	Marin	Tomko	08-030302020102	1487		1517	
302	"	Stephanus	Nicola	Sarachin	08-030302010205	1477		1482	
184	"	Symon	Marinus	Symcus	08-020302010801	1478		1489	
144	"	Symoneto	Piero	Symcus	08-020302010101	1425		1470	
329	"	Thoma	Bernardus	Tomko	08-030302020701	1488		1490	Period
311	"	Thomas	Marin	Tomko	08-030302020101	1465		1501	
347	"	Zupan	Marinus		08-03030208	1420		1464	
221	"	Çohan	Vlachussa	Luxa	08-0303010203	1425		1465	

[4] *Specchio*: fo. 390. Insufficient information. No likely candidate in Mahnken's genealogies.
[5] *Specchio*: fo. 390v. Insufficient information. No likely candidate in Mahnken's genealogies.
[6] *Specchio*: fo. 378. Mahnken gives the date of death as 1488.

ID (1)	Surname (2)	Name (3)	Father (4)	Grandfather (5)	Hackenberg Number (6)	Entry year (7)	(8)	End year (9)	(10)
247	Bona	Çugno	Luxa		08-03030104	1407		1460	
362	Bonda	Andrea			09-02	1407		1442	
365	"	Andreas	Tripho	Andrea	09-020102	1454	1stOff	1488	
371	"	Marinus	Tripho	Andrea	09-020106	1470		1490	LastOff
373	"	Maroe	Andrea		09-0202	1435		1447	
374	"	Nixa	Andrea		09-0203	1435		1485	
368	"	Raphael	Tripho	Andrea	09-020103	1464		1482	
363	"	Tripho	Andrea		09-0201	1425		1465	
366	"	Triphon	Andreas	Tripho	09-02010201	1489		1490	Period
405	Buchia	Andreas	Marinus	Dobre	10-01010103040303	1474		1485	
404	"	Benedictus	Marinus	Dobre	10-01010103040302	1473		1485	
397	"	Christophorus	Givcho	Dobre	10-01010103040203	1474		1510	
388	"	Dobre	Triphon		10-0101010304	1420		1456	
390	"	Dobruscho	Tripcho	Dobre	10-01010103040101	1460		1518	
403	"	Dobruschus	Marinus	Dobre	10-01010103040301	1470		1518	
396	"	Francischus	Givcho	Dobre	10-01010103040202	1473		1539	
394	"	Givcho	Dobre	Triphon	10-010101030402	1430		1478	LastOff
391	"	Johannes	Tripcho	Dobre	10-01010103040102	1472		1483[7]	
409	"	Junius	Dobre	Triphon	10-01010103040406	1451	1stOff	1488	
402	"	Marinus	Dobre	Triphon	10-010101030403	1446	Ballot	1482	
392	"	Natalis	Tripcho	Dobre	10-01010103040103	1466		1486	LastOff
406	"	Nicola	Marinus	Dobre	10-01010103040304	1483		1515	
389	"	Tripcho	Dobre	Triphon	10-01010103040401	1425		1477	
512	Caboga	Antonius	Nicola	Maroe	11-0405010405	1450		1464	
2448	"	Bernardus	Giovanni		11-01020101010201	1478		1490[8]	
443	"	Bernardus	Thomas	Nicolaus	11-01020101010501	1484		1505	
507	"	Blasius	Nicola	Maroe	11-040501040404	1431		1493	
456	"	Christophorus	Nicolaus	Giue	11-010201010115	1465		1489	LastOff
2473	"	Christophorus	Thomas	Nicolaus	11-01020101010504	1490		1535[9]	
524	"	Daniel	Marin	Daniel	11-040501050401	1488		1503	
519	"	Daniel	Maroe		11-04050105	1421		1461	
455	"	Franciscus	Nicolaus	Giue	11-010201010114	1465		1478	
510	"	Francisus	Blasius	Nicola	11-040501040403	1489		1525	
473	"	Franco	Çorçi	Givchus	11-030101010201	1450		1477	
486	"	Georgius	Nicola	Çorçi	11-03010101020701	1485		1494	
432	"	Giovanni	Nicolaus	Giue	11-010201010102	1434		1480	
474	"	Johannes	Franco	Çorçi	11-03010101020101	1484		1490	Period
439	"	Johannes	Martolo	Nicolaus	11-01020101010401	1488		1519	
517	"	Johannes	Nicola	Maroe	11-0405010408	1464		1490	LastOff
523	"	Marin	Daniel	Maroe	11-0405010504	1454	Ballot	1500	
475	"	Marinus	Franco	Çorçi	11-03010101020102	1486		1490	Period
525	"	Martoliça	Daniel	Maroe	11-0405010505	1454	1stOff	1473	LastOff
438	"	Martolo	Nicolaus	Giue	11-010201010104	1454	1stOff	1482	
434	"	Mathias	Giovanni	Nicolaus	11-01020101010202	1489		1532	
513	"	Nicola	Antonius	Nicola	11-040501040501	1478		1487	
503	"	Nicola	Maroe		11-04050104	1420		1457	
496	"	Nicola	Pasqual		11-0402020201	1424		1460	LastOff
485	"	Nicola	Çorçi	Givchus	11-030101010207	1448		1490	Period
508	"	Nicolaus	Blasius	Nicola	11-040501040401	1482		1486	
430	"	Nicolaus	Giue		11-010201010101	1407		1453	
445	"	Nicolaus	Thomas	Nicolaus	11-01020101010503	1489		1490	Period
495	"	Pasqual	Nichola		11-0402020202	1434		1449	
497	"	Pasqualis	Nicola	Pasqual	11-040202020101	1477		1524	
442	"	Thomas	Nicolaus	Giue	11-010201010105	1454	1stOff	1494	
472	"	Çorçi	Givchus		11-0301010102	1411		1468	
529	Calich	Dobre	Junius	Dobre	12-010101	1449		1457	

[7] *Specchio*: fo. 389v. No death year given in Mahnken.
[8] *Specchio*: fo. 390v. No death year given in Mahnken.
[9] *Specchio*: fo. 392v. No death year given in Mahnken.

ID (1)	Surname (2)	Name (3)	Father (4)	Grandfather (5)	Hackenberg Number (6)	Entry year (7)	(8)	End year (9)	(10)
528	Calich	Junius	Dobre		12-0101	1411		1457	
531	"	Michael	Junius	Dobre	12-010103	1443		1513[10]	
532	"	Nicola	Junius	Dobre	12-010104	1444		1450[11]	
530	"	Piero	Junius	Dobre	12-010102	1447	1stOff	1465	
533	"	Simon	Junius	Dobre	12-010105	1457		1487	
683	Crosio	Andrea	Michiel	Marinus	14-010802	1451	1stOff	1467	
2459	"	Dragoe	Andrea	Michiel	14-01080201[12]	1486		1490	Period
687	"	Georgius	Michiel	Marinus	14-010807	1467		1470	EntRel
670	"	Junius	Jacomo	Marinus	14-010106	1450		1500	
669	"	Marin	Jacomo	Marinus	14-010105	1426		1490	
682	"	Marin	Michiel	Marinus	14-010801	1452	1stOff	1469	LastOff
672	"	Marin	Çugno	Marinus	14-010201	1426		1451	
681	"	Michiel	Marinus		14-0108	1423		1445	
2474	"	Sarachinus	Mar(?)		14-[13]	1490		1518	
2315	Georgio	Aloisius	Šišmund	Junius	36-050202040210	1475		1479	
2341	"	Aloviz	Junius	Give	36-0502020410	1434		1481	
2313	"	Antonius	Šišmund		36-050202040208	1468		1500	
2323	"	Damian	Junius	Give	36-0502020408	1432		1458	
2239	"	Francho	Nixa		36-0101010408	1421		1466	
2302	"	Franciscus	Šišmund	Junius	36-050202040202	1460		1490	LastOff
2334	"	Franciscus	Nicho	Junius	36-050202040901	1472		1512	
2244	"	Giovanni	Maroe	Matheus	36-010103010102	1427		1463	
2324	"	Guigno	Damian	Junius	36-050202040801	1463		1479	
2300	"	Šišmund	Junius	Give	36-0502020402	1421		1471	LastOff
2248	"	Jacobus	Giovanni	Maroe	36-01010301010204	1476		1512	
2277	"	Jakob	Matheus		36-0101030107	1418		1462	
2329	"	Jeronimus	Damian	Junius	36-050202040806	1477		1490	
2301	"	Johannes	Šišmund	Junius	36-050202040201	1459		1527	
2342	"	Junius	Aloviz	Junius	36-050202041001	1480		1490	Period
2245	"	Junius	Giovanni	Maroe	36-01010301010201	1467		1512	
2307	"	Junius	Šišmund	Junius	36-050202040204	1464		1499	
2298	"	Junius	Maroe	Junius	36-050202040102	1452	1stOff	1467	LastOff
2235	"	Leonardo	Nixa		36-0101010407	1433		1449	
2238	"	Leonardus	Nicola	Leonardo	36-01010104070201	1489		1546	
2343	"	Lucas	Aloviz	Junius	36-050202041002	1479		1490	Period
2328	"	Marinus	Damian	Junius	36-050202040805	1468		1486	
2246	"	Marinus	Giovanni	Maroe	36-01010301010202	1471		1490	LastOff
2299	"	Marinus	Junius	Maroe	36-05020204010201	1476		1490	LastOff
2336	"	Marinus	Nicho	Junius	36-050202040903	1476		1490	
2296	"	Maroe	Junius	Give	36-0502020401	1419		1457	
2218	"	Maroe	Martholo	Nixa	36-010101040103	1438		1498	
2240	"	Martolus	Francho	Nixa	36-010101040801	1465		1476	LastOff
2219	"	Martolus	Maroe	Martholo	36-010101040010301	1481		1526	
2247	"	Matheus	Giovanni	Maroe	36-01010301010203	1474		1484	
2267	"	Matheus	Vlachusa	Matheus	36-010103010401	1452	1stOff	1525	
2256	"	Matko	Nikša	Matheus	36-010103010301	1433		1454	
2333	"	Nicho	Junius	Give	36-0502020409	1435		1490	Period
2237	"	Nicola	Leonardo	Nixa	36-010101040702	1465		1473	LastOff
2260	"	Nicola	Matko	Nikša	36-01010301030104	1470		1484	
2230	"	Nicola	Michael	Nixa	36-010101040501	1463		1503	
2325	"	Nicolo	Damian	Junius	36-050202040802	1463		1524	
2255	"	Nikša	Matheus		36-0101030103	1407		1460	

[10] *Specchio*: fo. 386. Mahnken gives the year of death as 1501.

[11] No year of death is given in Mahnken or can be located in any source. Since Nicola neither held office, nor was nominated for any, it is presumed that he died shortly after entering the Great Council.

[12] *Specchio*: fo. 391v, but no death year recorded. Not recorded in Mahnken's genealogies.

[13] *Specchio*: fo. 392v. Not recorded in Mahnken's genealogies and his genealogical position cannot be accurately determined. He might be the son of either Marin Michiel (ID 682) or Marin Jacomo (ID 669).

ID (1)	Surname (2)	Name (3)	Father (4)	Grandfather (5)	Hackenberg Number (6)	Entry year (7)	(8)	End year (9)	(10)
2303	Georgio	Sigismund	Franciscus	Sigismund	36-05020204020201	1489		1515	
2264	"	Stephano	Nikša	Matheus	36-010103010302	1445	1stOff	1475	
2274	"	Živan	Matheus		36-0101030106	1425		1464	
750	Getaldo	Jacobus	Mathio	Savinus	15-010202	1454		1505	
740	"	Jeronimo	Marin	Savinus	15-010103	1452		1465	
745	"	Johannes	Marin	Savinus	15-010108	1466		1486	
737	"	Marin	Savinus		15-0101	1425		1462	
2907	"	Marinus	Vita	Marin	15-01010703	1488		1557[14]	
749	"	Matheus	Savolin	Mathio	15-01020101	1480		1518	
747	"	Mathio	Savinus		15-0102	1422		1447	
738	"	Savolin	Marin	Savinus	15-010101	1431		1455	LastOff
748	"	Savolin	Mathio	Savinus	15-010201	1449	1stOff	1466	
744	"	Vita	Marin	Savinus	15-010107	1454	Ballot	1505	
1184	Gondola	Andreas	Marinus	Benedetto	17-01020304040403	1488		1539	
1153	"	Antonius	Marin	Nicolinus	17-01020304010107	1484		1478	LastOff
1210	"	Antonius	Çugno	Givcho	17-03030102010302	1480		1534	
1177	"	Benedetto	Marin	Nifficus	17-0102030404	1419		1446	
2469	"	Benedictus	Jo(?)	M(?)	17-[15]	1489		1534	
1149	"	Benedictus	Marin	Nicolinus	17-01020304010103	1470		1518	
1113	"	Benedictus	Pietro	Benko	17-01010203010101	1463		1490	Period
1182	"	Benko	Marinus	Benedetto	17-01020304040401	1471		1490	LastOff
1245	"	Bernardinus	Nicola	Marin	17-03030102030405	1467		1508	
1192	"	Damian	Marin	Nifficus	17-0102030406	1427		1445	
1207	"	Damiano	Givcho	Jacobus	17-030301020102	1429		1479	
1150	"	Daniel	Marin	Nicolinus	17-01020304010104	1477		1488	LastOff
1126	"	Federico	Johannes	Federicus	17-01010203040401	1487		1519	
1160	"	Franciscus	Giovane	Nicolinus	17-01020304010403	1477		1505	
1247	"	Franciscus	Nicola	Marin	17-03030102030406	1468		1525	
1157	"	Giovane	Nicolinus	Marin	17-010203040104	1433		1489	
1252	"	Giovanni	Marin	Jacobus	17-030301020308	1433	1stOff	1480	
1204	"	Givcho	Jacobus		17-0303010201	?		1442	
1249	"	Hieronymo	Marin	Jacobus	17-030301020305	1433		1482	
1170	"	Jacobus	Nicola	Nicolinus	17-01020304010801	1483		1486	LastOff
1256	"	Jacobus	Paladin	Marin	17-03030102030902	1489		1530	
1209	"	Jacobus	Çugno	Givcho	17-03030102010301	1472		1483	
1228	"	Jacomo	Marin	Jacobus	17-030301020301	1440		1473	
1223	"	Jacomo	Paladin	Jacobus	17-03030102020201	1431		1481	
1125	"	Johannes	Federicus	Petrus	17-010102030404	1467		1496	
2463	"	Johannes	Givcho	Jacobus	17-030301020110[16]	1488		1540	
1243	"	Johannes	Nicola	Marin	17-03030102030403	1464		1507	
1154	"	Joseph	Marin	Nicolinus	17-01020304010108	1484		1522	
1173	"	Junius	Marin	Junius	17-01020304020101	1477		1490	Period
1227	"	Marin	Jacobus		17-0303010203	1408		1441	
1229	"	Marin	Jacomo	Marin	17-030301020301	1465		1525[17]	
1172	"	Marin	Junius	Marin	17-010203040201	1407		1486	
1199	"	Marin	Matheus	Marin	17-01020304090	1465	1474		
1146	"	Marin	Nicolinus	Marin	17-01020304010	1428	1462		
1130	"	Marinco	Federicus	Petrus	17-010102030405	1460	Ballot	1475	
1217	"	Marino	Givcho	Jacobus	17-030301020108	1445	1stOff	1511	
1187	"	Marino	Nicola	Benedetto	17-01020304040601	1489		1490	Period
1181	"	Marinus	Benedetto	Marin	17-010203040404	1439		1495	
1162	"	Marinus	Giovane	Nicolinus	17-01020304010405	1488		1517	
1127	"	Marinus	Johannes	Federicus	17-01010203040402	1488		1504	
1239	"	Marinus	Nicola	Marin	17-03030102030401	1454	Ballot	1485	
1198	"	Matheus	Marin	Nifficus	17-0102030409	1426		1468	

[14] *Specchio*: fo. 392. No death year given in Mahnken.
[15] *Specchio*: fo. 392. Not recorded in Mahnken's genealogies and there is insufficient evidence to place him accurately. [16] *Specchio*: fo. 392. Not recorded in Mahnken's genealogies.
[17] *Specchio*: fo. 387v. Mahnken gives the year of death as 1495.

ID (1)	Surname (2)	Name (3)	Father (4)	Grandfather (5)	Hackenberg Number (6)	Entry year (7)	(8)	End year (9)	(10)
1242	Gondola	Michael	Nicola	Marin	17-03030102030402	1454		1490	Period
1166	"	Michael	Nicolinus	Marin	17-010203040105	1430		1459[18]	
1251	"	Michiel	Marin	Jacobus	17-030301020307	1459	Ballot	1463	
1186	"	Nicola	Benedetto	Marin	17-010203040406	1455		1482	
1238	"	Nicola	Marin	Jacobus	17-030301020304	1428		1482	
1169	"	Nicola	Nicolinus	Marin	17-010203040108	1436		1489	
1260	"	Nicola	Paulus		17-030301060 3	1411		1469	
1235	"	Nicolaus	Jacomo	Marin	17-03030102030105	1464		1515	
1148	"	Nicolaus	Marin	Nicolinus	17-01020304010102	1465		1526	
1240	"	Nicolaus	Marinus	Nicola	17-0303010203040101	1489		1542	
1158	"	Nicolinus	Giovane	Nicolinus	17-01020304010401	1486		1490	Period
1147	"	Nicolinus	Marin	Nicolinus	17-01020304010101	1464		1489	LastOff
1176	"	Nixa	Marin	Nifficus	17-0102030403	?		1446	
1254	"	Paladin	Marin	Jacobus	17-030301020309	1432		1489	
1216	"	Paladino	Givcho	Jacobus	17-030301020107	1451		1505[19]	
1250	"	Paulus	Marin	Jacobus	17-030301020306	1444	1stOff	1478	LastOff
1248	"	Petrus	Nicola	Marin	17-03030102030407	1472		1482	
1152	"	Stephanus	Marin	Nicolinus	17-01020304010106	1484		1525	
1208	"	Çugno	Givcho	Jacobus	17-030301020103	1427		1475	
2461	Goçe	Aloisio	Marinus	Aloisius	18-0401010201030801	1487		1525	
770	"	Aloisius	Clemens		18-040101020103	1413		1457	
792	"	Aloisius	Georgius	Aloisius	18-0401010201030701	1488		1522	
846	"	Alovise	Vitcho	Ludovicus	18-04010102020201	?		1457[20]	
823	"	Alovise	Çorçi	Clemens	18-04010102020405	?		1455	
854	"	Alovisio	Johannes	Ludovicus	18-04010102020402	1453		1482	
986	"	Alvise	Çuan		18-040101020909	?		1445	
810	"	Ambrosia	Marinus	Zorzi	18-0401010201040104	1487		1523	
1049	"	Andreas	Polo	Nixa	18-04010305010104	1454		1497	
1011	"	Antonio	Clemens	Viticus	18-040101040103	1411		1448	
1014	"	Antonius	Marino	Antonio	18-0401010401030201	1471		1520	
972	"	Bartholo	Çuan		18-040101020904	1427		1497	
812	"	Bernardus	Marinus	Zorzi	18-0401010201040106	1487		1515	
983	"	Blasius	Stephano	Zuan	18-04010102090803	1473		1494	
911	"	Clemens	Federico	Raphael	18-04010102060507	1467		1511	
880	"	Clemens	Marin	Raphael	18-04010102060202	1427		1482	
1020	"	Clemens	Marino	Antonio	18-0401010401030203	1480		1489	LastOff
994	"	Clemens	Vitticus	Clemens	18-04010104010102	1434		1465	
1012	"	Climento	Antonio	Clemens	18-04010104010301	1433		1482	
1024	"	Climento	Marin	Clemens	18-04010104010401	1452		1495	
1053	"	Damian	Polo	Nixa	18-04010305010107	1450	1stOff	1515	
773	"	Dragoe	Aloisius	Clemens	18-04010102010303	1425		1498	
862	"	Dragoe	Jacheta	Ludovicus	18-04010102020604	1474		1510	
919	"	Dragoe	Raphael		18-040101020610	1429		1477	
828	"	Dragoe	Çorçi	Clemens	18-04010102010406	1450	1stOff	1482	
897	"	Federico	Raphael		18-040101020605	1419		1457	
938	"	Francescho	Marino	Nicola	18-04010102080105	1467		1498	
1048	"	Francesco	Polo	Nixa	18-04010305010103	1440		1473	
955	"	Francescus	Raphael	Nicola	18-04010102080404	1479		1490	Period
895	"	Francho	Marin	Raphael	18-04010102060206	1451	1stOff	1508	
869	"	Franciscus	Jacheta	Ludovicus	18-04010102020605	1477		1503	
814	"	Franciscus	Marinus	Zorzi	18-0401010201040108	1490		1543	
839	"	Franciscus	Çorçi		18-04010102010412	1465		1492	
791	"	Georgius	Aloisius	Clemens	18-04010102010307	1457		1483	
807	"	Georgius	Marinus	Zorzi	18-0401010201040101	1476		1489	LastOff
824	"	Georgius	Nicola	Zorzi	18-0401010201040401	1476		1490	LastOff
827	"	Giovanni	Nicola	Zorzi	18-0401010201040404	1477		1512	

[18] The wedding of Michael in 1459 is the last known mention. He held no offices and was nominated for none.

[19] *Specchio*: fo. 385v. Mahnken gives the year of death as 1506.

[20] *Specchio*: fo. 382v. No death year given in Mahnken.

ID (1)	Surname (2)	Name (3)	Father (4)	Grandfather (5)	Hackenberg Number (6)	Entry year (7)	(8)	End year (9)	(10)
857	Goçe	Jacheta	Ludovicus	Maroe	18-040101020206	1420		1454[21]	
859	"	Jachxa	Jacheta	Ludovicus	18-04010102020602	1466		1470	LastOff
953	"	Jacomo	Raphael	Nicola	18-04010102080402	1467		1493	
973	"	Johannes	Bartholo	Zuan	18-04010102090401	1464		1482	
1001	"	Johannes	Marin	Vitticus	18-0401010401010303	1484		1519	
965	"	Johannes	Nicolaus	Paulus	18-0401010208060302	1482		1532	
1057	"	Johannes	Nixa		18-040103050103	1429		1456	LastOff
976	"	Johannes	Raphael	Zuan	18-04010102090501	1467		1473	
981	"	Johannes	Stephano	Zuan	18-04010102090801	1471		1502	
918	"	Junius	Sigismundo	Raphael	18-04010102060904	1477		1490	
885	"	Luca	Nicola	Marin	18-0401010206020501	1478		1490	LastOff
954	"	Lucha	Raphael	Nicola	18-04010102080404	1474		1482	
941	"	Luxa	Nicola		18-040101020802	1439		1464	
1023	"	Marin	Clemens	Viticus	18-04010104040104	1433		1461	
1074	"	Marin	Nicola	Symeon	18-04010305020302	1448	1stOff	1492	
876	"	Marin	Raphael		18-04010102060602	1414		1447	
1067	"	Marin	Symeon	Marince	18-04010305020302	1407		1442	
998	"	Marin	Vitticus	Clemens	18-04010104010103	1447	1stNom	1468	
967	"	Marin	Çuan		18-040101020901	1412		1442	
1013	"	Marino	Antonio	Clemens	18-04010104010302	1430		1489	
932	"	Marino	Nicola		18-040101020801	1425		1446	
1072	"	Marino	Simcho	Nicola	18-0401030502030103	1480		1490	Period
800	"	Marinus	Aloisius	Clemens	18-04010102010308	1452	1stOff	1483	
775	"	Marinus	Dragoe	Aloisius	18-0401010201030302	1487		1510	
923	"	Marinus	Dragoe	Raphael	18-04010102061004	1489		1511	
825	"	Marinus	Nicola	Çorçi	18-0401010201040402	1481		1526	
878	"	Marinus	Raphael	Marin	18-0401010206020101	1472		1495	
806	"	Marinus	Çorçi	Clemens	18-04010102010401	1433		1482	
1077	"	Martinus	Nicola	Symeon	18-04010305020305	1463		1478	
2952	"	Michiel	Çuan		18-040101020911	?		1445	
808	"	Natalis	Marinus	Çorçi	18-0401010201040102	1481		1526	
858	"	Nicola	Jacheta	Ludovicus	18-04010102020601	1466		1505	
1059	"	Nicola	Johannes	Nixa	18-04010305010302	1442	1stOff	1482	
942	"	Nicola	Luxa	Nicola	18-04010102080201	1472		1502	
884	"	Nicola	Marin	Raphael	18-04010102060205	1435		1474	
1041	"	Nicola	Polo	Nixa	18-04010305010101	1426		1456	
949	"	Nicola	Raphael	Nicola	18-04010102080401	1468		1518	
1070	"	Nicola	Simcho	Nicola	18-0401030502030101	1477		1477[22]	
1068	"	Nicola	Symeon		18-04010305020303	1421		1465	
822	"	Nicola	Çorçi	Clemens	18-04010102010404	1443	1stOff	1477	
847	"	Nicolaus	Alovise	Vitcho	18-0401010202020101	1475		1502	
963	"	Nicolaus	Paulus	Nicola	18-04010102080603	1467		1490	LastOff
856	"	Nixa	Ludovicus		18-04010102020205	1432		1473	
802	"	Orsatus	Marinus	Aloisius	18-0401010201030802	1488		1514	
935	"	Paladino	Marino	Nicola	18-04010102080103	1467		1485	LastOff
947	"	Paladino	Nicola		18-040101020803	?		1453	
813	"	Paulus	Marinus	Zorzi	18-0401010201040107	1487		1509	
960	"	Paulus	Nicola		18-040101020806	1420		1452	LastOff
1042	"	Paulus	Nicola	Polo	18-04010305010101	1473		1519	
849	"	Piero	Vitcho	Ludovicus	18-04010102020203	1443		1501	
901	"	Raphael	Federico	Raphael	18-04010102060504	1457		1515	
861	"	Raphael	Jacheta	Ludovicus	18-04010102020603	1473		1507	
877	"	Raphael	Marin	Raphael	18-04010102060201	1429		1482	
937	"	Raphael	Marino	Nicola	18-04010102080104	1464		1508	
948	"	Raphael	Nicola		18-040101020804	1434		1465	
886	"	Raphael	Nicola	Marin	18-0401010206020502	1484		1531	

[21] *Specchio*: fo. 382v. Mahnken records the year of death as 1464. Jacheta held his last office in 1452 (*Specchio*: s.v. *Pregato*).

[22] Except for note of entry into the Great Council (*Specchio*: fo. 391v), there is no further information about Nicola.

ID (1)	Surname (2)	Name (3)	Father (4)	Grandfather (5)	Hackenberg Number (6)	Entry year (7)	(8)	End year (9)	(10)
950	Goçe	Raphael	Nicola	Raphael	18-0401010208040101	1490		1532	
830	″	Raphael	Çorçi	Clemens	18-04010102010407	1456		1465	
974	″	Raphael	Çuan		18-040101020905	1436		1455	
914	″	Sigismundo	Raphael		18-040101020609	1424		1475	
1069	″	Simcho	Nicola	Symeon	18-04010305020301	1448	1stOff	1466	
980	″	Stephano	Çuan		18-040101020908	1432		1453	
1017	″	Stephanus	Antonius	Marino	18-04010104010302 01	1488		1558	
1000	″	Stephanus	Marin	Vitticus	18-0401010401010302	1473		1479	
995	″	Vita	Clemens	Vitticus	18-0401010401010201	1471		1513	
870	″	Vitchus	Jacheta	Ludovicus	18-04010102020606	1477		1482	
1028	″	Vladislav	Clemens	Viticus	18-040101040105	1423		1489	
1051	″	Çiovanne	Polo	Nixa	18-04010305010106	1427		1456	
805	″	Çorçi	Clemens		18-040101020104	1407		1462	
966	″	Çuan	Maroe		18-0401010209	1419		1445	
1083	″	Çuanne	Symeon		18-04010305020204	1438		1455	
690	Grade	Biaso	Marinus		19-0201010101	?		1441	
724	″	Geronimus	Çugno	Mateus	19-04010104020106	1440		1494	
733	″	Giacomo	Mateus		19-040101040204	1432		1451	LastOff
708	″	Junius	Marin	Zugno	19-04010104020102 01	1485		1525	
707	″	Marin	Çugno	Mateus	19-04010104020102	1450	1stOff	1497	
694	″	Marinus	Biasio	Marinus	19-020101010104	1455		1499	
704	″	Mateus	Junius		19-0401010402	1407		1444	
725	″	Paulus	Geronimus	Zugno	19-04010104020106 01	1488		1538	
695	″	Petrus	Biasio	Marinus	19-020101010105	1457		1499	
718	″	Stephanus	Çugno	Mateus	19-04010104020104	1463		1490	LastOff
697	″	Çugno	Marinus		19-0201010102	1430		1479	
705	″	Çugno	Mateus	Junius	19-040101040201	1409		1462	
1278	Luca	Baptista	Nixa	Zuane	20-010303	1474		1483	
1270	″	Batista	Zuane		20-0102	1445	1stOff	1479	LastOff
2467	″	Gaspar	Batista	Zuane	20-010205[23]	1489		1532	
1273	″	Johannes	Batista	Zuane	20-010203	1484		1550	
1276	″	Johannes	Nixa	Zuane	20-010301	?		1450	LastNom
1274	″	Marin	Batista	Zuane	20-010204	1488		1517	
1280	″	Michael	Nixa	Zuane	20-010305	1481		1510	
1272	″	Nicolaus	Batista	Zuane	20-010202	1483		1546	
1275	″	Nixa	Zuane		20-0103	1443		1465	
1279	″	Nunciatus	Nixa	Zuane	20-010304	1477		1531	
1337	Lucari	Blasio	Michiel	Giovanni	21-03110102	1481		1490	Period
1339	″	Francesco	Michiel	Giovanni	21-03110104	1489		1490	Period
1334	″	Giovanni	Michael		21-0311	1418		1473	
1288	″	Hieronymo	Michiel	Nicola	21-03010103	1472		1507	
1307	″	Jacobus	Marco	Petrus	21-03040404	1486		1538	
1298	″	Jacomo	Petrus	Michael	21-030402	1428		1441	
1336	″	Johannes	Michiel	Giovanni	21-03110101	1477		1490	LastOff
1343	″	Lorenzo	Giovanni	Michael	21-031104	1443	1stOff	1480	
1338	″	Marco	Michiel	Giovanni	21-03110103	1484		1490	Period
1303	″	Marco	Petrus	Michael	21-030404	1429		1484[24]	
1322	″	Marin	Michael	Nicola	21-0308	?		1450	
1324	″	Marin	Nicola	Marin	21-03080101	1484		1522[25]	
1305	″	Marinus	Marco	Petrus	21-03040402	1481		1520	
1315	″	Marinus	Petrus	Michael	21-030406	1434		1472	LastOff
1326	″	Martolo	Marin	Michael	21-030802	1454	1stOff	1498	
1335	″	Michiel	Giovanni	Michael	21-031101	1450	1stOff	1492	
1285	″	Michiel	Nicola	Michael	21-030101	1438		1465	LastOff
1345	″	Natalis	Lorenzo	Giovanni	21-03110402	1477		1521	
1323	″	Nicola	Marin	Michael	21-030801	1448		1492	
1358	″	Nicola	Paulus	Nicola	21-04030201	1476		1490	Period

[23] *Specchio*: fo. 392. Not recorded in Mahnken's genealogies.
[24] *Specchio*: fo. 384v. Mahnken records the death year as 1483.
[25] *Specchio*: fo. 392. Mahnken records the death year as 1512.

ID (1)	Surname (2)	Name (3)	Father (4)	Grandfather (5)	Hackenberg Number (6)	Entry year (7)	(8)	End year (9)	(10)
1306	Lucari	Paladinus	Marco	Petrus	21-03040403	1481		1490	Period
1314	"	Paladinus	Petrus	Michael	21-030405	1423		1484	
1325	"	Pasqualis	Nicola	Marin	21-03080102	1488		1498	
1357	"	Paulus	Nicola	Stefanus	21-040302	1444	1stOff	1484	
1344	"	Petrus	Lorenzo	Giovanni	21-03110401	1476		1490	Period
1304	"	Petrus	Marco	Petrus	21-03040401	1476		1486	
1361	"	Petrus	Paulus	Nicola	21-04030204	1485		1490	Period
1296	"	Petrus	Çubriano	Petrus	21-03040102	1464		1499	
1299	"	Pietro	Jacomo	Petrus	21-03040201	1463		1490	LastOff
2433	"	Simon			21-[26]	1461		1463	LastOff
1355	"	Stephanus	Nicola	Stefanus	21-040301	1429		1479	
1359	"	Stephanus	Paulus	Nicola	21-04030202	1481		1490	Period
1294	"	Çubriano	Petrus	Michael	21-030401	?		1441	
1385	Martinussio	Franciscus	Nicola	Micoçius	22-030101020502	1464		1488	
1372	"	Martinusso	Nicola		22-020501090103	1425		1441	LastOff
1386	"	Michael	Nicola	Micoçius	22-030101020504	1477		1481	LastOff
1383	"	Nicola	Micoçius		22-030101020205	1429		1460	
1369	"	Nicola	Çugno	Nicola	22-02050109010202	1473		1485	
1370	"	Paulus	Çugno	Nicola	22-02050109010203	1474		1524	
2436	"	Theodorus	Nicola	Micoçius	22-030101020503	1465		1495[27]	
1367	"	Çugno	Nicola		22-020501090102	1427		1473	
1462	Mençe	Andrea	Giovanni	Micus	23-050402010103	1442		1459	
1494	"	Antonio	Lampriça	Maroe	23-060401020304	1429		1489[28]	
1488	"	Antonius	Maroe	Lampriça	23-06040102030102	1473		1519[29]	
1402	"	Biasio	Marinus	Vlachussa	23-010306020103	1434		1482	
1464	"	Christophorus	Andrea	Giovanni	23-05040201010302	1477		1483	
1436	"	Damian	Johannes		23-0110030101	1411		1476	
1439	"	Damianus	Simon	Damian	23-01100301010102	1476		1486	
1408	"	Francesco	Marinus	Vlachussa	23-010306020106	1454	Ballot	1470	
2444	"	Franciscus	Matcho		23-06040102030201[30]	1476		1524	
1459	"	Giovanni	Micus		23-0504020101	1410		1457	
1430	"	Giovanni	Nicola	Vlachussa	23-010306020206	1439		1481	
1463	"	Johannes	Andrea	Giovanni	23-05040201010301	1475		1510	
1449	"	Johannes	Damian	Johannes	23-011003010105	1463		1508	
1485	"	Lampriça	Maroe		23-0604010203	1422		1442	LastOff
1487	"	Laurentius	Maroe	Lampriça	23-06040102030101	1472		1496	
1491	"	Laurentius	Matcho	Lampriça	23-06040102030203	1472		1488	LastOff
1403	"	Marinus	Biasio	Marinus	23-010306020301	1472		1529	
1447	"	Marinus	Damian	Johannes	23-011003010103	1460		1466	
1486	"	Maroe	Lampriça	Maroe	23-060401020301	1422		1473	
1496	"	Maroe	Piero	Maroe	23-060401020401	1427		1489	
1489	"	Matcho	Lampriça	Maroe	23-060401020302	1438		1457	
1475	"	Nichola	Andre		23-0601050202	?		1441	
1416	"	Nicola	Blasio	Marinus	23-01030602010302	1473		1523	
1407	"	Nicola	Marinus	Vlachussa	23-010306020105[31]	1428		1454	
1415	"	Nicola	Nicola	Vlachussa	23-01030602020201	1444	1stOff	1490	Period
1414	"	Nicola	Vlachussa		23-0103060202	1421		1465	
1446	"	Nicolaus	Damian	Johannes	23-011003010102	1450	Ballot	1466	
1490	"	Nicolaus	Matcho	Lampriça	23-06040102030202	1473		1518	
1421	"	Orsolin	Nicola	Vlachussa	23-010306020204	1436	Ballot	1497	
1465	"	Petrus	Andrea	Giovanni	23-05040201010303	1479		1522	
1497	"	Petrus	Maroe	Piero	23-06040102040101	1472		1508	

[26] *Specchio*: fo. 387. Insufficient information. No likely candidate in Mahnken's genealogies.

[27] *Specchio*: fo. 387v. Mahnken records the death year as 1496.

[28] *Specchio*: fo. 385. No death year given in Mahnken.

[29] *Specchio*: fo. 390. Mahnken records the death year as 1513.

[30] *Specchio*: fo. 389v. Cf. *Act. Maior*. 13: fo. 173v and *Act. Maior*. 15: fo. 59v. No genealogical entry is given in Mahnken.

[31] Not shown in correct genealogical position in Mahnken.

ID (1)	Surname (2)	Name (3)	Father (4)	Grandfather (5)	Hackenberg Number (6)	Entry year (7)	(8)	End year (9)	(10)
1498	Mençe	Savinus	Maroe	Piero	23-06040102040102	1480		1511	
1504	"	Savolin	Piero	Maroe	23-060401020405	1454	1stOff	1505	
1438	"	Sigismundus	Simon	Damian	23-01100301010101	1477		1527	
1437	"	Simon	Damian	Johannes	23-011003010101	1443	1stOff	1506	
2440	"	Stephano	Nicola		23-010306020209	1467		1500	
1453	"	Tibalto	Give		23-0110030104	1435		1461	
1393	Mlaschagna	Blasius	Nicoliça	Theodorus	24-010102	1482		1489	LastOff
1390	"	Nicoliça	Theodorus		24-0101	1428		1463	
1391	"	Theodorus	Nicoliça	Theodorus	24-010101	1472		1493	
1525	Palmota	Georgius	Nicola	Zore	25-01010101	1477		1501	
1533	"	Johannes	Zore	Nicho	25-010103	1434		1482	
1536	"	Nicola	Johannes	Zore	25-01010302	1469		1483	
1526	"	Nicola	Nicola	Zore	25-01010102	1475		1518	
1524	"	Nicola	Zore	Nicho	25-010101	1431		1485	
2455	"	Nicolaus	Johannes	Zore	25-01010305[32]	1480		1490	LastOff
1537	"	Stephan	Johannes	Zore	25-01010303	1484		1490	Period
1534	"	Zore	Johannes	Zore	25-01010301	1465		1512	
1523	"	Zore	Nicho		25-0101	1410		1441	
1605	Poça	Aloysius	Christophorus	Nicola	26-010102010202	1454	1stOff	1511	
1568	"	Andreas	Nicolaus	Zuicus	26-010101010208	1429		1456	
1585	"	Antonio	Gauže	Saucus	26-010105010104	1430		1443	
1625	"	Bernardus	Polo	Nicola	26-020102010308	1472		1482	
1578	"	Biasio	Gauže	Saucus	26-01010501010101	1412		1442	LastOff
1565	"	Carolus	Polo	Nicolaus	26-01010101020702	1478		1522	
1606	"	Christophorus	Aloysius	Christophorus	26-02010201020201	1489		1517	
1601	"	Christophorus	Nicola		26-0201020102	1425		1450	LastNom
1650	"	Domenico	Nicola		26-0201020109	1429		1472	
1598	"	Dominicus	Nicola	Ruschus	26-02010201010302	1484		1521	
1612	"	Dominicus	Polo	Nicola	26-020102010301	1455		1478	
1649	"	Dominicus	Çovan	Nicola	26-020102010808	1468		1489	LastOff
1615	"	Franciscus	Polo	Nicola	26-020102010302	1449	1stOff	1496	
1642	"	Franciscus	Çovan	Nicola	26-020102010802	1459		1490	LastOff
1624	"	Georgius	Polo	Nicola	26-020102010307	1474		1487	
1550	"	Giovanni	Nicolaus	Zuicus	26-010101010201	1421		1475	
1641	"	Johannes	Nicola	Çovan	26-02010201080101	1484		1550	
1587	"	Marinus	Antonio	Gauze	26-01010501010402	1464		1465	
1643	"	Marinus	Çovan	Nicola	26-020102010803	1457		1495	
1562	"	Michael	Nicolaus	Zuicus	26-010101010206	1426		1492	
1621	"	Michael	Polo	Nicola	26-020102010304	1459		1490	Period
1602	"	Nicola	Christophorus	Nicola	26-020102010201	1450	1stOff	1465	
1626	"	Nicola	Polo	Nicola	26-020102010309	1472		1512	
1596	"	Nicola	Ruschus	Nicola	26-020102010103	1452	1stOff	1496	
1640	"	Nicola	Çovan	Nicola	26-020102010801	1454	1stOff	1490	Period
1549	"	Nicolaus	Çuicus		26-01010101102	1407		1455	
1564	"	Pandulphus	Polo	Nicolaus	26-01010101020701	1476		1497	
1616	"	Paulus	Franciscus	Polo	26-02010201030201	1487		1486	LastOff
2457	"	Paulus	Nicol		26-[33]	1485		1490	Period
1648	"	Paulus	Çovan	Nicola	26-020102010807	1459		1497	
1638	"	Piero	Nicola		26-0201020107	?		1444	
1555	"	Piero	Nicolaus	Zuicus	26-010101010202	1423		1476	
1611	"	Polo	Nicola		26-0201020103	1432		1465	
1563	"	Polo	Nicolaus	Zuicus	26-010101010207	1435		1486	
1597	"	Ruschus	Nicola	Ruschus	26-02010201010301	1477		1490	LastOff
1554	"	Simon	Giovanni	Nicolaus	26-01010101020104	1476		1505	
1607	"	Vitchus	Christophorus	Nicola	26-020102010203	1466		1495	
1639	"	Çovan	Nicola		26-0201020108	?		1444	
1657	Proculo	Jakob	Nalcus		27-0104	1432		1467	

[32] *Specchio*: fo. 391. Not included in Mahnken's genealogy.

[33] *Specchio*: fo. 391v. Not recorded in Mahnken's genealogy and there is insufficient information to locate him accurately.

ID (1)	Surname (2)	Name (3)	Father (4)	Grandfather (5)	Hackenberg Number (6)	Entry year (7)	(8)	End year (9)	(10)
1654	Proculo	Michael	Piero	Nalcus	27-010201	1464		1490	Period
1652	"	Micho	Nalcus		27-0101	1414		1459	
1655	"	Natalis	Piero	Nalcus	27-010202	1466		1512	
1661	"	Nicolaus	Jakob	Nalcus	27-010404	1477		1517	
1653	"	Piero	Nalcus		27-0102	1425		1462	
1673	Prodanello	Jacomo	Nikša		28-020202	1429		1465	
1696	"	Jacomo	Theodoro		28-0508	?		1449	
1676	"	Marin	Nikša		28-020204	1460		1466	
1674	Prodanello	Nicolaus	Jacomo	Nichola	28-02020201	1488		1552	
1688	"	Nicolo	Piero	Theodoro	28-050204	1453	Ballot	1494	
1685	"	Theodoro	Piero	Theodoro	28-050203	1448		1505	
1747	Ragnina	Andreas	Lorenzo	Nicola	29-0101030704	1472		1483	
1759	"	Andreas	Marinus		29-050204	1436		1451	
1726	"	Biasio	Nicola	Maroe	29-01010306	1423		1452	
1731	"	Blasius	Nicola	Biasio	29-010103060104	1490		1505	
1743	"	Cesar	Nicola	Lorenzo	29-010103070102	1481		1490	Period
1709	"	Dimitri	Nicola	Maroe	29-01010304	1421		1458	
1715	"	Franciscus	Dimitri	Nicola	29-0101030406	1464		1471	
1749	"	Franciscus	Lorenzo	Nicola	29-0101030706	1476		1536	
1722	"	Hieronymus	Dimitri	Nicola	29-0101030410	1472		1483	
2465	"	Hieronymus	Nicola	Lorenzo	29-010103070101[34]	1488		1507	
1764	"	Jacobus	Andreas	Marinus	29-05020403	1472		1490	
1733	"	Johannes	Biasio	Nicola	29-0101030602	1450	1stOff	1481	
1744	"	Johannes	Lorenzo	Nicola	29-0101030702	1459		1460	LastOff
1742	"	Laurentius	Nicola	Lorenzo	29-010103070103	1489		1521[35]	
1740	"	Lorenzo	Nicola	Maroe	29-01010307	1424		1457	
1760	"	Marinus	Andreas	Marinus	29-05020401	1466		1507	
1717	"	Marinus	Dimitri	Nicola	29-0101030408	1467		1521	
1745	"	Marinus	Lorenzo	Nicola	29-0101030703	1470		1489	LastOff
1728	"	Marinus	Nicola	Biasio	29-010103060101	1480		1513	
1718	"	Matheus	Dimitri	Nicola	29-0101030409	1472		1506	
1734	"	Mathias	Biasio	Nicola	29-0101030603	1457		1478	
1727	"	Nicola	Biasio	Nicola	29-0101030601	1444		1479	
1710	"	Nicola	Dimitri	Nicola	29-0101030401	1446	1stOff	1479[36]	
1741	"	Nicola	Lorenzo	Nicola	29-0101030701	1453	1stOff	1512[37]	
1763	"	Nicolaus	Andreas	Marinus	29-05020402	1469		1496	
1713	"	Petrus	Dimitri	Nicola	29-0101030404	1459		1463	
1765	"	Simon	Andreas	Marinus	29-05020404	1472		1502	
1803	Resti	Aloisius	Andreas	Micocius	30-01020903	1473		1518	
1791	"	Alovisius	Micocius		30-010206	1425		1459	
1800	"	Andreas	Micocius		30-010209	1433		1466	
1794	"	Benedetto	Micocius		30-010208[38]	1432		1454	
1786	"	Clemens	Nicola	Micocius	30-01020304	1455		1490	LastOff
1847	"	Daniel	Nicola	Pasche	30-0202010302	1473		1490	LastOff
1773	"	Federicus	Michoč	Maroe	30-0102020102	1477		1481[39]	
1832	"	Francho	Michiel		30-01040604	1441		1476	
1783	"	Franciscus	Michiel	Nicola	30-0102030104	1487		1490	Period
1842	"	Gauze	Michiel	Pasche	30-0202010104	1452	1stOff	1502	
1809	"	Ilia	Symon	Marinus	30-01040103	1428		1482	
1777	"	Johannes	Maroe	Micocius	30-01020204	1429		1494	
1781	"	Johannes	Michiel	Nicola	30-0102030102	1486		1494[40]	

[34] *Specchio*: fo. 392. Not recorded in Mahnken's genealogies.
[35] *Specchio*: fo. 392. No death year given in Mahnken.
[36] *Specchio*: fo. 385. No death year given in Mahnken.
[37] *Specchio*: fo. 386. Mahnken records the death year as 1511.
[38] There are two places where a Benedetto Resti appears in *Specchio*: fos. 382v and 386. Only one Benedetto appears in Mahnken's genealogies and the office-holding records also indicate that there is only one Benedetto whose career ended in 1454 (cf. *Specchio*: s.v. *Procuratori de la Croma*).
[39] *Specchio*: fo. 390v. No death year given in Mahnken.
[40] *Specchio*: fo. 391v. No death year given in Mahnken.

ID (1)	Surname (2)	Name (3)	Father (4)	Grandfather (5)	Hackenberg Number (6)	Entry year (7)	(8)	End year (9)	(10)
1774	Resti	Johannes	Michoč	Maroe	30-0102020103	1486		1494	
2462	"	Judicus	Nicole		30-[41]	1487		1525	
1825	"	Junius	Mathio	Marinus	30-01040404	1452		1506	
1808	"	Marin	Symon	Marinus	30-01040102	1408		1443	LastOff
2458	"	Marinus	Junius		30-0104040401[42]	1486		1490	Period
1772	"	Marinus	Michoč	Maroe	30-0102020101	1473		1524	
1816	"	Marinus	Paolo	Marinus	30-01040301	1454		1457	
1806	"	Marinus	Syme		30-0104	?		1443	
1770	"	Maroe	Micocius		30-010202	1421		1464	
1790	"	Martoliza	Giovanni	Micocius	30-01020501	1460		1490	LastOff
1801	"	Michael	Andreas	Micocius	30-01020901	1467		1509	
1795	"	Michael	Benedetto	Micocius	30-01020801	1465		1484	
1828	"	Michiel	Marinus	Syme	30-010406	?		1443	
1779	"	Michiel	Nicola	Micocius	30-01020301	1446	1stOff	1472	LastOff
1838	"	Michiel	Pasche	Matheus	30-02020101	1435		1443	
1771	"	Michoć	Maroe	Micocius	30-01020201	1446	1stOff	1466	
1833	"	Nicola	Michiel		30-01040605	1454	Ballot	1486	
1780	"	Nicola	Michiel	Nicola	30-0102030101	1477		1481	LastOff
1845	"	Nicola	Pasche	Matheus	30-02020103	1435		1454	
1811	"	Nicola	Symon	Marinus	30-01040105	1425		1443	LastOff
2468	"	Nicolaus	Clemens	Nicola	30-0102030401[43]	1489		1518	
1815	"	Paolo	Marinus		30-010403	1420		1456	LastOff
1846	"	Pasqua	Nicola	Pasche	30-0202010301	1468		1519	
1839	"	Pasqual	Michiel	Pasche	30-0202010101	1452	1stOff	1456	LastOff
1776	"	Simon	Maroe	Micocius	30-01020203	1449	1stOff	1466	
1848	"	Stephanus	Nicola	Pasche	30-0202010303	1476		1487	
1857	"	Valcho	Clemens	Valchus	30-03010201	1433		1482	
1859	"	Vitcho	Clemens	Valchus	30-03010203	1433		1442	
1853	"	Vitcho	Valchus	Vita	30-030101	1410		1448	
1911	Saraca	Bernardo	Ilcho	Nicola	31-0604010101	1471		1500	
1892	"	Giovanni	Ruscus		31-060102	1421		1457	
1910	"	Ilcho	Nicola	Helia	31-06040101	1429		1478	
1925	"	Illio	Matcho		31-060602	1426		1455[44]	
1919	"	Johannes	Naocho	Nicola	31-0604010202	1485		1490	LastOff
1881	"	Marin	Nicola	Percus	31-02010207	1430		1494	
1880	"	Marinus	Paulus	Nicola	31-0201020602	1487		1490	Period
1928	"	Matheus	Illio	Matcho	31-06060203	1468		1523	
1905	"	Mathio	Nicola	Ruscus	31-06010402	1445		1482	
1872	"	Michiel	Nicola	Percus	31-02010203	1426		1482	
1917	"	Naocho	Nicola	Helia	31-06040102	1448	1stOff	1494	
1924	"	Nicola	Matcho		31-060601	1421		1470	
1879	"	Nicola	Paulus	Nicola	31-0201020601	1477		1490	Period
1869	"	Nicola	Percus		31-020102	1422		1459	
1901	"	Nicola	Ruscus		31-060104	1417		1463	
1929	"	Nicolaus	Illio	Matcho	31-06060204	1472		1478	LastOff
1930	"	Paladin	Illio	Matcho	31-06060205	1473		1522	
1878	"	Paulus	Nicola	Percus	31-02010206	1432		1465	
1918	"	Petrus	Naocho	Nicola	31-0604010201	1481		1490	LastOff
1874	"	Ruscus	Michiel	Nicola	31-0201020302	1480		1532	
1884	"	Simon	Nicola		31-02010210	1452	Ballot	1482	
1940	Sorgo	Andrea	Micho		32-01050102010101	1434		1465	
2061	"	Andreas	Francho		32-0604030502	1447	1stOff	1499	
1962	"	Andreas	Lucha	Andrascus	32-01050102010501	1445		1465	
2027	"	Biasio	Laurentius		32-0604030401	1421		1456	
2092	"	Biasio	Piero		32-0604030606	1437		1476	

[41] *Specchio*: fo. 392. Does not appear in Mahnken's genealogies and there is insufficient evidence to place him accurately. [42] *Specchio*: fo. 391v. Not recorded in Mahnken's genealogies.

[43] *Specchio*: fo. 392. Not recorded in Mahnken's genealogies.

[44] *Specchio*: fo. 382v. Mahnken has death year as 1457.

ID (1)	Surname (2)	Name (3)	Father (4)	Grandfather (5)	Hackenberg Number (6)	Entry year (7)	(8)	End year (9)	(10)
1992	Sorgo	Damiano	Juncho		32-0108020406	1410		1453	
1949	"	Dragoe	Marinus		32-01050102010201	1423		1460	EntRel
2063	"	Franchus	Andreas	Francho	32-060403050202	1471		1507	
2460	"	Franciscus	Biasio	Piero	32-060403060604[45]	1487		1499	
2052	"	Francus	Çove	Francho	32-060403050103	1466		1483	
2033	"	Jacobus	Biasio	Laurentius	32-060403040104	1464		1465	
2003	"	Jacobus	Damiano	Juncho	32-010802040608	1472		1481	
1990	"	Jacomo	Juncho		32-010802040'5	1407		1451	
2043	"	Jacomo	Laurentius		32-0604030403	1432		1454	
1971	"	Johannes	Lucha		32-01050102010504	1457		1513	
1996	"	Junius	Damiano	Juncho	32-010802040604	1455		1491	
2007	"	Junius	Pasqual	Juncho	32-010802040901	1457		1509	
2028	"	Laurentius	Biasio	Laurentius	32-060403040101	1451		1490	Period
2076	"	Lucas	Stephano	Piero	32-060403060108	1471		1490	LastOff
2442	"	Lucas	Andreas	Lucha	32-0105010201050101	1473		1506	
1965	"	Marinus	Andreas	Lucha	32-0105010201050103	1483		1525	
1952	"	Marinus	Dragoe	Marinus	32-0105010201020103	1457		1464	LastOff
1973	"	Marinus	Lucha	Andrascus	32-01050102010506	1429		1460	
1969	"	Michiel	Lucha	Andrascus	32-01050102010502	1454	1stOff	1490	
2001	"	Natalis	Damiano	Juncho	32-010802040606	1457		1509	
2038	"	Nicola	Biasio	Laurentius	32-060403040109	1476		1503	
2084	"	Nicola	Piero		32-0604030605	1418		1466	
2071	"	Nicola	Stephano	Piero	32-060403060103	1473		1491	
2080	"	Nicolinus	Urso	Piero	32-060403060302	1473		1490	
1964	"	Nixa	Andreas	Lucha	32-0105010201050102	1472		1487	
2041	"	Orsatus	Biasio	Laurentius	32-060403040111	1479		1490	Period
2002	"	Pasqual	Damiano	Juncho	32-010802040607	1464		1482	
2006	"	Pasqual	Juncho	Marinus	32-0108020409	1411		1454	
2029	"	Pasqualis	Laurentius	Biasio	32-060403040102	1482		1490	Period
2037	"	Petrus	Biasio	Laurentius	32-060403040108	1474		1503	
2085	"	Piero	Nicola	Piero	32-060403060501	1481		1490	LastOff
2068	"	Stephano	Piero		32-0604030601	1432		1455	
2039	"	Stephanus	Biasio	Laurentius	32-060403040110	1478		1490	Period
2059	"	Stephanus	Çove	Francho	32-06040305107	1488		1522	
2088	"	Thomas	Nicola	Piero	32-060403060504	1473		1506	
2057	"	Thomas	Çove	Francho	32-060403050105	1469		1492	
2096	"	Thomaso	Vlacussa		32-06040307	1407		1447	
2078	"	Urso	Piero	Vlacussa	32-0604030603	?		1448	
2034	"	Valchus	Biasio	Laurentius	32-060403040105	1467		1535	
1997	"	Vladissav	Junius	Damiano	32-01080204060401	1488		1517	
2049	"	Çove	Francho		32-060403050501	1431		1475	
2104	Tudisio	Francisco	Nichola		33-01030502	1423		1483	
2099	"	Giovane	Nichola		33-01030501	1423		1466	
2106	"	Johannes	Francisco	Nicola	33-0103050202	1477		1500	
2100	"	Junius	Giovane	Nicola	33-0103050101	1460		1494	
2105	"	Nicola	Francisco	Nicola	33-0103050201	1473		1490	LastOff
2114	Volçe	Andreas	Johannes		34-0201	1411		1444	
2143	"	Franciscus	Michel	Johannes	34-020607	1471		1488	LastOff
2141	"	Jacobus	Michel	Johannes	34-020605	1467		1493	
2110	"	Johannes	Andreas	Macus	34-010101	1410		1471	
2120	"	Johannes	Marin	Andreas	34-02010203	1489		1517	
2137	"	Juhane	Michel	Johannes	34-020601	1408		1455	
2117	"	Marin	Andreas	Johannes	34-020102	1430		1476	
2138	"	Marinus	Michel	Johannes	34-020602	1454	Ballot	1491	
2136	"	Michel	Johannes		34-0206	1428		1474	
2148	"	Nicola	Johannes		34-0207	1426		1482	
2129	"	Paladinus	Andreas	Johannes	34-020110	1446	1stOff	1489[46]	
2142	"	Paulus	Michel	Johannes	34-0200606	1468		1494	

[45] *Specchio*: fo. 391v. Not recorded in Mahnken's genealogies.
[46] *Specchio*: fo. 386. No death year given in Mahnken.

ID (1)	Surname (2)	Name (3)	Father (4)	Grandfather (5)	Hackenberg Number (6)	Entry year (7)	(8)	End year (9)	(10)
2118	Volçe	Stephanus	Marin	Andreas	34-02010201	1476		1519	
2115	"	Çouanne	Andreas	Johannes	34-020101	1444	1stOff	1482	
2198	Zamagna	Bartol	Biasio	Martolus	35-020301	1446	1stOff	1518	
2197	"	Biasio	Martolus		35-0203	1419		1464	
2174	"	Christophorus	Stephanus	Ursius	35-010111	1455		1490	Period
2464	"	Franciscus	Orsatus	Biasio	35-020304011[47]	1488		1490	Period
2158	"	Helias	Marin	Stephanus	35-01010204	1471		1505	
2471	"	Jacobus	Christophorus	Stephanus	35-01011102[48]	1489		1521	
2153	"	Marin	Stephanus	Ursius	35-010102	1438		1480	
2207	"	Martolus	Orsato	Martolus	35-020501	1467		1490	LastOff
2181	"	Martolus	Stepe		35-02	1409		1451	
2168	"	Martolus	Stephanus	Ursius	35-010109	1446		1499	
2201	"	Michael	Biasio	Martolus	35-020303	1460		1473	
2187	"	Michael	Vita	Michiel	35-02010401	1476		1490	Period
2182	"	Michiel	Martolus		35-0201	1423		1466	
2188	"	Nicola	Vita	Michiel	35-02010402	1480		1522	
2206	"	Orsato	Martolus		35-0205	1432		1488	
2151	"	Orsato	Stephanus	Ursius	35-010101	1425		1477	
2202	"	Orsatus	Biasio	Martolus	35-020304	1464		1512	
2193	"	Paulus	Michiel	Martolus	35-020108	1464		1484	
2159	"	Silvester	Marin	Stephanus	35-01010205	1482		1494	
2175	"	Stephanus	Christophorus	Stephanus	35-01011101	1488		1525	
2154	"	Stephanus	Marin	Stephanus	35-01010201	1469		1510	
2150	"	Stephanus	Ursius		35-0101	1407		1460	
2186	"	Vita	Michiel	Martolus	35-020104	1447		1482	
652	Zrieva	Aelius	Lampre	Illia	13-020204030901	1483		1520	
633	"	Andreas	Illia		13-0202040302	1427		1468	LastOff
618	"	Andreas	Maroe	Johannes	13-020204010201	1467		1501	
577	"	Andreas	Martolo	Junius	13-0101040112	1457		1485	
643	"	Andreas	Nicola	Illia	13-020204030602	1448	1stOff	1490	Period
646	"	Antonius	Nicola	Illia	13-020204030604	1487		1490	Period
657	"	Bartolom	Illia		13-0202040310	1450		1493	
566	"	Bartolus	Jacomo		13-010104010601	1470		1525	
576	"	Blasius	Martolo	Junius	13-0101040111	1457	EntYr	1490	Period
626	"	Franco	Johannes		13-0202040105	1448	1stOff	1458	LastOff
570	"	Francus	Nicolinus		13-010104010801	1485		1521	
2470	"	Gabriel	Stephanus		13-010104011004[49]	1489		1490	Period
555	"	Giovane	Martoliça		13-010101010501	1412		1454	
634	"	Helias	Andreas	Illia	13-020204030201	1471		1482	
631	"	Helias	Mathia	Illia	13-020204030101	1467		1486	
642	"	Helias	Nicola	Illia	13-020204030601	1471		1501	
602	"	Hieronymus	Orsatus	Giovanni	13-02010101010303	1488		1490	Period
2452	"	Jacobus	Stephanus		13-010104011002[50]	1479		1517	
565	"	Jacomo	Martolo	Junius	13-0101040106	1441		1482	
547	"	Johannes	Aloise	Martoliça	13-010101010103	1444		1462	
627	"	Johannes	Franco	Johannes	13-020204010501	1476		1489	LastOff
543	"	Johannes	Martol	Aloise	13-01010101010101	1477		1497	
606	"	Junius	Marinus		13-0201010103	1411		1450	
600	"	Junius	Orsatus	Giovanni	13-02010101010301	1480		1490	LastOff
651	"	Lampre	Illia		13-020204030309	1449		1487	
2450	"	Ma(?)	S(?)	Jo(?)	13-[51]	1478		1490	Period

[47] *Specchio*: fo. 392. Not recorded in Mahnken's genealogies.

[48] *Specchio*: fo. 392v. Not recorded in Mahnken's genealogies.

[49] *Specchio*: fo. 392. Not recorded in Mahnken's genealogies.

[50] *Specchio*: fos. 390v, 489: s.v. *Capitanio de la ponta*. Cf. *Act. Maior.* 15: fos. 40v, 245. Not recorded in Mahnken's genealogies.

[51] *Specchio*: fo. 390v. Not sufficient information to locate this individual. He is clearly differentiated from Martoliza Stephanus (ID 2449) who entered the Great Council four days earlier on 3 December 1478 (ibid.).

ID (1)	Surname (?)	Name (3)	Father (4)	Grandfather (5)	Hackenberg Number (6)	Entry year (7)	(8)	End year (9)	(10)
637	Zrieva	Marcus	Andreas	Illia	13-020204030204	1474		1509	
2996	"	Marcus	Maroe	Johannes	13-020204010207[52]	1476	EntYr	1518	
609	"	Marinus	Junius	Marinus	13-020101010303	1444		1500	
586	"	Marinus	Zugno	Michie	13-010104030102	1454[53]		1465	LastOff
617	"	Maroe	Johannes		13-0202040102	1426		1501	
542	"	Martol	Aloise	Martoliça	13-010101010101	1444	1stOff	1462	
2449	"	Martoliza	Stephanus		13-010104011001	1478		1520[54]	
630	"	Mathio	Illia		13-0202040301	1432		1466	
645	"	Michael	Nicola	Illia	13-020204030603	1477		1485	LastNom
636	"	Nicola	Andreas	Illia	13-020204030203	1472		1482	
641	"	Nicola	Illia		13-0202040306	1444	1stOff	1469	LastOff
567	"	Nicolinus	Jacomo		13-010104010602	1481		1512	
569	"	Nicolinus	Martolo	Junius	13-0101040108	1437		1494	
599	"	Orsatus	Giovanni	Marinus	13-020101010103	1450	1stOff	1505	
659	"	Paladinus	Illia		13-0202040311	1457		1459	
656	"	Pasqua	Lampre	Illia	13-020204030905	1482		1483	
611	"	Petar	Junius	Marinus	13-020101010305	1457		1490	Period
549	"	Piero	Aloise	Martoliça	13-010101010104	1429		1462	
2699	"	Stephano	Nicola	Junius	13-0101040405	1442		1495[55]	
573	"	Stephanus	Martolo	Junius	13-0101040110	1448		1485	
655	"	Troian	Lampre	Illia	13-020204030904	1477		1493	
660	"	Troianus	Illia		13-0202040312	1445		1453	
610	"	Vochsa	Junius	Marinus	13-020101010304	1445		1446[56]	
582	"	Çugno	Michiel		13-0101040301	1432		1485	

[52] *Specchio*: fo. 390. Not recorded in Mahnken's genealogies.

[53] There is a discrepancy concerning this man. In one place the *Specchio* lists him as entering the Great Council in February 1464 (fo. 387), but elsewhere he is recorded as holding office in both 1457 and 1459 (ibid.: s.v. *Castellan de Stagno* and *Castellan de quelmar, Castello de supra*) and he is nominated for a seat on the Small Council in 1465 (*Act. Maior.* 12: fo. 230). I assume the entry date in the *Specchio* is an error.

[54] *Specchio*: fo. 390v. No death year given in Mahnken.

[55] *Specchio*: fo. 385. Mahnken records the year of death as 1496.

[56] No year of death is given in Mahnken or can be located in any source. Since he neither held office nor was nominated for any, it is presumed that he died shortly after entering the Great Council.

BIBLIOGRAPHY

Archival Sources: Historijski arhiv u Dubrovniku, Dubrovnik

Acta Consilii Maioris
  (6) 1440–1442; (7) 1442–1445; (8) 1445; (9) 1449–1453; (10) 1453–1456; (11) 1457–1460;
  (12) 1460–1466; (13) 1466–1472; (14) 1477–1483; (15) 1485–1491
Acta Consilii Rogatorum
  (7) 1438–1441; (8) 1441–1443; (9) 1444–1446; (10) 1446–1448; (11) 1448–1454;
  (12) 1451–1452; (13) 1452–1453; (14) 1454–1456; (15) 1456–1460; (16) 1460–1461;
  (17) 1461–1463; (18) 1463–1466; (19) 1466–1467; (20) 1468–1470; (21) 1470–1472;
  (22) 1473–1476; (23) 1476–1478; (24) 1481–1485; (25) 1485–1488; (26) 1489–1492
Acta Minoris Consilii
  (8) 1438–1441; (9) 1441–1443; (10) 1444–1446; (11) 1446–1448; (12) 1448–1450; (13)
  1451–1455; (14) 1455–1459; (15) 1459–1462; (16) 1462–1466; (17) 1466–1469; (18)
  1470–1472; (19) 1473–1475; (20) 1475–1478; (21) 1478–1481; (22) 1482–1486; (23)
  1486–1490
Cathasthicum
  (3) *Case del comune de Ragusi e terreni e affitti 1481*; (6) *Verficazione e divisioni delle terre
  dello stato 1440 (accopiavit Joh. Laur. Reginus de Feltre)*
Diversa Cancellariæ
  (62) 1450–1451; (63) 1451–1452
Diversa Notariæ
  (24) 1440–1441; (25) 1441–1442; (26) 1442–1443; (27) 1443–1444
Liber Dotium Notariæ
  (6) a. *Dotium* 1439–1450, b. *Venditiones* 1439–1450; (7) a. *Dotium* 1460–1472, b. *Venditiones*
  1460–1472; (8) a. *Dotium* 1472–1485, b. *Venditiones* 1473–1495
Manuali Practici del Cancelliere
  (1) *Indice Magistrature ed officiali (nune Specchio del Magior Consiglio dictum)* 1440–1492;
  (8) *Ceremoniale*; (11) *Liber Viridis*; (12) *Liber Croceus*
Pacta Matrimonialia
  (1) 1447–1453; (2) 1453–1464; (3) 1495–1503; (4) 1503–1513; (5) 1513–1520
Privata
  (1) *Dare de Avere Polo de Pozza 1446*; (2) *Dare ed Avere Jacobo de Gondola 1457*
Testamenta de Notaria
  (13) 1437–1445; (14) 1445–1451; (15) 1451–1456; (16) 1456–1458; (17) 1456–1462; (18)
  1462–1465; (19) 1465–1466

194   *Bibliography*

Printed Sources

ANDERSON, R. (1963). Changing Kinship in Europe. *Kroeber Anthropological Society Papers*, 28: 1–47.

AZO (1966). *Summa super codicem*. Turin: ed. M. Viora.

BAXTER, P. and ALMAGOR, U. (1978). Observations about Generations. In J. La Fontaine (ed.), *Sex and Age as Principles of Social Differentiation*. London, New York, and San Francisco: Academic Press.

BERITIĆ, L. (1978). *The City Walls of Dubrovnik*. Dubrovnik: Društvo prijatelja dubrovačke starine.

BIEGMAN, N. (1967). *The Turco-Ragusan Relationship*. The Hague and Paris: Mouton.

BIERSACK, A. (1989). Local Knowledge, Local History: Geertz and Beyond. In L. Hunt (ed.), *The New Cultural History*. Berkeley, Los Angeles, and London: University of California Press.

BISCHOFF, B. (1990). *Latin Palaeography: Antiquity and the Middle Ages*. (Trans. D. Ó Cróinín and D. Ganz.) Cambridge: Cambridge University Press.

BOHOLM, Å. (1992). The Coronation of Female Death: The Dogaressa of Venice. *Man* (NS), 27: 91–104.

BOURDIEU, P. (1977). *Outline of a Theory of Practice*. Cambridge: Cambridge University Press.

BOŽIĆ, I. (1948). Ekonomski i Društveni Razvitak Dubrovnika u XIV–XV Veku. *Istoriski Glasnik*, 1–2: 21–66.

——(1973). Filip de Diversis i njegovo djelo. *Dubrovnik*, 3: 75–80.

——(1983). *Filip de Diversis opis Dubrovnika*. Dubrovnik: Časopis 'Dubrovnik'.

BRAUDEL, F. (1972–3). *The Mediterranean and the Mediterranean World in the Age of Philip II*. London: Collins.

BURKE, P. (1987). *The Historical Anthropology of Early Modern Italy*. Cambridge: Cambridge University Press.

CAPPELLI, A. (1973). *Dizionario di abbreviature Latine ed Italiane*. 6th edn. Milan: Ulrico Hoepli.

CARSTEN, J. and HUGH-JONES, S. (1995). Introduction. In J. Carsten and S. Hugh-Jones (eds.), *About the House: Lévi-Strauss and Beyond*. Cambridge: Cambridge University Press.

CARTER, F. (1968–9). Balkan Exports through Dubrovnik 1358–1500: A Geographical Analysis. *Journal of Croatian Studies*, 9–10: 133–59.

——(1971a). The Woollen Industry of Ragusa (Dubrovnik) 1450–1550: Problems of a Balkan Textile Centre. *Textile History*, 2: 3–27.

——(1971b). The Commerce of the Dubrovnik Republic, 1500–1700. *Economic History Review*, 24: 370–94.

——(1972). *Dubrovnik (Ragusa), A Classic City-State*. London and New York: Seminar Press.

CHOJNACKI, S. (1973). In Search of the Venetian Patriciate: Families and Factions in the Fourteenth Century. In J. R. Hale (ed.), *Renaissance Venice*. London: Faber and Faber.

——(1985). Kinship Ties and Young Patricians in Fifteenth-Century Venice. *Renaissance Quarterly*, 38: 240–70.

——(1986). Political Adulthood in Fifteenth-Century Venice. *American Historical Review*, 91: 791–810.

——(1990). Marriage Legislation and Patrician Society in Fifteenth-Century Venice. In B. S. Bachrach and D. Nicholas (eds.), *Law, Custom and the Social Fabric in Medieval Europe: Essays in Honor of Bryce Lyon*. Kalamazoo: Western Michigan University.

——(1994). Social Identity in Renaissance Venice: The Second *Serrata*. *Renaissance Studies*, 8: 341–58.

CIPPOLA, C. (1956). *Money, Prices and Civilization in The Mediterranean World, Fifth to Seventeenth Century*. Princeton: Princeton University Press.

CLARKE, P. (1991). *The Soderini and the Medici: Power and Patronage in Fifteenth-Century Florence*. Oxford: Clarendon Press.

COHN, B. (1981). Anthropology and History in the 1980s. *Journal of Interdisciplinary History*, 12: 227–52.

COMAROFF, J. and COMAROFF, J. (1992). *Ethnography and the Historical Imagination*. Boulder, San Francisco, and Oxford: Westview Press.

COTRUGLI, B. (1573). *Della mercatura e del mercante perfetto*. Venice: Elefanta, 1573. A reprinting of the first (Cavtat) edition. Ed. Z. Muljačić. Dubrovnik: DTS, 1989.

ĆIRKOVIĆ, S. (1979). Dubrovčani Kao Poduzetnici u Rudarstvu Srbije i Bosne. *Acta Historico-Œconomica Iugoslaviæ*, 6: 1–20.

——(1987). Unfulfilled Autonomy: Urban Society in Serbia and Bosnia. In B. Krekić (ed.), *Urban Society of Eastern Europe in Premodern Times*. Berkeley: University of California Press.

ČUČKOVIĆ, V. (1963). Epitropi u Starom Dubrovačkom Pravim. *Godišnjak Pravnog Fakulteta (Sarajevo)*, 11: 257–74.

——(1977). O Odredbi Dubrovačkog Statuta de Concordio Inter Virum et Uxorem Schepatos. *Godišnjak Pravnog Fakulteta (Sarajevo)*, 25: 441–51.

——(1983). Porodica i porodični odnosi u srednjovjekovnom Dubrovniku. *Godišnjak Pravnog Fakulteta (Sarajevo)*, 31: 267–82.

DAVIS, J. (1989). The Social Relations of the Production of History. In E. Tonkin, M. McDonald, and M. Chapman (eds.), *History and Ethnicity*. London: Routledge.

DAVIS, R. (1962). *The Rise of the English Shipping Industry in the Seventeenth and Eighteenth Centuries*. London: Macmillan.

DELILLE, G. (1985). *Famille et propriété dans le royaume de Naples, XV*ᵉ*–XIX*ᵉ. Rome and Paris: École Française de Rome.

DINIĆ-KNEŽEVIĆ, D. (1972). Homo sui juris. *Godišnjak Filizofskog Fakulteta u Novom Sadu*, 15: 27–32.

——(1974). *Položaj Žena u Dubrovniku u XIII i XIV Veku*. Belgrade: Srpska Akademija Nauka i Umetnosti.

——(1982). *Tkanine u privredi srednjovjekovnog Dubrovnika*. Belgrade: Srpska Akademija Nauka i Umetnosti.

DIVERSIS DE QUARTIGIANIS DE LUCCA, P. DE (1880–2) [1440]. Situs Ædificiorum, Politiæ et Laudabilium Consuetudinum Inclytœ Civitatis Ragusii. Ed. with notes by Y. Brunelli. *Programma dell' I.R. Ginnasio Superiore in Zara*, 23: 3–54 (1880), 24: 3–48 (1881), 25: 3–36 (1882).

DRUCKER-BROWN, S. (1989). Mamprusi Installation Ritual and Centralisation: A Convection Model. *Man* (NS), 24: 485–501.

DUMONT, L. (1970). *Homo Hierarchicus*. Chicago and London: University of Chicago Press.

ELDER, F. (1934). *Glossary of Medieval Terms of Business (Italian Series 1200–1600)*. Cambridge, Mass.: Medieval Academy of America.

ELTON, G. R. (1967). *The Practice of History*. Sydney: Sydney University Press.

EVANS-PRITCHARD, E. E. (1940). *The Nuer*. Oxford: Clarendon Press.

FEELEY-HARNIK, G. (1985). Issues in Divine Kingship. *Annual Review of Anthropology*, 14: 273–313.

FINE JR., J. (1987). *The Late Medieval Balkans: A Critical Survey from the Late Twelfth Century to the Ottoman Conquest*. Ann Arbor: University of Michigan Press.

FINLAY, R. (1978). The Venetian Republic as a Gerontocracy: Age and Politics in the Renaissance. *Journal of Medieval and Renaissance Studies*, 8: 157–78.

——(1980a). Politics and History in the Diary of Marino Sanuto. *Renaissance Quarterly*, 23: 585–98.

——(1980b). *Politics in Renaissance Venice*. London: Ernest Benn.

FORTES, M. (1945). *The Dynamics of Clanship among the Tallensi*. London: Oxford University Press for the International African Institute.

——(1949). *The Web of Kinship among the Tallensi*. London: Oxford University Press for the International African Institute.

——(1953). The Structure of Unilineal Descent Groups. *American Anthropologist*, 55: 17–41.

——(1958). Introduction. In J. Goody (ed.), *The Developmental Cycle in Domestic Groups*. Cambridge: Cambridge University Press.

——(1962). Ritual and Office in Tribal Society. In M. Gluckman (ed.), *Essays on the Ritual of Social Relations*. Manchester: Manchester University Press.

——(1969). *Kinship and the Social Order*. Chicago: Aldine.

——(1970). Descent, Filiation and Affinity. In M. Fortes, *Time and Social Structure and Other Essays*. London: Athlone Press.

——(1984). Age, Generation, and Social Structure. In D. Kertzer and J. Keith (eds.), *Age and Anthropological Theory*. Ithaca: Cornell University Press.

FREIDENBERG, M. (1967). Kin Groups in Dalmatian Croatia, 11th–16th Centuries. *Sovetskaia Etnografiia*, 1: 68–79.

FULLER, C. and PARRY, J. (1989). 'Petulant Inconsistency'? The Intellectual Achievement of Edmund Leach. *Anthropology Today*, 5: 11–14.

GELČIĆ, M. (1955). 'Dubrovačka Trgovina Solju u XIV Veku. *Zbornik Filozofskog Fakulteta* (Belgrade), 3: 95–153.

GIDDENS, A. (1984). *The Constitution of Society*. Cambridge: Polity Press.

GIERKE, O. VON (1987). [1900]. *Political Theories of the Middle Age*. (Trans. F. W. Maitland.) Cambridge: Cambridge University Press.

GINZBURG, C. (1983). *The Night Battles: Witchcraft and Agrarian Cultures in the Sixteenth and Seventeenth Centuries*. (Trans. J. and A. Tedeschi.) London: Routledge & Kegan Paul.

GLUCKMAN, M. (1955). *The Judicial Process among the Barotse of Northern Rhodesia*. Manchester: Manchester University Press.

GOLDTHWAITE, R. (1980). *The Building of Renaissance Florence*. Baltimore and London: Johns Hopkins University Press.

GOODY, J. (1966). Introduction. In J. Goody (ed.), *Succession to High Office*. Cambridge: Cambridge University Press.

——(1983). *The Development of the Family and Marriage in Europe*. Cambridge: Cambridge University Press.

—— (1990). *The Oriental, the Ancient and the Primitive*. Cambridge: Cambridge University Press.

GRENDLER, P. (1989). *Schooling in Renaissance Italy: Literacy and Learning 1300–1600*. Baltimore and London: Johns Hopkins University Press.

GRUBB, J. (1988). *Firstborn of Venice: Vicenza in the Early Renaissance State*. Baltimore and London: Johns Hopkins University Press.

—— (1994). Memory and Identity: Why Venetians Didn't Keep Ricordanze. *Renaissance Studies*, 8: 375–87.

GRUJIĆ, N. (1977). Les Villas de Dubrovnik aux XVe et XVIe siècles. *Revue de l'art*, 115: 42–51.

GUERREAU-JALABERT, A. (1981). Sur les structures de parenté dans l'Europe médiévale. *Annales ESC* 36: 1028–49.

HACKENBERG, R. (1967). Parameters of an Ethnic Group: A Method for Studying the Total Tribe. *American Anthropologist*, 69: 478–92.

HAJNAL, J. (1965). European Marriage Patterns in Perspective. In D. Glass and D. Eversley (eds.), *Population in History*. London: Edward Arnold.

HAMMEL, E. (1957). Serbo-Croatian Kinship Terminology. *Kroeber Anthropological Society Papers*, 16: 45–75.

—— and WACHTER, K. (1977). Primonuptiality and Ultimonuptiality: Their Effects on Stem-Family-Household Frequencies. In R. Lee (ed.), *Population Patterns in the Past*. London: Academic Press.

HÉRITIER, F. (1981). *L'Exercise de la parenté*. Paris: Gallimard/Le Seuil.

HERLIHY, D. (1972). The Generation in Medieval History. *Viator*, 5: 346–64.

—— (1988). Tuscan Names, 1200–1530. *Renaissance Quarterly*, 41: 561–82.

—— and KLAPISCH-ZUBER, C. (1985). *Tuscans and Their Families: A Study of the Florentine Catasto of 1427*. New Haven and London: Yale University Press.

HRABAK, B. (1952). Dubrovačka Naseobina u Kapaoničkom Rudniku Belo Brdo. *Ogledi*.

JONES, P. (1956). Florentine Families and Florentine Diaries in the Fourteenth Century. *Papers of the British School at Rome*, 24 (NS 11): 183–205.

KENT, D. (1975). The Florentine *Reggimento* in the Fifteenth Century. *Renaissance Quarterly*, 28: 575–638.

—— (1978). *The Rise of the Medici: Faction in Florence 1426–1434*. Oxford: Oxford University Press.

KENT, D. and KENT, F. W. (1981). A Self Disciplining Pact Made by the Peruzzi Family of Florence (June 1433). *Renaissance Quarterly*, 34: 337–55.

—— (1982). *Neighbours and Neighbourhood in Renaissance Florence: The District of the Red Lion in the Fifteenth Century*. Locust Valley, NY: J. J. Augustin.

KENT, F. (1977). *Household and Lineage in Renaissance Florence*. Princeton: Princeton University Press.

KIRSHNER, J. (1978). Pursuing Honor While Avoiding Sin: The Monte Delle Doti of Florence. *Quaderni de 'Studi Senesi'*, 41: 1–82.

KLAPISCH-ZUBER, C. (1985). *Women, Family, and Ritual in Renaissance Italy*. (Trans. L. G. Cochraine.) Chicago and London: University of Chicago Press.

—— (1988a). Le Genealogie Fiorentine. In C. Klapisch-Zuber, *La famiglia e le donne nel Rinascimento a Firenze*. Bari: Editori Laterza.

—— (1988b). L'invenzione del passato familiare a Firenze. In C. Klapisch-Zuber, *La famiglia e le donne nel Rinascimento a Firenze*. Bari: Editori Laterza.

KLAPISCH-ZUBER, C. (1991). Kinship and Politics in Fourteenth-Century Florence. In D. Kertzer and R. Saller (eds.), *The Family in Italy*. New Haven and London: Yale University Press.

——(1994). Albero genealogicao e costruzione della parentela nel Rinascimento. *Quaderni storici*, 86: 405–20.

KOKOLE, S. (1996). Cyraicus of Ancona and the Revival of Two Forgotten Ancient Personifications in the Rector's Palace of Dubrovnik. *Renaissance Quarterly*, 49: 225–69.

KOSTRENČIĆ, M. (1973). *Lexicon Latinitatis Medii Ævi Iugoslaviæ*. Zagreb: Historijskog Instituta Jugoslavia.

KREKIĆ, B. (1964). Contribution to the Study of the Pronoia in Medieval Serbia. Reprinted in B. Krekić, *Dubrovnik, Italy and the Balkans in the Late Middle Ages*. London: Variorum Reprints, 1980.

——(1966). Ragusa e gli Aragonesi verso la metà del XV secolo. Reprinted in B. Krekić, *Dubrovnik, Italy and the Balkans in the Late Middle Ages*. London: Variorum Reprints, 1980.

——(1972). *Dubrovnik in the 14th and 15th Centuries: A City Between East and West*. Norman: University of Oklahoma Press.

——(1976). I mercanti e produttori toscani de panni de lana a Dubrovnik (Ragusa) nella prima metà del Quattrocento. Reprinted in B. Krekić, *Dubrovnik, Italy and the Balkans in the Late Middle Ages*. London: Variorum Reprints, 1980.

——(1978). Contributions of Foreigners to Dubrovnik's Economic Growth in the Late Middle Ages. *Viator*, 9: 375–94.

——(1979). Italian Creditors in Dubrovnik (Ragusa) and the Balkan Trade, Thirteenth through Fifteenth Centuries. Reprinted in B. Krekić, *Dubrovnik, Italy and the Balkans in the Late Middle Ages*. London: Variorum Reprints, 1980.

——(1986). O problemu koncentracije vlasti u Dubrovniku u XIV i XV vijeku. *Zbornika Radova Vizantoloskog Instituta*, 24–5: 397–406.

——(1987a). Developed Autonomy: The Patricians in Dubrovnik and Dalmatian Cities. In B. Krekić (ed.), *Urban Society of Eastern Europe in Premodern Times*. Berkeley, Los Angeles, and London: University of California Press.

——(1987b). Abominandum crimen: Punishment of Homosexuals in Renaissance Dubrovnik. *Viator*, 18: 337–45.

——(1994). *Miscellanea* from the Cultural Life of Renaissance Dubrovnik. *Byzantinische Forschungen*, 20: 133–51.

——(1995). On the Latino-Slavic Cultural Symbiosis in Late Medieval and Renaissance Dalmatia and Dubrovnik. *Viator*, 26: 321–32.

KUEHN, T. (1981). Women, Marriage, and 'Patria Potestas' in Late Medieval Florence. *Tijdschrift voor rechtsgeschiedensis*, 49: 127–47.

——(1982a). 'Cum Consensu Mundualdi': Legal Guardianship of Women in Quattrocento Florence. *Viator*, 13: 309–33.

——(1982b). *Emancipation in Late Medieval Florence*. New Brunswick: Rutgers University Press.

——(1987). Some Ambiguities of Female Inheritance Ideology in the Renaissance. *Continuity and Change*, 2: 11–36.

——(1991). A Reconsideration of Self-Disciplining Pacts among the Peruzzi of Florence. In T. Kuehn, *Law, Family, and Women: Toward a Legal Anthropology of Renaissance Italy*. Chicago and London: University of Chicago Press.

KUPER, A. (1982). Lineage Theory: A Critical Retrospect. *Annual Review of Anthropology*, 11: 71–95.

——(1993). The 'House' and Zulu Political Structure in the Nineteenth Century. *Journal of African History*, 34: 469–87.

LANE, F. (1940). The Mediterranean Spice Trade: Its Revival in the Sixteenth Century. *American Historical Review*, 45: 581–90.

——(1964). Tonnages, Medieval and Modern. *Economic History Review*, Second Series, 17: 213–33.

——(1971). The Enlargement of the Great Council of Venice. In J. Rowe and W. H. Stockdale (eds.), *Florilegium Historiale: Essays Presented to Wallace K. Ferguson*. Toronto: University of Toronto Press.

——(1973). *Venice: A Maritime Republic*. Baltimore and London: Johns Hopkins University Press.

LANE, F. and MUELLER, R. (1985). *Money and Banking in Medieval and Renaissance Venice. Vol. 1, Coins and Moneys of Account*. Baltimore and London: Johns Hopkins University Press.

LEACH, E. R. (1970) [1954]. *Political Systems of Highland Burma: A Study of Kachin Social Structure*. London: Athlone Press (a reprinting incorporating the 1964 edition's 'Introductory Note').

——(1971). *Pul Eliya, A Village in Ceylon: A Study of Land Tenure and Kinship*. Cambridge: Cambridge University Press.

LEE, R. (1978). Models of Preindustrial Dynamics with Applications to England. In C. Tilly (ed.), *Historical Studies of Changing Fertility*. Princeton: Princeton University Press.

LE ROY LADURIE, E. (1978). *Montaillou: Cathars and Catholics in a French Village, 1294–1324*. (Trans. B. Bray.) London: Scolar Press.

——(1979). *The Territory of the Historian*. (Trans. B. and S. Reynolds.) Hassocks: Harvester.

LETUNIĆ, B. (1989). *Obnova Dubrovnika 1979–1989*. Dubrovnik: Zavod za obnovu Dubrovnika.

LÉVI-STRAUSS, C. (1966). *The Savage Mind*. Chicago: University of Chicago Press.

——(1969). *The Elementary Structures of Kinship*. (Trans. J. Bell, J. von Sturmer, and R. Needham.) Boston: Beacon Press.

——(1983). The Social Organization of the Kwakiutl. In C. Lévi-Strauss, *The Way of the Masks*. London: Jonathan Cape.

LLOYD, C. (1993). *The Structures of History*. Oxford: Blackwell.

MACLEAN, I. (1980). *The Renaissance Notion of Woman*. Cambridge: Cambridge University Press.

MAHNKEN, I. (1960). *Dubrovački Patricijat u XIV Veku*. Belgrade: Srpska Akademija Nauka i Umetnosti.

MARTIN, J. (1981). Genealogical Structures and Consanguineous Marriage. *Current Anthropology*, 22: 401–12.

MASON, K. O. *et al.* (1973). Some Methodological Issues in Cohort Analysis of Archival Data. *American Sociological Review*, 47: 242–58.

MINEO, E. I. (1995). Formazione delle élites urbane nella Sicilia del tardo medioevo: matrimonio de sistemi di successione. *Quaderni storici*, 88: 9–41.

MITCHELL, J. (1967). On Quantification in Social Anthropology. In A. L. Epstein (ed.), *The Craft of Social Anthropology*. London: Tavistock.

MITIĆ, I. (1973). Konzulati i konzularna služba starog Dubrovnika. Dubrovnik: Historijski Institut Jugoslavenske Akademije Znanosti i Umjetnosti u Dubrovniku.

MOLHO, A. (1978). Visions of the Florentine Family in the Renaissance. Journal of Modern History, 50: 304–11.

——(1994). Marriage Alliance in Late Medieval Florence. Cambridge and London: Harvard University Press.

MOLHO, A. et al. (1994). Genealogia e parentado. Memorie del potere nella Firenze tardo medievale. Il caso de Giovanni Rucellai. Quaderni storici, 86: 365–403.

MOLS SJ, R. (1974). Population in Europe 1500–1700. In C. Cipolla (ed.), The Fontana Economic History of Europe. Vol. 2, The Sixteenth and Seventeenth Centuries. London: Collins/Fontana Books.

MUIR, E. (1981). Civic Ritual in Renaissance Venice. Princeton: Princeton University Press.

MUNN, N. (1983). Gawan Kula: Spatiotemporal Control and the Symbolism of Influence. In J. W. Leach and E. R. Leach (eds.), The Kula: New Perspectives on Massim Exchange. Cambridge: Cambridge University Press.

——(1986). The Fame of Gawa: A Symbolic Study of Value Transformation in a Massim (Papua New Guinea) Society. Cambridge and New York: Cambridge University Press (Lewis Henry Morgan Lectures, 1976).

NEDELJKOVIĆ, B. (1984). Liber Viridis. Belgrade: Srpska Akademija Nauka i Umetnosti.

ORIGO, I. (1963). The Merchant of Prato. Harmondsworth: Penguin Books.

PADGETT, J. and ANSELL, C. (1993). Robust Action and the Rise of the Medici, 1400–1434. American Journal of Sociology, 98: 1259–1319.

PARETO, V. (1963). The Mind and Society: A Treatise on General Sociology. 4 vols. (Trans. A. Bongiorno and A. Livingston.) New York: Dover Publications.

PARSONS, T. (1949). The Structure of Social Action. Glencoe: The Free Press.

PELZER, A. (1966). Abréviations Latines Médiévales: Supplément au dizionario de Abbreviature Latine ed Italiane de Adriano Cappelli. 10th edn. Paris: Béatrice-Nauwelaerts.

PETERS, E. (1960). The Proliferation of Segments in the Lineage of the Bedouin of Cyrenaica. Journal of the Royal Anthropological Institute, 90: 29–53.

PETROVICH, M. (1974). A Mediterranean City-State: A Study of Dubrovnik Elites, 1592–1667. University of Chicago Ph.D. thesis.

PHILLIPS, M. (1987). The Memoir of Marco Parenti: A Life in Medici Florence. Princeton: Princeton University Press.

POPOVIĆ, M. (1959). La penetrazione dei mercanti Pratesi a Dubrovnik (Ragusa) nell prima metà del XV secolo. Archivio storico italiano 117: 503–21.

POPOVIĆ-RADENKOVIĆ, M. (1957–8). Le relazioni commerciali fra Dubrovnik (Raguse) e la Puglia nel periodo angioino (1266–1442). Archivio storico per le province napoletane, NS 37–8.

PULLAN, B. (1971). Rich and Poor in Renaissance Venice. Oxford: Basil Blackwell.

QUELLER, D. (1986). The Venetian Patriciate: Reality Versus Myth. Urbana and Chicago: University of Illinois Press.

REŠETER, M. (1924–5). Dubrovačka numizmatika. 2 vols. Belgrade: Srpska Akademija Nauka.

——(1929a). Dubrovačko Veliko Vijeće. Dubrovnik, 1: 3–10.

——(1929b). Popis Dubrovačkijeh Vlastoeskijeh Porodica. Glasnik Dubrovačkog Učenog Drustva 'Sveti Vlaho', 1: 1–11.

REŠETER, P. (1891–2). Zecca della Repubblica de Ragusa. Bullettino di Archeologia e Storia Dalmata, supplement.

RHEUBOTTOM, D. (1987). Computers and the Political Structure of a Fifteenth-Century City-State (Ragusa). In P. Denley and D. Hopkin (eds.), *History and Computing*, Manchester: University of Manchester Press.

——(1988). 'Sisters First': Betrothal Order and Age at Marriage in Fifteenth-Century Ragusa. *Journal of Family History*, 13: 359–76.

——(1990). Hierarchy of Office in Fifteenth-Century Ragusa. *Bulletin of the John Rylands University Library of Manchester*, 72: 155–67.

——(1994). Genealogical Skewing and Political Support: Patrician Politics in Fifteenth-Century Ragusa (Dubrovnik). *Continuity and Change*, 9: 369–90.

RODGERS, W. L. (1982). Estimal Functions of Age, Period, and Cohort Effects. *American Sociological Review*, 38: 774–87.

ROLLER, D. (1951). *Dubrovački Zanati u XV. i XVI. Stoljeću.* Zagreb: Jugoslavenska Akademija Znanosti i Umjetnosti (Građa za Gospodarsku Povijest Hrvatske, Knjiga 2).

ROSALDO, R. (1980). *Ilongot Headhunting 1883–1974: A Study in Society and History.* Stanford: Stanford University Press.

RUGGIERO, G. (1985). *The Boundaries of Eros: Sex, Crime and Sexuality in Renaissance Venice.* New York and Oxford: Oxford University Press.

SALLER, R. (1987). Men's Age at Marriage and its Consequences in the Roman Family. *Classical Philology*, 82: 21–34.

SCHEFFLER, H. (1986). The Descent of Rights and the Descent of Persons. *American Anthropologist*, 88: 339–50.

SEGALEN, M. (1991). *Fifteen Generations of Bretons: Kinship and Society in Lower Brittany 1720–1980.* Cambridge: Cambridge University Press.

SKINNER, Q. (1988). Political Philosophy. In C. B. Schmitt and Q. Skinner (eds.), *The Cambridge History of Renaissance Philosophy.* Cambridge: Cambridge University Press.

SMITH, M. (1960). *Government in Zazzau, 1800–1950.* London: Oxford University Press for the International African Institute.

——(1974). *Corporations and Society.* London: Duckworth.

SMITH, R. (1981). The People of Tuscany and their Families in the Fifteenth Century: Medieval or Mediterranean? *Journal of Family History*, 6: 107–28.

SPREMIĆ, M. (1971). *Dubrovnik i Aragonci (1442–1495).* Belgrade: Zavod za idavanje udzbenika.

STONE, L. (1987). Prosopography. In *The Past and the Present Revisited.* London: Routledge & Kegan Paul.

STUARD, S. (1976). Women in Charter and Statute Law: Medieval Ragusa/Dubrovnik. In S. Stuard (ed.), *Women in Medieval Society.* Philadelphia: University of Pennsylvania Press.

——(1981). Dowry Increase and Increments in Wealth in Medieval Ragusa (Dubrovnik). *Journal of Economic History*, 41: 795–811.

——(1983). Urban Domestic Slavery in Medieval Ragusa. *Journal of Medieval History*, 9: 155–71.

——(1992). *A State of Deference: Ragusa/Dubrovnik in the Medieval Centuries.* Philadelphia: University of Pennsylvania Press.

SUNDT, E. (1980). *On Marriage in Norway.* Cambridge: Cambridge University Press.

ŠUNDRICA, Z. (1973). Šetjna kroz arhiv (2). *Dubrovnik*, 3.

TADIĆ, J. (1948). Organizacija Dubrovačkog Pomorstva u XVI Veku. *Istoriski časopis*, 1–2.

——(1955). La Port de Raguse au commerce méditerranéen du XVIe siècle. *Rissunti Delle*

Comunicazione, Vol. VII (X Congresso Internazionale di Scienze Storiche, Rome, 1955). Florence: G. C. Sansoni.

TADIĆ, J. (1958). Le Port de Raguse et sa flotte au XVIe siècle. In M. Mollat (ed.), *Le Navire de l'économie maritime du moyen-age au XVIIIe siècle principalement en Méditerranée*. Paris: SEVPEN.

——(1968). Venecija i Dalmacija u Srednjem Veku. *Jugoslovenski Istoriski časopis*, 3–4: 6–17.

TURNER, V. (1957). *Schism and Continuity in an African Society: A Study of Ndembu Village Life*. Manchester: Manchester University Press.

VISCEGLIA, M. (1993). Un groupe social ambigu: Organisation, stratégies et représentations de la noblesse napolitaine XVIe–XVIIIe siècles. *Annales ESC*, 1993: 4: 819–51.

VIDOVIĆ, R. (1984). *Pomorski Rječnik*. Split: Logos.

WACHTER, K. and LASLETT, P. (1978). Measuring Patriline Extinction for Modeling Social Mobility in the Past. In K. Wachter with E. Hammel and P. Laslett (eds.), *Statistical Studies of Historical Social Structure*. New York, San Francisco, and London: Academic Press.

WEBER, M. (1968). *Economy and Society: An Outline of Interpretive Sociology*. 3 vols. New York: Bedminster Press.

WRIGLEY, E. A. (1981). The Prospects for Population History. *Journal of Interdisciplinary History*, 12: 207–26.

WURTHMANN, W. (1989). The Council of Ten and the Scuole Grande in Early Renaissance Venice. *Studi Veneziani*, 18: 15–66.

INDEX